COMRADES BEYOND THE COLD WAR

/ AFRICAN
/ ARGUMENTS

African Arguments is a series of short books about contemporary Africa and the critical issues and debates surrounding the continent. The books are scholarly and engaged, substantive and topical. They focus on questions of justice, rights and citizenship; politics, protests and revolutions; the environment, land, oil and other resources; health and disease; economy: growth, aid, taxation, debt and capital flight; and both Africa's international relations and country case studies.

Managing Editor, Stephanie Kitchen

Series editors

Adam Branch
Eyob Gebremariam
Ebenezer Obadare
Portia Roelofs
Jon Schubert
Nicholas Westcott
Nanjala Nyabola

TYCHO VAN DER HOOG

Comrades Beyond the Cold War

North Korea and the Liberation of Southern Africa

IAI International African Institute

OXFORD
UNIVERSITY PRESS

Oxford University Press is a department of the
University of Oxford. It furthers the University's objective
of excellence in research, scholarship, and education
by publishing worldwide.

Oxford New York

Auckland   Cape Town   Dar es Salaam   Hong Kong   Karachi
Kuala Lumpur   Madrid   Melbourne   Mexico City   Nairobi
New Delhi   Shanghai   Taipei   Toronto

With offices in

Argentina   Austria   Brazil   Chile   Czech Republic   France   Greece
Guatemala   Hungary   Italy   Japan   Poland   Portugal   Singapore
South Korea   Switzerland   Thailand   Turkey   Ukraine   Vietnam

Oxford is a registered trade mark of Oxford University Press
in the UK and certain other countries.

Published in the United States of America by
Oxford University Press
198 Madison Avenue, New York, NY 10016

Copyright © Tycho van der Hoog, 2025

All rights reserved. No part of this publication may be reproduced,
stored in a retrieval system, or transmitted, in any form or by any means,
without the prior permission in writing of Oxford University Press,
or as expressly permitted by law, by license, or under terms agreed with
the appropriate reproduction rights organization. Inquiries concerning
reproduction outside the scope of the above should be sent to the
Rights Department, Oxford University Press, at the address above.

You must not circulate this work in any other form
and you must impose this same condition on any acquirer.
Library of Congress Cataloging-in-Publication Data is available

ISBN: 9780197811108

Printed in the United Kingdom

For Kuki Noordam

CONTENTS

Preface	ix
Abbreviations	xv
Introduction: Comrades Beyond the Cold War	1

PART ONE
BLOOD
DIPLOMATIC TIES

Prologue: Freedom Fighters	19
1. Solidarity: The Southern African Struggle	23
2. Competition: Korean Rivalry for Recognition	37
3. Diplomacy: African Presidents in Pyongyang	55
4. Doctrine: Juche Ideology in Africa	71
5. Development: South–South Cooperation	85
Epilogue: Microphone Revolution	97

PART TWO
BULLETS
MILITARY COOPERATION

Prologue: The Barrel of a Gun	103
6. War: The Battlefields of Africa	107
7. Weapons: North Korean War Experience	119

CONTENTS

8. Training: Achieving Power, 1960–1980 — 129

9. Victory: Consolidating Power, 1980–2000 — 141

10. Survival: Maintaining Power, 2000–2020 — 161

Epilogue: Party–Military Complex — 175

PART THREE
BRONZE
CULTURAL HERITAGE

Prologue: A Monumental Relationship — 181

11. Myth: Patriotic History from Pyongyang — 185

12. Nations: A Family Affair — 195

13. Violence: Romanticising the Revolution — 205

14. Heroism: The Founding Fathers — 215

15. Money: Nationalism as a Business Model — 227

Epilogue: A Liberation Lens — 235

Conclusion: Power to the Party — 239

Note on Archives — 251

Notes — 259

Primary Sources — 297

References — 307

Index — 327

PREFACE

Note of gratitude

This book is based on my PhD thesis, which I defended in 2024. I wish to express my gratitude to the African Studies Centre Leiden for supporting this project, and to Hankuk University of Foreign Studies and Seoul National University for awarding me visiting fellowships in South Korea. I am particularly indebted to my supervisors, Jan-Bart Gewald and Remco Breuker. Thank you for believing in this book, for supporting me throughout the challenging research process and for your mentorship.

Several ideas from this book were presented at conferences and workshops held at: the Basler Afrika Bibliographien, the British International Studies Association, the East–West Center and the National Committee on North Korea, Hankuk University of Foreign Studies, the Korea Economic Institute, Korea University, Leiden University, London School of Economics, Sciences Po, University of Basel, University of Edinburgh, University of Groningen, University of Melbourne, University of Oxford and the University of Tübingen. I am grateful to the organisers for the opportunity to present my work and I wish to thank the participants for their input.

Sections and earlier versions of some of the chapters in this book were published elsewhere. Parts of Chapter 3 overlap with a publication from the International Institute for Asian Studies,[1] parts of Chapter 4 appeared in an edited volume of Leiden

PREFACE

University Press,[2] parts of Chapter 5 appeared in the Policy and Research Paper Series of the North Korea Economic Forum[3] and parts of Chapters 10 and 15 appeared in the Academic Paper Series of the Korea Economic Institute.[4] The third part of this book (on heritage) builds upon my MA thesis *Monuments of Power*.[5] I want to thank the responsible editors for their help in publishing my work.

My research would not have been possible without the encouragement and advice of many people. In particular, I would like to pay homage to the wonderful comrades that make up the PhD Cave, the Southern Africa Writing Group and the Ponzi Scheme Book Club. At the International African Institute and Hurst, I am indebted to Stephanie Kitchen, Alice Clarke, Olivia Ralphs, Niamh Drennan, Daisy Leitch and Michael Dwyer. Anna Yeadell did a stellar job in editing the manuscript.

Note on style

There are multiple systems for the transliteration of Korean into Latin script. Both North Korea and South Korea use different romanisation schemes, and the field of Korean Studies has not settled on a single convention. For the use of Korean terms in this book, I have been inspired by Brian Myers' distinction between the 'outside track' and the 'inside track' of North Korean propaganda.[6]

For Korean terms that are part and parcel of North Korea's 'outside track' of propaganda, I have decided to use the transcription into English that is preferred by the North Korean state and therefore most widely known: Kim Il Sung instead of Kim Ilsŏng, Pyongyang instead of P'yŏngyang and Juche instead of Chuch'e. However, for Korean terms that are not necessarily meant for public consumption and mainly appear within the 'inside track' of North Korean propaganda, I use the McCune-Reischauer system for romanisation. The titles of the archival sources that I found in the Diplomatic Archives of South Korea are deliberately not romanised, with the aim to aid other researchers who wish to access the same files.

In Korea, family names come before first or given names. Kim Jong Un is thus 'Chairman Kim' and not 'Chairman Un' as the

PREFACE

American Secretary of State Mike Pompeo erroneously said in 2018.[7] However, when people (usually academics) express their names in English form I have adopted this order.

Recent Southern Africa history is a complex and oftentimes confusing medley of changing statehood and abbreviations. 'How does one name the past I write about?', mused the historian Luise White in relation to Zimbabwe: this country had four different names between 1898 and 1980.[8] Moreover, Zimbabwe hosted multiple liberation movements that competed and cooperated in different constellations throughout time: Zimbabwe African People's Union (ZAPU) and Zimbabwe People's Revolutionary Army (ZIPRA), Zimbabwe African National Union (ZANU) and Zimbabwe African National Liberation Army (ZANLA) and so on. This was applicable to the entire Southern African region. In pursuit of clarity, I use the names of independent African states even when I describe the colonial era ('Namibia' instead of 'South West Africa'). Furthermore, I choose not to expand on the abbreviations in the text ('SWAPO', instead of 'South West Africa People's Organisation'). Instead, I have supplied a separate abbreviation key.

Note on poetry

During my undergraduate studies in history at Leiden University, I enrolled in a course on historical theory and was pleasantly surprised that the professor in charge recited a poem at the end of each lecture. Ever since, I have been sensitive to the ways that poetry can hold up a mirror to our world.

Poetry is an integral part of North Korean society, where it is one of the most common forms of state-sanctioned propaganda.[9] North Korean leaders such as Kim Il Sung and Kim Jong Il wrote epic poems about the liberation of the nation. Poetry is widely distributed across the masses and sometimes turned into revolutionary films.[10] The life trajectory of Jang Jin Sung exemplifies the importance that North Korea attaches to the literary arts. Jang was one of Kim Jong Il's favoured poets and had

PREFACE

thus earned unparalleled protection and privilege in Pyongyang before he defected to South Korea in the early 2020s.[11]

Poetry also became an important dimension of the liberation struggles in Southern Africa. Important liberation figures, such as Agostinho Neto in Angola and Christopher Okigbo in former Biafra, were famed poets. Most exiled liberation movements published magazines to promote their organisations, and virtually all publications included poems written by their members. FRELIMO used poetry in the literacy campaigns in their military camps, and Eduardo Mondlane called this 'the seeds of a national culture'.[12] A book about the relationship between 'exile poetry' and politics is waiting to be written.

It is no coincidence that Frantz Fanon wrote about the 'poetry of revolt' in his book *Wretched of the Earth*.[13] Poetry was a useful tool to question the status quo and to reimagine a new world. This made poets dangerous in the eyes of colonisers. Poetry was often repressed by colonial governments. Don Mattera, a South African poet who was banned by the apartheid state, placed under house arrest and tortured, captured the tension between poets and oppressive regimes in the following lines:

> The poet must die
> His murmuring threatens their survival
> His breath could start the revolution;
> He must be destroyed[14]

To honour this dimension of liberation history, I have included three poems from Southern Africa in this book.[15] The poems are intended to reflect the three themes of 'Blood', 'Bullets' and 'Bronze'. The first part of this book ('Blood') explains how African liberation movements turned to Asia for moral and material support. Mvula ya Nangolo's poem 'Robben Island' is dedicated to the Namibian activist Andimba Toivo ya Toivo, who was detained for 18 years on the prison island. Ya Nangolo describes the distance between the Western world and the atrocities that occurred in Africa, and the hypocrisy of Western leaders.

The second part of this book ('Bullets') elaborates on the guerrilla warfare that marked much of Southern Africa's

PREFACE

recent history. Jorge Rebelo's 'Poem for a Militant' is similar to many poems that I encountered in the magazines of liberation movements during my archival research. Strong and militaristic, it describes the desire to fight for freedom. The third part of this book ('Bronze') explores the North Korean memorials that are used to commemorate the liberation struggles. Jofre Rocha's 'Poem of Return' encapsulates the complicated feelings of a post-war world. The final verse, which describes the fallen heroes 'with a wingless stone in hand / and a thread of anger snaking from their eyes' reminds me of the cemeteries that North Korea built in Southern Africa to commemorate the fallen heroes of the wars for independence.

ABBREVIATIONS

AAPSO	Afro-Asian Peoples' Solidarity Organization
ANC	African National Congress
AREMA	Antoko Revolisionera Malagasy
BNP	Basotho National Party
CCM	Chama Cha Mapinduzi
CIA	Central Intelligence Agency
DPRK	Democratic People's Republic of Korea (North Korea)
FLN	Front de libération nationale
FNLA	Frente Nacional de Libertação de Angola
FOIA	Freedom of Information Act
FRELIMO	Frente de Libertação de Moçambique
KOMID	Korea Mining Development Trading Corporation
LGBT	Lesbian, Gay, Bisexual, and Transgender
MAAN	Memorial António Agostinho Neto
MK	Umkhonto we Sizwe
MOP	Mansudae Overseas Projects
MPLA	Movimento Popular de Libertação de Angola
NAM	Non-Aligned Movement
NATO	North Atlantic Treaty Organization

ABBREVIATIONS

OAU	Organisation of African Unity
PLAN	People's Liberation Army of Namibia
RENAMO	Resistência Nacional Moçambicana
ROK	Republic of Korea (South Korea)
SACP	South African Communist Party
SADC	Southern African Development Community
SPUP	Seychelles People's United Party
SWAPO	South West Africa People's Organisation
TANU	Tanganyika African National Union
UK	United Kingdom
UN	United Nations
UNIP	United National Independence Party
UNITA	União Nacional para a Independência Total de Angola
UNSC	United Nations Security Council
US	United States
WPK	Workers' Party of Korea
ZANLA	Zimbabwe African National Liberation Army
ZANU	Zimbabwe African National Union
ZANU-PF	Zimbabwe African National Union-Patriotic Front
ZAPU	Zimbabwe African People's Union
ZIPRA	Zimbabwe People's Revolutionary Army

INTRODUCTION

COMRADES BEYOND THE COLD WAR

It was 1982 and Kim Il Sung was the centre of attention at his birthday party. The founding president of North Korea had invited his closest friends for an evening of luxury and delight. Dozens of people gathered in a large, festive hall to enjoy an abundance of gifts, exquisite food and entertainment. Suddenly, the founding president of Zambia, Kenneth Kaunda, stepped forward and serenaded the Great Leader. Kaunda was a central figure of the Frontline States in Africa, a coalition of independent nations that supported Southern African liberation movements in their fight for freedom. Kim Il Sung, seated in a large chair and surrounded by half-empty glasses of wine, smiled while he listened to Kaunda's rendition of *Tiyende Pamodzi*, the legendary song of Zambia's liberation struggle. At the climax of the song, Kaunda shouted the national slogan of his country: 'One Zambia, One Nation!' And then, to Kim's great joy, he added: 'One Korea, One Nation!'[1]

Kaunda stands in a long line of African visitors to Pyongyang. During the Cold War, virtually all leaders of liberation movements and governments in Southern Africa travelled to North Korea in search of support. Footage of Kaunda's 1982 journey can be found on YouTube, taped from North Korean television. In his birthday speech, the Great Leader said he was 'deeply moved' by the support from his 'brothers and comrades-in-arms'. He vowed that

1

this was 'the age of independence' and that North Korea would make 'every effort to strengthen unity and solidarity among the independent forces of the world'.[2] The North Korean government used the visits from African leaders for domestic propaganda, as it reminded the local population of their important role in global affairs.

In 2012, precisely 30 years after Kaunda's visit to Pyongyang, a busload of North Korean labourers arrived in Windhoek. They entered the capital city of Namibia to construct a museum that commemorates the history of Namibia's liberation struggle.[3] I stumbled upon this building by accident, shortly after it opened its doors to the public, and wondered why African history was displayed through North Korean aesthetics.[4] So much of Namibia's postcolonial landscape is designed by North Korea—other examples include the presidential palace, the defence headquarters and a cemetery for national heroes—that Windhoek's city centre might as well be nicknamed Little Pyongyang.[5]

Namibia is a remarkable case, but far from unique. In recent years, similar-looking monuments of power have emerged in and around the former Frontline States, including in Angola, Botswana, Congo, Mozambique, Zimbabwe and other countries.[6] African governments use North Korean monuments for domestic propaganda, as it reminds their citizens of their important role in the struggle for independence.

The juxtaposition between these two events provides an intriguing contrast: an African song in North Korea and a North Korean museum in Africa—separated by 30 years but connected through the common theme of liberation.

This book explores North Korea's influential role in the liberation of Southern Africa and describes how African states repay this historical aid today. Specifically, it examines the question of how political elites in Southern Africa benefitted from North Korean support, from 1960 until 2020. Contrary to existing scholarship, I argue that the end of the Cold War did not terminate the fraternal ties between both parties, but merely changed the nature of the African–North Korean alliance. Hence, African and North Korean elites remain comrades beyond the Cold War.

INTRODUCTION

A revolutionary alliance

The brotherhood between African and North Korean revolutionaries emerged from the ruins of World War II. The establishment of the United Nations system in 1945 marked the beginning of a new global order, which was heavily contested by two powerful developments from the outset: first, the ideological competition between the Western Bloc and the Eastern Bloc, and second, the campaigns for self-determination that led to the emancipation of new nation states. The Cold War and decolonisation were two major tectonic plates that shifted global politics, and Southern Africa was a region heavily impacted by the ensuing ruptures.

While, in the 1960s, most of the African continent was liberated from colonialism, Southern Africa remained largely under the yoke of colonial and settler governments.[7] National liberation movements led the resistance against white minority rule, but these organisations were heavily repressed and pushed into exile, often in the Frontline States. The region was only fully liberated when the first democratic elections in South Africa were held, in 1994. Until then, dozens of liberation movements negotiated and fought for freedom.

Julius Nyerere, the founding president of Tanzania, identified two routes to independence for African liberation movements. Like Zambia, Tanzania was a Frontline State that harboured exiled revolutionaries from neighbouring countries.[8] Nyerere's nickname was *Mwalimu*, a Swahili word for teacher, and the words of this towering figure in the struggle for freedom carried weight. The teacher instructed African nationalists that majority rule could either be obtained from 'a conference or out of a battlefield'.[9] For both routes, diplomacy or war, African liberation movements depended on the support of international allies.[10]

In an entirely different part of the globe, another kind of struggle was taking place in East Asia. The conclusion of World War II led to the end of Japanese colonial rule over Korea, but immediately resulted in the division of the peninsula. The Republic of Korea (South Korea; ROK) was supported by the United States and most of the Western world, while the Democratic People's Republic of Korea (DPRK; North Korea) was backed by the Soviet Union and China.[11] The Korean War (1950–53) ended in a stalemate that only reinforced the original division.[12] Both Koreas desired recognition as the sole legitimate government on the peninsula and therefore needed allies beyond the superpowers. This resulted in a vigorous diplomatic competition for support that spanned the entire globe, but perhaps became most intense in Africa.

The decolonisation of the African continent presented an unequalled opportunity for inter-Korean rivalry. The division of the Korean peninsula coincided with an African 'moment of seeming national possibility ... when at times new states were recognised every week'.[13] The two Koreas understood that each new African state was a potential new ally and deployed different strategies to gain a foothold in the continent. North Korea, in contrast to its southern rival, supported African liberation movements in the years before independence, and this aid arrived at a time when these movements needed it the most.

North Korea offered African liberation movements support for both paths to power identified by Nyerere: the conference and the battlefield. Through diplomacy, doctrine and development aid, Africans and North Koreans actively sought to change the global order. In addition, North Korea armed and trained African freedom fighters in African states, particularly in the field of presidential security. This book is organised with Nyerere's words in mind, as the first part examines the diplomatic dimension and the second part discusses the military dimension of African–North Korean relations.

Conventional histories view the conclusion of the Cold War as the end of an era. The dissolution of the Soviet Union, a financial benefactor of Pyongyang, plunged North Korea into a crisis. A large-scale famine, known as the Arduous March, crushed the economic and social structures of the state.[14] Kim Il Sung passed away in 1994, and his successor and son, Kim Jong Il, no longer had the money to bankroll elaborate programmes in the African continent. Since 2006, North Korea has been heavily sanctioned

INTRODUCTION

by the United Nations. From that perspective, the end of the Cold War severely disrupted African–North Korean relations.

However, the construction of North Korean monuments all over Africa during the twenty-first century reveals that African–North Korean interactions are ongoing. By hiring North Korean art studios, African governments pay back the aid that North Korea offered in the previous century—this contemporary connection is examined in the third part of this book. Despite the largest UN sanctions regime in history, North Korean diplomats continue to engage in a wide range of illicit activities in Africa, from selling forced labour and military hardware to the highest bidder, to smuggling gold and ivory. This historical study is therefore relevant to understanding contemporary African–North Korean relations.

* * *

The main argument of this book is that *liberation* (and not the Cold War) is the leitmotif for African–North Korean relations, as the transition from anticolonial struggles to postcolonial politics is characterised by continuity not change. My approach is based on three assumptions that underpin the analysis of this book.

First, political culture in Southern Africa transcends national boundaries, which is a legacy of the exile dimension of the struggle for liberation. Most Southern African ruling parties are rooted in anticolonial movements that operated in a regional system of politics. In that sense, this book builds upon the work of Jan-Bart Gewald, who argues that Southern Africa must be viewed as a single whole on account of its deep economic and social entanglements.[15] It is therefore imperative to view African–North Korean ties through a transnational lens, rather than maintaining the methodological convention of using bilateral case studies.

Second, we must shift our lens from states to regimes. Today, the majority of states in Southern Africa are ruled by political regimes that are rooted in liberation movements. As a general rule, when independence was finally secured, the victorious liberation movements were transformed into political parties and elected to office. Inspired by the work of Henning Melber, this book conceptualises these 'liberation governments' as the main unit of analysis.[16] Liberation governments continue to govern Angola (MPLA), Mozambique (FRELIMO), Namibia (SWAPO), South Africa (ANC), Tanzania (CCM) and Zimbabwe (ZANU-PF), while they governed Malawi (MCP) and Zambia (UNIP) for the first 30 years of independence.[17] During and after the Cold War, North Korea primarily offered support to the political elites of these liberation governments. I argue that it therefore makes much more sense to analyse ZANU–North Korean relations instead of Zimbabwean–North Korean relations, and the same goes for the majority of states in Southern Africa.

Third, the standard periodisation of African history and the Cold War distorts a proper understanding of African–North Korean interactions. The distinction between colonial and postcolonial eras is relatively irrelevant for the study of liberation governments, which underlines Stephen Ellis' critique of the standard periodisation of African history as artificial.[18] Moreover, a Cold War lens obscures the existence of contemporary African–North Korean exchanges.[19] In short, the liberation struggle in Southern Africa is not a thing of the past—it is very much an ongoing process. Today, African governments are under increasing internal and external opposition and use North Korean aesthetics and military expertise to legitimise and defend their enduring rule.

African agency

During the Cold War, a burgeoning field of research was devoted to communist engagements with Africa. This scholarship was primarily motivated by the fear of a communist revolution in the rapidly decolonising African continent, which would lead to the inevitable marginalisation of the 'Free World'. This corpus targets the big three of the Communist Bloc—China, the Soviet Union and, to a lesser extent, Cuba. The fact that North Korea hardly features in these accounts gives the false impression that there were few North Korean–African interactions.[20]

While there is another strand of literature that describes North Korean foreign policy during the Cold War, most studies gloss over

INTRODUCTION

Africa and focus instead on inter-Korean relations or general East–West rivalry.[21] Only a handful of publications explicitly consider North Korean relations with African states.[22] Published between 1978 and 1991, these authors naturally embrace a Cold War perspective.

In recent years, benefitting from the availability of new archival material, the study of North Korean foreign policy has made a revival. This line of inquiry is mainly published from the United States and is based on a number of implicit assumptions. Most of this research covers North Korea's relations with the entire globe; it is primarily based on Western diplomatic sources; and it remains firmly rooted within a Cold War time frame. As a consequence, Africa again features little or is dealt with rather superficially.

Charles Armstrong's landmark study on North Korea's international relations, *Tyranny of the Weak: North Korea and the World* (2013), only devotes four pages to Africa, with a small case study of Ethiopia.[23] *Tyranny of the Weak* is no longer suitable for teaching since it was discovered that Armstrong plagiarised the work of Balázs Szalontai, and Cornell University Press has subsequently taken the book out of print.[24] In contrast, Benjamin Young's *Guns, Guerrillas, and the Great Leader: North Korea and the Third World* (2021) provides a compelling and useful analysis of North Korea's foreign policy. Yet, Young's global scope, over-reliance on Western sources and Cold War time frame obscures both African agency and contemporary developments in African–North Korean engagements.[25]

A niche in the study of North Korean foreign policy is strongly related to an American-infused security paradigm of terrorism. Focused specifically on the military relations of North Korea, this body of works adopts a global scope. Alongside Asia and Latin America, the examination of North Korea's military export regularly features the African continent.[26] However, North Korean motives are, again, central to such analyses. The fact that a landmark study repeatedly describes the leader of Mozambique as 'President Michael' instead of President Machel does not inspire much confidence in the ability of this subfield to grasp local African contexts.[27]

In addition, North Korea's contemporary involvement in Africa has led to the publication of several policy papers that detail its illicit engagements with the continent. In contrast to the aforementioned scholarship, which is situated in the Cold War time frame, this strand of work draws attention to the ways that North Korean diplomats today abuse their diplomatic privileges by facilitating a wide array of criminal activities.[28] Although these papers provide fascinating insights, they deal with the present and hardly consider the past.

The question therefore remains how the former strand of historically informed scholarship (which focuses on the Cold War) can be connected to the strand of contemporary policy analysis (which focuses on recent developments). Moreover, the study of North Korean foreign policy is obsessed by North Korean motives for cooperation. The main problem with this approach is that it ignores African agency.

Most literature of African–North Korean interactions reduces the African continent to a chessboard of geopolitics, where African nations are mere pawns in a global game for influence. According to a 1975 book about the communist influence in Africa, South Africa is a 'coveted prize for communist imperialists and their leftist collaborators' because of its strategic position. The authors literally describe South Africa as 'a key piece on the global chessboard of power'.[29] This is a fitting illustration of a persistent trend in which African actors are rendered voiceless. As the North Korea-centred approach dominates the scholarship of the past 40 years, we know little of how African actors shape their interactions with the DPRK. It is time to reconsider this.

* * *

This book is consciously centred around African agency. Far too often, Africa's role in international relations has been viewed from the perspective of external actors, which reduces 'Africa as a supplicant actor' in global politics.[30] Solomon Dersso, for example, argues that the Cold War turned Africa into 'an object of manipulation, a theatre in which the countries in the West

INTRODUCTION

prosecuted their ideological and geo-strategic battles against the Soviet'.[31] As such, the agency of African states and Africans has often been overlooked or diminished.[32] 'It is high time that we approach Africa's international relations from a different perspective', argue William Brown and Sophie Harman.[33]

The point of departure throughout this book is the question of how ruling elites in Southern Africa benefited from their connections with North Korea. In contrast to the existing body of scholarship that revolves around North Korean motives for cooperation, this book takes a different approach with regard to focus, sources and time frame. First, instead of a broad focus on the 'Third World' or 'Global South' (or the 'Majority World'), this book zooms in on Africa, in particular the liberation governments of Southern Africa. Second, African primary source material takes centre stage. Third and last, the scope of this book consciously cuts through the Cold War time frame and connects the past to the present. This is why the third part of this book is important: the presence of North Korean monuments in Africa signifies the continuing relevance of African–North Korean relations.

A global paper trail

A transnational history requires a transnational approach. I have spent a combined total of about a year travelling across Africa, Asia, Europe and the United States, trudging around archives and libraries. The research for this book was significantly influenced by Covid-19, which erupted at the start of my project. The pandemic forced me to complement fieldwork with alternative modes of research, including the use of digital repositories, swapping archival data with fellow researchers and collaborating with research assistants.[34] With the help of many people, this book draws on novel declassified material from 32 different archives from four continents. These primary sources are supplemented by secondary literature, a select number of interviews and open-source data.

The global paper trail that I doggedly pursued throughout my studies stopped at the borders of North Korea. Researchers have no chance of gaining unfettered access to people and archives in

9

North Korea. Nevertheless, plenty of esteemed colleagues within Korean Studies travel to Pyongyang on guided tours, accompanied by government minders. Personally, I have strong moral objections to the Disneyfication of a country that maintains concentration camps. Moreover, security issues are a real risk. I saw this up close when the head of a research project on North Korean forced labour, which I participated in as a project researcher, was threatened by Kim Jong Un's regime.[35] For foreign visitors, the problem is not so much entering Pyongyang, but leaving Pyongyang—on your own accord.

Nevertheless, the refusal to travel to North Korea does not necessarily mean that academic research is impossible. The absence of evidence is not the evidence of absence. Most notably, interviewing North Korean exiles and utilising open-source data can yield tremendous insights and compensates for a lack of engagement with the North Korean state. The remainder of this section discusses three categories of source material and three related limitations of my research.

The first pillar of this book is archival research. The majority of my empirical analysis is based on recently declassified archival sources that have hardly been featured elsewhere, if at all. This includes African source material (scattered across party archives, university archives, and exiled archives, where research is a laborious but rewarding challenge), Korean source material (primarily from the Diplomatic Archives in South Korea, which provides a fascinating insight into the inter-Korean competition in Africa during the Cold War) and Western source material (primarily from national archives of the United Kingdom and the United States, whose embassies in Africa closely monitored North Korean activities). At the end of the book, I have included a more technical discussion of the primary source material that I have found in the archives.

The benefit of a multi-archival approach is not only a richness in data, but also the triangulation of certain events. For example, the description of the Pyongyang Conference of 1987 in Chapter 2 is based on source material from two African, a South Korean, and British and American archives. The limitation of my approach is a

INTRODUCTION

lack of engagement with primary sources from Lusophone Africa. Although I found original MPLA sources in the Nordic Africa Institute, in Sweden, and FRELIMO sources in the University of the Western Cape, in South Africa, practical reasons related to time and funding prevented me from conducting extensive research in Portuguese-language archives.

Interviews were originally intended as the second major pillar of this research project, alongside archival data. The memories of African freedom fighters who had encountered North Koreans during their years of exile and thereafter would have been a useful addition to the written record. North Korea is a sensitive issue in Southern Africa, and finding participants would have required long stints of dedicated fieldwork and trust-making. Unfortunately, the border closures, travel bans and infection risks that resulted from the Covid-19 pandemic ruled out an ambitious oral history project.

Nevertheless, this book benefits from lengthy conversations with two former diplomats who have experienced the inner workings of Pyongyang. James Hoare joined the East Asian Desk of the British Foreign Office in 1969 and was subsequently stationed in Seoul, Beijing and Pyongyang. In addition, a defected North Korean diplomat, who requested anonymity, told me the most remarkable stories about his travels through Africa during the 1980s as we sat in a little café in downtown Seoul. His deep knowledge of the North Korean Ministry of Foreign Affairs was remarkable. The testimonies of both men provide greater insights into the politics of the Cold War.

The third pillar of this book is a creative approach to the physical and digital footprints of North Korea in Africa. The aforementioned North Korean monuments in Africa can be viewed as source material in their own right. Tangible heritage sites are not only evidence of North Korea's presence in foreign lands, but also contain a narrative that presents certain stories and forgets others. The third part of this book provides a meta-analysis of North Korean heritage in Africa based on a reading of these monumental narratives.

COMRADES BEYOND THE COLD WAR

In addition to physical footprints in Africa, North Korea also leaves digital footprints on the internet: North Korean art studios and military companies publish their catalogues online, while North Korean operatives in Africa are active on Facebook. Open-source intelligence techniques (OSINT) present contemporary historians with new ideas to locate and analyse digital source material. Such tools are pioneered by non-governmental organisations and investigative reporters and have yet to find their way into the toolbox of ordinary historians, who are accustomed to paper archives.[36] However, OSINT can be highly useful for the study of the recent past: the third part of this book partly relies on it.

The main limitation of this final approach is an overreliance on North Korea's 'outside track' of information. State-produced propaganda does not reveal much about the inner workings of the government. Moreover, the focus on elites obscures the experiences of ordinary people.

About the book

This book describes 60 years of engagement between Southern Africa and North Korea through a thematic, three-pronged approach. The first part, organised around the theme of 'Blood', considers the diplomatic ties between African and North Korean elites that emerged at the nexus of African decolonisation and the Cold War. Part Two, organised around the theme of 'Bullets', highlights how African elites benefited from North Korean military support before, during and after the victory of independence. The third part, organised around the theme of 'Bronze', explores the cultural heritage of the liberation struggle by discussing the North Korean monuments that have emerged in Southern Africa in recent years.

Readers may detect a deliberate sequence throughout the book. Diplomatic ties, as described in the first part, led to military cooperation, as described in the second part. The themes of 'Blood' and 'Bullets' symbolise the two routes Nyerere identified for African liberation movements that desired independence: diplomacy and warfare. North Korea offered support for both

INTRODUCTION

options. Throughout the twentieth century, in meeting halls and on the battlefield, anti-imperialist forces in Africa and Korea were collaborating to bend the course of history in their favour. The final and third part, which is primarily set in the twenty-first century, looks back at this bygone era. The North Korean memorials in Africa are a direct outcome of the diplomatic friendship between North Korean and African leaders, and often celebrate the wars for independence.

* * *

The first part of the book, Chapters 1 through 5, examines how African freedom fighters forged intimate connections with a hereditary regime in the northern half of the Korean peninsula. The first two chapters introduce the main characters of this book. Chapter 1 sets the scene in Southern Africa, the last part of the continent to be liberated from colonialism and white settler-rule. African liberation movements were often pushed into exile and became dependent on the solidarity of foreign sponsors. Chapter 2 pivots to the Korean peninsula and considers the competition between the DPRK and the Republic of Korea for international recognition as the true Korea. Both Koreas launched elaborate diplomatic campaigns in Africa to garner support among newly independent nations.

Chapters 3 through 5 cover the practical outcomes of the African–North Korean diplomatic ties that were forged in the 1960s. Chapter 3 is centred around the successful invitation diplomacy of North Korea and analyses the journeys of several first-generation Southern African presidents to Pyongyang. A significant number of African elites flocked to Pyongyang in search of support, education and training. Chapter 4 describes the establishment of North Korean ideological centres in Africa. The state ideology of North Korea, Juche, made the country distinct from the major communist powers and therefore appealing to non-aligned African nations. Juche Study Centres allowed ordinary Africans to learn about the wonders of North Korea through books, films, exhibitions and discussions. Chapter 5 explores the largely unknown history of North Korean development aid in Africa. In the spirit of South–South cooperation, North Korean experts established experimental Juche farms in Africa; in return, African leaders praised North Korea's plans for reunification of the peninsula.

The main impact of North Korea's activities in Africa was not the establishment of farms, but the proliferation of arms. The second part of this book, Chapters 6 through 10, therefore revolves around military cooperation. Chapter 6 describes the liberation wars that defined Southern Africa in the twentieth century. When peaceful campaigns for independence were repressed by minority governments, some African liberation movements turned to violent revolution. As most Western countries refused to offer them weapons and training, many organisations looked East for support. Chapter 7 describes how North Korea, with its colonial history and anti-imperialist credentials, positioned itself as a natural ally for African freedom fighters. Military exports became a key component of North Korea's foreign policy, and the country became a major player in the global arms market.

Chapters 8 to 10 narrate the story of how Africans benefited from North Korean military support. Chapter 8 examines how exiled liberation movements received support in the years leading up to independence. African guerrilla fighters underwent basic training in North Korean camps in the Frontline States, while advanced training was offered to talented cadres in North Korea. Chapter 9 subsequently describes what happened after the victory of independence, when North Korea offered internal regime support for newly established governments. The best documented example is the notorious Fifth Brigade in Zimbabwe, but this chapter uncovers how virtually all neighbouring states were trained in the dark arts of presidential security. Chapter 10 brings us to the present, at a time when the governments of Southern African states and North Korea are desperately clinging to power. Despite United Nations sanctions prohibiting military cooperation, trade is ongoing and African armies continue to depend on North Korean services.

INTRODUCTION

The third part, Chapters 11 through 15, is centred around heritage. Despite its current isolated position in global affairs, North Korea is hired by African governments to design and construct some of the most eye-catching public buildings in Africa, including a 120-metre-tall memorial, a cemetery in the shape of two AK-47s and a history museum. Chapter 11 describes how African liberation governments turned the narratives of liberation into myths that glorify their status as revolutionaries. It is a model of African patriotic history that is well suited to North Korean visual aesthetics.

The next three chapters explore what the import of North Korean aesthetics means for the display of African history. What stories are revealed or concealed through these monuments? Chapter 12 analyses how nations are defined in party-centric terms that are organised around the notion of family: the leaders are the fathers of the nation, the citizens are their children and counter-voices become outcasts. Chapter 13 considers the role of violence in the memorialisation of the struggle. North Korean monuments emphasise the need for continuous revolution that protects the gains from early colonial and late colonial warfare. Chapter 14 is centred around heroism and scrutinises the gendered dimensions of African–North Korean memorial culture.

Chapter 15 discusses the economic dimension of African–North Korean relations. Similar to military trade, African heritage is a profitable business model for North Korea. Monuments justify the enduring rule of African liberation governments, but also signify the importance of foreign currency for North Korea's government. Economic activities in Africa are a lifeline for the increasingly isolated elites in Pyongyang. The monuments therefore symbolise the strategies of survival for both African and North Korean regimes.

15

PART ONE

BLOOD

DIPLOMATIC TIES

Just how far is Robben Island from a black child at play?
What forces take his father there with all the world between?
Oh! Mother caution your warrior son again
or else he'll show his might

Just how far is Robben Island from the United Nations headquarters?
Have I time to ponder now when patriots are drilling fast?
Spears are flying and the shields are once more bloody
for the drums of war are beating again

Just how far is Robben Island from the London Stock Exchange?
You couldn't hear my talking war drums
for uselessly loud is the enemy's cannon roar

Just how far is Robben Island from the Yankee's White House?
I have no sight for I do not speak languages so foreign
the stars and zebra stripes are dazzling me
the US President speaks—his foreign secretary cheats

Then just how far is Robben Island from the field of Waterloo?
A few bushes away
a village or two in between
and the warrior son will take you there.

— 'Robben Island', by Mvula ya Nangolo, Namibia

PROLOGUE

FREEDOM FIGHTERS

As Namibia's colourful national flag was hoisted for the first time on Independence Day, 21 March 1990, thousands of elated Namibians celebrated the victory of liberation by singing their new anthem. 'Freedom's fight we have won', the spectators roared, 'glory to their bravery, whose blood waters our freedom'.[1] The sentiments of the new anthem echo those of SWAPO's 'freedom songs', sung during the struggle, such as 'Many rivers of blood will flow', which asserted that the Namibian people must continue to suffer for the just cause of freedom.[2]

The combination of freedom and blood is a recurring theme in the discourse of Southern African liberation movements. For SWAPO, the history of resistance in Namibia is 'written in blood'.[3] The Revolutionary Government of Angola in Exile similarly proclaimed that its people were 'writing history with their blood so that one day Angola can be free and independent'.[4] A Zambian official observed in 1975 that 'our oppressed brothers' in Namibia, Angola, Zimbabwe and Mozambique 'have written the history of their independence struggle in blood'. He announced that 'Zambian blood is part of the ink with which that history is being written'.[5]

Blood became a symbol of sacrifice during the era of liberation. Robert Mugabe, the leader of ZANU and later president of

Zimbabwe, mourned the death of his comrades by proclaiming that 'their blood shall forever water the seed of our revolution'.[6] One of ZANU's most prominent struggle songs is named *Zimbabwe Ndeye Ropa*, meaning 'Zimbabwe is born of blood'.[7] The MPLA of Angola celebrated the 'irrigation of our battlefields with the blood of the best sons of our peoples'.[8] The SACP, a fundamental ally of the ANC, asserted that they would 'continue to water the tree of freedom in our land, if necessary, with our own blood'.[9] The ANC called the people 'the lifeblood of our revolution'.[10] The SWAPO leadership declared that they were 'prepared to cross many rivers of blood in our march to freedom, independence and national liberation'.[11] Samora Machel, the leader of FRELIMO and later president of Mozambique, said that 'the blood of our people was not shed only to free the land from foreign domination', but also to 'reconquer our Mozambican personality ... to create a new society'.[12] Machel believed that Africa offered 'her blood and sacrifices ... for the general cause of humanity': as Africa was liberating herself, she was simultaneously liberating the world.[13]

Blood also symbolises the comradeship that freedom fighters found on the path to liberation. The term comrade, Machel explained, is a word 'bathed in blood and sacrifices'.[14] At the Non-Aligned Summit in Zimbabwe, in 1986, Machel introduced Mugabe as 'an outstanding personality, a comrade and friend ... Mugabe stands for us Mozambicans as a symbol of solidarity forged by the struggles of our peoples and sealed in blood'.[15] When the MPLA leader, José Eduardo dos Santos, visited his Zambian UNIP comrades, he stressed that their ties were not just based on friendship—'they are also blood ties'.[16] Comrades are people that fight and suffer for freedom, together.

Blood is an equally significant theme in North Korean propaganda. Kim Il Sung credited himself with writing the opera *Sea of Blood*, a story of indigenous defiance against the colonial Japanese occupation of Korea.[17] *Sea of Blood*, which premiered in 1971, became a cornerstone of North Korean nationalism and is regarded as one of the Five Great Revolutionary Operas. The story exemplifies the virtues of Juche and was later adapted into a novel and a film.[18] Every North Korean has been exposed

PROLOGUE

to its revolutionary contents—and so have a number of African leaders. When Agostinho Neto visited Pyongyang in the 1970s (before Angolan independence), he was not only welcomed with a rendition of the MPLA anthem, but he was also treated by Kim to a private screening of *Sea of Blood*.[19]

Sacrifice and comradeship are noble values in the pursuit of freedom and therefore have positive connotations. On the other hand, the word blood is associated with ethnic nationalisms that are based on exclusionary definitions of race. North Korea is a society founded on the idea of a pure Korean race, and Brian Myers, a renowned expert on ideology and propaganda, argues that North Korea's political ideology is closer to fascism than to communism.[20] This is different from Southern Africa. Although race is key to understanding Southern African history, and recent years have seen an increase in xenophobic politics, the rule of African liberation governments cannot be defined as *Blut und Boden*.

For the conceptualisation of this book, blood, ultimately, stands for solidarity. Not just between anticolonial movements within Southern Africa, but especially between African and North Korean freedom fighters, who, despite vastly different backgrounds, came to regard each other as blood brothers. This explains why African leaders were comfortable in Pyongyang, so much so that the Zambian president sang his liberation song and the president of Botswana danced in front of an exuberant crowd. As a result, North Korean books were translated into Swahili and Afrikaans and distributed across the continent. In time, experimental North Korean farms in Africa were established to showcase the benefits of practical collaboration between the oppressed peoples of the world.

The following five chapters describe how Africans and North Koreans were brought together by the powerful force of solidarity, how they navigated internal and external power struggles, exchanged ideas and eventually became allies in search of freedom.

21

1

SOLIDARITY

THE SOUTHERN AFRICAN STRUGGLE

In retrospect, a revolution always seems like an eruption, observes the writer Namwali Serpell in her great Zambian novel *The Old Drift*. Revolution is commonly understood as 'a massive upheaval that overturns everything, flips the tables, shatters the sky, fractures the earth'. Yet, in truth, 'no one talks about how long a revolution takes or how boring it can be, how it can slowly chew time with grinding teeth before gulping it down at once'.[1]

Between 1960 and 1990, Southern Africa was a region engulfed in revolution. The end of World War II unleashed a whirlwind of nationalist campaigns for self-determination while colonial empires crumbled. As the Cold War came to an end, the region regained its political freedom. So, within half a century, the political conditions in Southern Africa had changed completely.

The African nationalists, these agents of change, characterised their campaigns for independence as a *struggle*—and that is exactly what it was. For outsiders, the political turnaround in Southern Africa may seem remarkably fast; yet, for the people in the midst of the struggle, it was often painfully long. The burden of a century of colonial occupation weighed heavily on those that made history.

Anticolonial campaigns could last decades, as was the case in South Africa—which only held its first democratic elections in 1994.

During the decades of decolonisation, the eyes of the world were fixed upon Southern Africa. As the region captured international headlines, powerful external forces sought to influence the unfolding events. This chapter highlights a crucial dimension in the fight for freedom, namely, solidarity. The first section provides a historical summary of the occupation of Southern Africa and introduces the national liberation movements that opposed the racially divided status quo. The chapter then zooms out to examine African solidarity, most notably the Frontline States and the Liberation Committee. Finally, the chapter considers the global implications of African decolonisation through a discussion of the United Nations and the necessity for Afro-Asian solidarity.

The occupation and liberation of Southern Africa

Most of the African continent had achieved independence by the 1960s—except for Southern Africa, the last region in the world to remain colonised. A loose coalition of white minority governments ignored the thundering calls for liberation and 'stubbornly held on to power': the Portuguese Empire controlled Angola and Mozambique, Ian Smith's settler regime governed Rhodesia (modern Zimbabwe), and the Nasionale Party ruled South Africa and Namibia with an iron fist.[2]

South Africa is the key to unlocking the various interwoven liberation struggles of the entire Southern African region. Its unwavering commitment to apartheid determined events far beyond its borders. South Africa had incorporated South West Africa (modern Namibia) as an unofficial fifth province and backed Smith's minority rule in Rhodesia. When Angola and Mozambique suddenly became independent in 1975 (an outcome of the Carnation Revolution in Portugal that overthrew the *Estado Novo* regime), and were subsequently plunged into civil wars, South Africa interfered by supporting armed groups that opposed the newly elected African governments.[3] The result was a complicated

SOLIDARITY

mix of prolonged guerrilla wars across the Southern Africa region, a messy history that is explored in more detail in Chapter 6.

African resistance to minority rule was organised through national liberation movements, the protagonists of this book. Every revolution needs its administrators. Liberation movements were complex organisations with extensive bureaucracies that gradually came to mirror the states they vowed to overthrow. Their civil servants were essentially revolutionaries with business cards. Long before independence, the most successful African liberation movements operated as proto-states: led by a president and a central committee that acted as a cabinet, these organisations coordinated various departments, small armies and foreign missions that functioned as informal embassies.[4] When SWAPO opened an office in India in 1986 (four years before Namibian independence), Sam Nujoma called it a 'SWAPO Embassy'.[5] During the struggle, the ANC had more foreign missions than the South African apartheid government.[6]

In response to their fight to introduce majority rule, African liberation movements were banned, oppressed and persecuted. This only added fuel to the fire. Numerous freedom fighters poured into exile in the Frontline States (such as Zambia and Tanzania), where the most powerful liberation movements established headquarters and camps. Most, if not all, key figures in the struggle passed through these camps at a certain point in time, and some lived there for years on end.

In these exile camps, national liberation movements were able to govern their own citizens and exercise the traditional functions of a state for the first time: the rule of law, the monopoly of violence and the administration of public institutions such as schools and hospitals.[7] 'The nature of our struggle', according to the ANC, 'calls upon us to exercise some of the functions of an embryonic state. We have our army, we have our security, we already express the beginnings of a new popular sovereignty'.[8] When the journalist Lisa Distelheim visited an ANC camp near Lusaka (Zambia), she described the movement as a 'state within a state waiting to go home'. The camp included a radio station, a publishing house, a clinic and a farm.[9] Similarly, Machel called the

25

liberated areas during the Mozambican struggle 'a school in the exercise of power'. In these areas, FRELIMO 'gained experience in alternatives of government ... They were the decisive factor in the transformation of the struggle into a revolutionary struggle'.[10]

For anticolonial movements, the route to freedom was uncertain. As captured in Serpell's novel, it could take years or even decades before a revolution was successful in securing independence. The time spent in limbo was a daunting challenge, trapped between a shackled past and a liberating future. As these movements organised themselves into proto-states,[11] it was a time of both imagining new and different worlds and of day-to-day survival and power struggles.

* * *

The decolonisation of Southern Africa is a transnational history marked by complex regional dynamics of cross-border interactions between national liberation movements.[12] This was largely the result of exile: examples include the camps and headquarters of liberation movements that were scattered across the region, the party conferences that were organised on foreign soil and the ad hoc diplomatic or military alliances between anticolonial movements.[13] Even their propaganda was transnational: published from exile, the public messaging of liberation movements often contained profiles, solidarity statements and interviews with leaders from fellow revolutionary organisations.

The historian Jan-Bart Gewald conceptualises Southern Africa as 'a single whole, albeit with different accents'. This region is bound together by deep cultural and economic structures that have been forged over the past thousand years.[14] The political history of decolonisation in Southern Africa only reinforces Gewald's observations. To reiterate, most of Southern Africa continues to be ruled by former liberation movements and thus shares a similar political culture, one that is rooted in the transnational struggles of the recent past.[15]

Within the parameters of this study, Tanzania is an integral part of Southern Africa. For African liberation fighters, its capital, Dar

SOLIDARITY

es Salaam, was a 'hub of decolonisation' where exiled nationalists could establish headquarters and camps.[16] Neto called the city 'one of the heroic capitals of African resistance to colonial and racist rule'.[17] The city operated as a 'gatekeeper' between African liberation movements and the outside world. 'New connections and channels for mobility could be forged, maintained and managed', notes the historian Eric Burton. This was especially true for relations between African revolutionaries and communist countries, which were dependent on hubs such as Dar es Salaam, as colonial countries cracked down on contacts with the Communist Bloc.[18]

Tanzania was one of the principal stages for the politics of African solidarity, and therefore a strategic place for North Korean investment.[19] As an exiled North Korean diplomat with working experience in Dar es Salaam told me, Tanzania became one of the core countries of North Korea's Africa policy: the two nations had 'a very close relationship'. Dar es Salaam hosted the largest North Korean embassy in Africa and the only one built by the North Koreans themselves. Among the approximately 40 staff members, a special diplomat was dispatched to forge relationships with Southern African liberation movements.[20] The two nations had established diplomatic relations in 1965, which was followed by a succession of visits and pledges for cooperation.[21] North Korea had 'singled out Tanzania among the developing countries as an area of special interest' and utilised the country as an entry point into the various liberation struggles in Southern Africa.[22]

African solidarity

The diplomacy of African liberation movements 'was crucial' to maintaining the 'flows of weapons, material aid, and humanitarian support' upon which the survival of said movements depended.[23] To a large extent, liberation movements launched these diplomatic efforts from Tanzania and other members of the Frontline States. During the Cold War, the Frontline States operated as a loose alliance of African states that opposed South African apartheid.

27

Through its summits and interpersonal relations, the group would 'shape Africa's position on decolonisation'.[24]

The Frontline States originated from informal consultations between Kenneth Kaunda and Julius Nyerere in the 1960s on the question of how to support liberation movements in neighbouring countries. When other leaders joined, this group became known as the Mulungushi Club.[25] In 1969, these leaders produced the Lusaka Manifesto, a statement that outlined the African strategy to challenge South Africa. In the words of the Zimbabwean nationalist Nathan Shamuyarira, the Lusaka Manifesto became a 'rallying point for all African states, moderate and radical'.[26] Chapter 6 discusses the Manifesto and subsequent African policy documents in further detail.

The Frontline States gradually expanded as a deterrent against South Africa. Formally established by name in 1975, the group originally consisted of Botswana, Lesotho, Tanzania and Zambia, and in subsequent years incorporated Angola, Mozambique and Zimbabwe.[27] This created a liberated zone that stretched roughly from the Indian Ocean to the Atlantic Ocean. The Frontline States found themselves in a precarious position, as their expressions of solidarity were punished by South Africa's strategies of destabilisation. Kaunda described Zambia's predicament as 'sitting at the edge of an active volcano whose lava spills beyond its crater'.[28]

In addition to the Frontline States, the Liberation Committee was a key factor in the support of African liberation movements. Established by the Organisation of African Unity in 1963, the Liberation Committee was headquartered in Dar es Salaam and mobilised political support and material resources for exiled nationalists.[29] Machel, the leader of FRELIMO, stated that the Liberation Committee was 'above all an essential instrument of African solidarity'.[30] At a 1975 meeting of the OAU, Machel characterised the organisation as a 'blood bank'.[31] He reminisced about how Tanzanian people would queue up in hospitals to donate blood to Mozambican people and claimed that 'Tanzanian blood saved many Mozambican lives'.[32]

SOLIDARITY

However, Machel's powerful prose cannot disguise the fact that there was also a strong degree of competition between liberation movements for recognition. For each colonised territory in Southern Africa there were multiple nationalist groups that were bitter rivals and competed with each other for funding and status.[33] The Liberation Committee tried to foster unity between rivalling groups but often failed.[34] Its ability to fund certain liberation movements and set aside others turbocharged intra-nationalist competition.

The liberation governments that are in power today were not always the obvious frontrunners in the past. Namibia's political history seems defined by SWAPO but, in truth, the nationalist campaign in Namibia was initially spearheaded by the rival SWANU, which was recognised by the OAU and was a member of the Afro-Asian People's Solidarity Organisation.[35] The SWAPO diplomat Andreas Shipanga described his 'horror' at discovering that he was not allowed to attend the opening ceremony of an AAPSO conference in Havana (Cuba), in 1965. After 'flying halfway round the world' he was stopped at the entrance of the conference venue because it was the rival SWANU that was identified as the representative of the Namibian struggle, instead of SWAPO. Shipanga was 'furious' that he missed Fidel Castro's speech but decided to make the most of his time in Cuba (no doubt helped by the Cubans stocking a 'fresh bottle of Bacardi rum' in his room every day).[36]

The fortunes of liberation movements could easily change. The main difference between SWANU and SWAPO was the decision to pick up arms against South Africa. The Liberation Committee and other benefactors favoured nationalist organisations that were willing to wage war on the battlefield and sidelined organisations that confined themselves to conference rooms. Fanuel Kozonguizi, a founding member of SWANU, said that 'SWAPO's single asset in the battle for recognition was their declaration of an armed struggle in 1966'.[37] SWANU was expelled from AAPSO in 1967 and lost OAU recognition in 1968.[38] Kozonguizi no longer received a stipend from the Liberation Committee, as one of the OAU officials argued that 'we have neither time nor money for movements that do not produce results'.[39] Abruptly, SWAPO became the leading light of the Namibian struggle.

Similar examples can be found across the Southern African region. In Zimbabwe, for example, nationalist energies were initially channelled through ZAPU, led by Joshua Nkomo, but internal disputes impeded the organisation. The historian Stuart Doran describes how gradually 'tensions morphed into open hostility' among the ZAPU leadership, and when the rift reached a climax in Dar es Salaam, Mugabe and others left the party and formed ZANU. The schism between the two parties came to define much of Zimbabwe's liberation struggle.[40] It was ultimately ZANU that would win the first democratic elections in Zimbabwe, in 1980, and the party would subsequently use its state power and North Korean help to crush ZAPU (more on this in Chapter 9).

The Liberation Committee clearly had its limits. It had to navigate complicated nationalist rivalries—not only with regard to Namibia and Zimbabwe, but also in the case of Angola, Mozambique and South Africa. Furthermore, the Liberation Committee was incapable of meeting the material and financial needs of the liberation movements. This is illustrated by a military budget that SWAPO submitted to the OAU in 1967 (for a total sum of 65,000 British pounds). In the conclusion, SWAPO stressed that 'the financial assistance we receive from the Committee is always far below our needs'.[41] In short, African liberation movements could not rely on African solidarity alone and had to search for alternative sources of support.

Global solidarity

The historian Alanna O'Malley describes how the UN 'enjoyed an unprecedented and unique moment of influence' around the time of African decolonisation and the Korean War, as the Afro-Asian Bloc within the organisation grew considerably. At the time, the UN developed an 'activist and interventionist' agenda, offering political support for African and Asian actors.[42]

For African liberation movements, the UN was a vital forum that offered funding, legitimacy and political capital. In Namibia, for example, nationalist Africans in the 1950s automatically 'looked to the UN for help in their struggle' and petitioned the world body to intervene on their behalf. The UN General Assembly later recognised SWAPO as 'the sole and authentic representative' of the Namibian nation, a status that greatly contributed to the credibility of the nationalist movement.[43] Lydia Walker argues that 'the prospect and presence' of a UN committee dedicated to Namibia 'completely shaped the Namibian independence struggle'.[44] SWAPO was not the only liberation movement that travelled to New York in search of support—the UN received numerous African liberation movements throughout the Cold War. Chapter 2 describes in more detail how North Korea approached the UN as a venue to cooperate with African actors. The Korean peninsula was the oldest Cold War affair debated in the UN General Assembly.[45]

The supranational power of the UN had its limits though because the world body ultimately consisted of national states that determined its policies. The historian Christopher Saunders shows that, in Namibia, the UN 'only played its role when the Western countries allowed it to do so'. While SWAPO 'never entirely lost faith' in the UN, it did have 'major doubts' about its effectiveness.[46] O'Malley argues that the UN 'itself became a contested battleground for different ideas and visions of world order'.[47]

As African solidarity was insufficient to support the needs of African liberation movements, and the United Nations was limited in its power, liberation movements became dependent on sponsorship from powerful countries in the West and the East. Consequently, they were inadvertently sucked into the vortex of Cold War tensions.

The Western and Eastern Blocs approached African decolonisation from entirely different angles. The stark difference in assistance from both parts of the world is well captured in diplomat Shipanga's testimony during a United States Senate hearing in 1982. During the 1960s, he had established several offices and military camps for SWAPO in exile and made the rounds at foreign embassies to rally support. He described that 'either it was because of great naiveté or some strange illusion' that he first tried to approach the Western Bloc, as he was met with 'open hostility and contempt' in Western missions in Dar es Salaam, Kinshasa, Accra, Cairo and Algiers. Finally, he knocked on the doors of Asian and socialist countries, who 'not only sympathised but also supported our struggle'.[48]

The relations between the Western world and Southern Africa were tense. The United States 'had an ambivalent attitude towards decolonisation' and was widely condemned in Southern Africa for linking Namibian decolonisation to the withdrawal of Cuban troops in Angola, a position that severely delayed Namibian independence.[49] Portugal and the United Kingdom were obviously tarnished by their own colonial exploits, while NATO countries supplied military hardware to Portugal and the apartheid regime of South Africa. Western indifference to the Southern African struggles is captured in Mvula ya Nangolo's poem, in which he laments the distance between Robben Island and the UN headquarters, the London Stock Exchange and the White House.[50]

As a side note, there was oftentimes a discrepancy between the position of Western states and (parts of) their populations. Citizens across the Western world and beyond established solidarity groups to support African anticolonial movements.[51] The Anti-Apartheid Movement (AAM) in particular became 'one of the most significant social movements during the post-war era'.[52] North Korea carefully studied the AAM's statutes, publications and staff in an attempt to understand the Southern African struggles.[53]

Whereas the doors of the Western world remained largely closed for African diplomats, the gates to the East were swung open, especially those in Asia. This moment in time was the breakthrough of Afro-Asian solidarity, an intercontinental alliance that emerged from the Bandung Conference of 1955. 'Bandung' was a key moment to 'discuss the possible futures of the postcolonial world', notes the historian Christopher J. Lee, and became the moniker of an era during which new networks were established between non-aligned countries.[54] In particular, the founding of the Afro-Asian People's Solidarity Organisation and the Non-Aligned Movement (NAM) presented novel opportunities for African liberation movements to find support among Asian states. Chapter

SOLIDARITY

2 elaborates upon the question of how AAPSO and NAM were used by North Korea to connect to African liberation movements.

Asian support for African liberation movements was often seen by Western stakeholders as evidence of communist indoctrination. In 1967, Kaunda proclaimed that he did not know 'whether to be angry or to laugh' at accusations that he was 'a man moving towards the East ... towards the communist camp'. He stressed that Zambian policy was informed by domestic principles and criticised Western hypocrisy: when he made four trips to the West he was not labelled as a capitalist, but when he made one trip to Peking he was immediately branded as a communist. 'We will get aid wherever it is available', Kaunda said, 'but we never allow those who give us aid to influence our thinking'.[55]

The driving force behind African liberation movements was a quest for self-determination, not ideological competition. Yet, such accusations became even stronger when African liberation movements accepted military aid from communist states in Asia, a tension that is further explored in Chapter 7. In reality, the Cold War lens is 'inadequate' for understanding the true meaning and extent of African–Asian encounters, including those between African liberation movements and North Korea.[56]

Conclusion

The twentieth century was an era of bold ideas. The 'Third World' must start 'a new history of Man', wrote Frantz Fanon in 1961.[57] People dreamt with unparalleled energy of new directions.[58] The age of revolution in Southern Africa, especially the decades between the 1960s and the 1990s, embodies this vigour.[59] Despite significant impediments, the Black majorities of Southern Africa successfully defied the 'South African-dominated security system for the preservation of minority rule' while navigating a bipolar international security system.[60]

The struggle was a formative experience, not just for the individuals within liberation movements, but for nations as a whole. Between the point of departure (the start of anticolonial resistance) and the final destination (the attainment of independence) was a period of time that represented endless opportunities to visualise a future world. The connections made with outside sponsors during these formative years would therefore have a lasting impact.

In Southern Africa today, the experience of the various intertwined liberation struggles of the twentieth century continue to define political culture.[61] Henning Melber describes the transformation of liberation movements into governments as a process in which the boundaries between party, government and state became blurred.[62] A crucial facet of African–North Korean history is that, unlike most Western actors, North Korea did not treat African liberation movements as non-state actors, but rather as states-in-waiting.

Gilbert Khadiagala argues that the Frontline States illustrate how 'small states have a knack for seizing opportunities to exploit changes in their immediate environments'.[63] This observation extends to non-state actors. African liberation movements navigated treacherous waters while securing recognition and funding. This included crushing internal disputes, lobbying for African support and accessing global funds of solidarity, all the while balancing an ever-increasing group of outside actors that intervened in the struggle, including the Frontline States, the OAU Liberation Committee, the United Nations, AAPSO, the NAM and foreign governments, among others.

In the end, African liberation movements realised that Asian support was inevitable, simply because African funding was insufficient and Western support was limited. The material support from non-African socialist countries 'far outstripped' what the Liberation Committee could offer.[64] Aid from countries such as North Korea was thus a necessary lifeline for African liberation movements, in a time of great need. Kim Il Sung believed that 'the road of national liberation' was the 'road of arduous struggle' and saw it as an 'important principle of foreign policy' to support African decolonisation.[65]

If liberation was the leitmotif of African–North Korean relations, then the Cold War was the background music—sometimes a bit louder, sometimes a bit softer, but ever present. The Cold War was shaping, but not driving, the interactions between the African

SOLIDARITY

liberation movements and their North Korean comrades. They did not see their alliance as a Cold War issue—only the outside world did.

Much of this chapter focused on the predicaments of African liberation movements, as the struggle in Southern Africa is key to understanding why they made a pact with North Korea. In the next chapter, we turn to the Korean peninsula.

2

COMPETITION

KOREAN RIVALRY FOR RECOGNITION

The Korean War was a devastating event in history. Historians have described it as 'quite possibly the most important event since World War II' and 'a defining moment of the Cold War'.[1] The Korean peninsula had been an independent, unified state for 500 years, before it was formally annexed by the Japanese Empire in 1910. The end of World War II liberated Korea from Japanese colonialism, but saw the peninsula immediately divided between Soviet and American occupation zones. The 1945 division was intended as a temporary solution, but in 1948 two separate governments were established in the northern and southern parts of Korea.[2]

In 1950, North Korea launched a military incursion into South Korea to unify the Korean people. Despite an initially highly successful invasion, the North Korean army (supported by the Soviet Union and China) was ultimately repulsed by a United Nations coalition led by the United States. With an estimated 3 million casualties, the conflict was terribly destructive.[3] The Korean War ended, in 1953, in a stalemate that simply reinforced the original division along the 38th parallel, which subsequently became the most heavily militarised border in the world.[4] Formally, both states are still at war and the memories of the violence continue to haunt Korean relations.[5]

Following the war, both Koreas sought international recognition as the legitimate government of the entire peninsula.[6] The UN General Assembly became a key battleground for recognition.[7] South Korea became a permanent observer at the UN General Assembly in 1948, North Korea followed a few years later, in 1973.[8] Yet, the question of who could become a full member was heavily contested. The British Foreign Office summarised this rivalry by observing that 'the North Koreans were to a large extent preoccupied with spitting in the eye of South Korea, and vice versa'.[9]

The African continent turned out to be crucial for UN debates about Korea.[10] At the start of the inter-Korean diplomatic rivalry in the 1950s, South Korea enjoyed a solid position within the UN. But in the early 1960s, the South Korean observer to the UN detected a 'change in atmosphere' in the UN General Assembly, which organised an annual debate about Korea. During the second half of the twentieth century, the UN membership doubled in size and many new members were recently liberated African countries.[11] There were only four African UN members in 1945, but this number had increased to 29 members by 1961: a staggering seven-fold increase.[12] In 1960 alone, 17 African states gained independence—a moment that became known as the 'Year of Africa'. African member states often supported North Korea instead of South Korea, a phenomenon that American diplomats called the 'African shift'.[13] Since the 1960s, Pyongyang had 'embarked on a hard-sell diplomatic campaign in Africa' and made several 'summer tours' or 'good-will missions' to African capitals to drum up support in the UN.[14]

The British Foreign Office noted in 1965 that North Korea's diplomatic gains may allow the country to 'ride into the UN on Africa's back'.[15] A year later, American diplomats railed against 'the confusion in the minds of many newer nations' and instructed all of its diplomatic missions in Africa to educate the locals on the virtues of South Korea.[16] But North Korea received more support from the continent in 1975, at a UN General Assembly vote on

COMPETITION

a resolution that was co-sponsored by several African states.[17] Pyongyang celebrated this as 'a great turning-point in the history of the United Nations'.[18] Jide Owoeye noted that 'Africans began to turn the table on the Korean question'—and the continent became the most important theatre for inter-Korean competition.[19]

This chapter investigates how both Koreas competed for African support in the diplomatic arena. The first part is dedicated to strategy and analyses the diverging foreign policy approaches of Seoul and Pyongyang. The second part focuses on multilateral diplomacy, especially the Afro-Asian solidarity fora that were established in the wake of the Bandung Conference. It argues that the Afro-Asian People's Solidarity Organisation and the NAM were new channels for engagement between African states and the Korean peninsula. The third part is a case study of the 1987 Pyongyang Conference, a story that encapsulates Korean competition for African support.

Korean competition

The political scientist Park Sang-Seek argues that 'it was the Koreans who took the initiative' in the formation of African–Korean relations. Yet, both Koreas adopted different 'diplomatic styles' in their efforts to charm African nations: Pyongyang focused primarily on cultural diplomacy, whereas South Korea depended upon trade diplomacy.[20] This rivalry reached a peak in the 1970s.[21]

In an effort to influence African governments, foreign states were obsessed with tabulating allegiances to determine whether African states were pro-North Korea or pro-South Korea. Endless lists and tables with the results of UN votes would circulate across the African Desks or East Asian Desks of the Ministries of Foreign Affairs in London, Washington D. C. and other places. This approach was adopted by scholars interested in Korean foreign policy. However, their focus on the delivery of Korean foreign policy in Africa overlooks the question of how African states received such policy.[22]

Bean counting does not capture the complex dynamics of diplomatic competition. The fact that, in 1977, South Korea had

39

diplomatic ties with 27 African countries while North Korea had relations with 42 African countries is interesting, but largely useless.[23] Diplomatic relations are not static and seldom reflect a dichotomous reading of politics. Most importantly, bean counting fails to understand why African states operate the way they do. The next section reviews why African states tended to favour North Korea instead of South Korea.

* * *

African countries valued North Korea's apparent independent position in the world. Its membership of the NAM made Pyongyang an appealing partner for African states that wanted to forge relations in spite of Western pressures.[24] In the 1980s, the United States tried to dissuade Mugabe from accepting North Korean military aid, but Zimbabwe dismissed American criticism by arguing that Zimbabwe did not take sides. From their perspective, 'North Korea was a genuine non-aligned country'.[25]

The same trick also worked in Malawi. In the 1960s, South Korean diplomats visited the strongly anti-communist president Hastings Banda and were 'rewarded by unsolicited assurance' that Malawi would be happy to recognise Seoul. The Americans were delighted with this result.[26] In the following years, Malawi 'consistently supported' the American position on the Korean question in the UN and maintained ties with South Africa.[27] However, when the press reported in 1982 that Banda had befriended North Korea, the British Foreign Office assumed that the Malawi News Agency had reported 'the wrong Korea' as the prospect of Malawian–North Korean relations would be 'very unlikely'.[28] The Americans also confidently said that they did not 'anticipate a sharp change from pro-Western foreign policies'.[29] But the British and the Americans were wrong as Malawi indeed recognised North Korea in 1982.[30] Much to South Korea's regret, cordial ties between both states ensued.[31] Banda's government defended its support for Pyongyang through its commitment to a non-aligned foreign policy—after all, North Korea was a non-aligned country.[32]

COMPETITION

Nevertheless, the West often assumes that North Korea was a satellite state of either China or the Soviet Union. Confusingly, a cursory reading of the diplomatic archives reveals that Western countries oftentimes labelled North Korea as both. In Zaire (Democratic Republic of Congo), Americans believed that a North Korean training mission for the exiled Angolan liberation movement FNLA was a vehicle for Chinese aid.[33] In Zimbabwe, South Korean diplomats thought that North Korea acted as a representative of the Soviet Union.[34] In Zambia, the British government branded North Korea 'the principal satellite of China'.[35] In Tanzania, however, British diplomats concluded that 'North Korea is reached via Moscow, not via Peking'.[36] Meanwhile, in Lesotho, their Foreign Office colleagues believed that the North Koreans were 'closer to the Chinese than to the Russians'.[37]

In practice, North Korea skilfully manoeuvred between both communist powers.[38] The Sino-Soviet split of 1961, when ideological differences caused a rift between the two giants, only strengthened North Korea's position in Africa as a safe alternative. Pyongyang executed a successful balancing act between Moscow and Beijing. Its independence from the Communist Bloc was emphasised through its adoption of Juche Thought as its guiding principle (an ideology that stressed self-reliance, further explained in Chapter 4).[39] Juche was 'an attractive concept for countries which are hostile to foreign investment'.[40] North Korea was further seen as distinct from the Communist Bloc because it was a former colony, unlike China or the Soviet Union (arguably, South Korea enjoyed the same status, but in the eyes of North Korea and others Seoul remained occupied by American troops).[41] North Korea's struggle credentials resonated with African countries that shared a similar experience of oppression. North Korea was therefore a welcome alternative for countries that were not keen on a large Chinese or Soviet presence, or wanted to stay out of the Sino-Soviet rivalry altogether.[42]

It is imperative to note that during the inception of African– North Korean relations, Kim Il Sung's country was commonly seen in an entirely different light than it is today. Presently, we view North Korea as a bleak dictatorship, devoid of any freedom

41

or happiness. In the 1960s, however, North Korea carried the promise of anti-imperialist aspirations and outperformed its southern neighbour in terms of economic wealth and political prestige. For African states, non-alignment made North Korea acceptable despite Western opposition, while Juche made North Korea an alternative to communist conflict. It was a peculiar but highly effective strategy to win over African hearts and minds.

* * *

South Korea became equally determined to forge relations with non-aligned African states, in an attempt to 'secure a diplomatic edge over North Korea'.[43] However, several strategic handicaps diminished Seoul's appeal to African states. First, in the early years of its diplomatic campaign in Africa, South Korea adopted what was known as a Hallstein Doctrine.[44] A Hallstein Doctrine (named after Walter Hallstein from the Federal Republic of Germany) envisioned a zero-sum game of diplomatic recognition: one does not maintain relations with a state that recognises your enemy. This rigid approach was not always to the benefit of the ROK. For instance, when North Korea established diplomatic relations with the Republic of Congo in 1965, South Korea was forced to break off its relations with Brazzaville.[45] In the 1970s, Seoul relinquished its Hallstein Doctrine and adopted a more flexible approach.[46]

Second, South Korean diplomacy was dependent upon support from the United States and the United Kingdom. Both countries had a vested interest in helping their ally but were despised by many African governments for their relations with apartheid South Africa and their colonial record.[47] Moreover, the presence of tens of thousands of American troops in Seoul raised African suspicion that South Korea was a 'puppet' of the US, as a Tanzanian diplomat professed to his American colleague in 1966.[48] In contrast, there were no Chinese or Soviet troops stationed permanently in North Korea.

Nevertheless, in a 1967 meeting between the South Korean and American officials, it became evident that 'the ROK needed US advice and assistance in countering North Korean initiatives'.[49] Soon, it became formal American policy 'to strengthen the international standing of the ROK ... and to prevent the DPRK from gaining diplomatic recognition'. The State Department urged its diplomatic posts around Africa 'to use what influence they can to counter these North Korean efforts'.[50] When the US was unable to help South Korea, they turned to the UK. A former British diplomat, who was stationed in Seoul during the Cold War, confirmed to me that the UK provided South Korea with intelligence, and advice and passed on messages to African governments.[51]

Seoul lacked sufficient funding to sway African countries to their side of the aisle and requested Western money to finance their diplomatic efforts in Africa. When South Korea tried to persuade Malawi to establish relations in 1964, the Korean ambassador argued that they would 'need US financial backing' to pay for the technical assistance he wanted to offer to Malawi.[52] In 1966, a South Korean diplomat complained in Washington D. C. that their ambition to invite African leaders to Seoul did not materialise because of 'a lack of funds'.[53] Nevertheless, Seoul recognised that its dependence on US support for its African missions 'could backfire' if it became public knowledge, on account of America's controversial status in the continent.[54]

Even though Western diplomats viewed North Korea as a Sino-Soviet satellite, Pyongyang was much better equipped to execute its own foreign policy when it came to African diplomacy. In fact, this book argues that, during the early Cold War, South Korea was closer to being a satellite state than North Korea.

Third, South Korea's global image was also tainted by its tumultuous domestic affairs. For most of the Cold War, South Korea was governed by a right-wing dictatorship that received widespread criticism for its human rights abuses. While North Korea could hardly be called a democracy, its brand in Africa was noticeably better at that time. Moreover, African countries recognised that South Korea's economy was stagnating, while North Korea developed rapidly—an appealing prospect for many young, postcolonial states.[55]

* * *

How did North Korea make sense of the messy, complicated situation in Southern Africa? Kim Il Sung publicly stated that he had 'been deeply concerned about ... Southern Africa for a long time', arguing that 'the situation is as tense as in our country'.[56] A former North Korean diplomat who worked closely with Kim counselled me on Pyongyang's Africa strategy. He explained that the North Korean Ministry of Foreign Affairs conducted extensive research on all liberation movements in Africa: screening, categorising and ranking them. The Ministry even had a special team dedicated to OAU affairs. The results were presented to Kim, who ultimately decided which movement to support. His personal ties to African leaders were an important dimension of North Korea's Africa policy. Kim saw these relationships through a transactional lens: if he helped get these leaders into power, they should help him with his plan to unify the Korean peninsula.[57]

Indeed, virtually all African anticolonial leaders who rose to power during the Cold War touted pro-North Korea lines in public fora. In a speech at the UN, Mozambique's president Machel called for the withdrawal of American forces from South Korea.[58] On several other public occasions, Machel supported reunification of the Korean peninsula 'on the basis of the various initiatives of the DPRK'.[59] At a conference of the NAM, Zambia's president, Kaunda, announced that 'Zambia stands for reunification of Korea' and demanded the 'total and unconditional withdrawal' of American troops from Seoul.[60] Angolan president dos Santos similarly 'expressed the Angolan's people solidarity' with North Korea's proposal to reunify Korea in public speeches.[61] Kim Il Sung's policies were also endorsed by the leaders of Botswana, Namibia, Tanzania and Zimbabwe, to name but a few.

The odd one out is South Africa. The ANC was the oldest and best-known liberation movement of the region; it faced the longest struggle of them all, but it seemed to have the fewest interactions with North Korea. Signs of a mutual friendship were revealed by Jacob Zuma, the ANC's former intelligence chief and president of South Africa. In a meeting in 2005 with the North Korean prime minister Yang Hyong Sop (Yang Hyŏngsŏp), Zuma 'highlighted the support the ANC had received during the anti-apartheid struggle'.

COMPETITION

The political scientist Don Geldenhuys suggests that the ANC therefore 'had political debts to repay'.[62] In the ANC archives in Cape Town, I found several cases of correspondence between North Korean diplomats and the ANC.[63] North Korea evidently expressed solidarity with the South African struggle.[64]

However, when I asked Ronnie Kasrils, the former intelligence chief of Umkhonto we Sizwe (MK; the ANC's armed wing) about ties to Pyongyang he curtly replied that at least MK 'never had any … relationship or assistance from North Korea'.[65] During my research in Seoul, an exiled North Korean diplomat told me that North Korean support for the ANC was mainly financial, material and mostly political—but not military. North Korean assistance to the ANC was primarily channelled through SWAPO and ZANU, with whom the ANC cooperated.[66] I can only speculate about the reasons why their relations with the ANC appear to have been weaker than elsewhere: perhaps the strong influence of the SACP on the ANC resulted in less interest in North Korean aid.[67]

Pragmatism was the commanding rationale behind North Korea's Africa strategy. Kim Il Sung was prepared to withdraw his support for certain liberation movements and endorse their rivals if he thought that he was backing a losing team.[68] The pragmatic motives behind North Korean–African ties are demonstrated in the cases of Angola and Zimbabwe.

North Korea had been interested in the Angolan liberation struggle since the 1960s and a number of Angolan nationals from different organisations were invited to Pyongyang.[69] Kim first decided to provide financial and military support to the FNLA, and, in 1971, a group of North Korean instructors provided military training for FNLA cadets in Congo.[70] Kinshasa served as the transit place for FNLA members who were en route to Pyongyang for advanced military training. However, when the United States began supporting the FNLA and UNITA, while the MPLA was gaining the upper hand, North Korea switched its allegiance to the latter. In 1975, North Korea established formal relations with the MPLA.[71]

In the Zimbabwean case, where ZAPU and ZANU competed for recognition, North Korea was unsure which group had a stronghold and adopted an ambivalent stance.[72] North Korea initially financed and trained ZAPU,[73] but ultimately decided to throw its weight behind ZANU.[74] The same occurred in other parts of Africa, for example in Congo or Uganda.[75] North Korea was not the only actor to do so: SWAPO, for instance, also switched its support from UNITA to the MPLA.[76] Pragmatism reigned throughout Southern Africa.

Afro-Asian solidarity

The division of the Korean peninsula coincided with the emergence of a new age of internationalism, which was turbocharged by the emergence of postcolonial states from dwindling empires. The formation of Afro-Asian political networks provided both Koreas with diplomatic opportunities beyond the realm of Western and Eastern power politics.[77]

Neither of the Koreas were present at the 1955 Afro-Asian Conference in Bandung (Indonesia), presumably because they were still reeling from the carnage of the Korean War, but they were quick to catch up. In the years following Bandung, the Afro-Asian People's Solidarity Organisation and the NAM were established as multilateral fora where Afro-Asian networks could be further developed. In 1965, Kim Il Sung travelled to Indonesia for the tenth anniversary of the Bandung Conference.[78] According to Andrei Lankov, this was the first time Kim publicly launched Juche as 'a basic ideological principle of North Korean politics'.[79]

With a stalemate in UN debates about the future of the Korean peninsula, Korean competition moved to these alternative international organisations. African participation in AAPSO and NAM promised opportunities for strengthening ties with anticolonial movements and getting the message out on Korean reunification. North Korea was manifestly much more successful in this regard than South Korea.

* * *

COMPETITION

Founded in 1958, in Cairo (Egypt), the Afro-Asian People's Solidarity Organisation was designed as a 'broadening and deepening of the "Bandung Spirit"'. The organisation was dedicated to non-aligned solidarity and decolonisation: Kaunda once said that 'the history of AAPSO is the history of liberation in Asia and Africa'.[80] The Permanent Secretariat included representatives of Egypt, India, Algeria, Russia and China, while its membership—consisting of political parties, liberation movements and solidarity committees—covered most of Africa and Asia.[81] North Korea managed to become a member; South Korea did not.

North Korea turned its participation in AAPSO into a major foreign policy success. As most African liberation movements were members or participated in AAPSO events, the organisation became a platform for North Korea to make meaningful connections to African delegates.[82] AAPSO conferences, which were attended by North Korean delegates, were regularly hosted by African countries, and there is a direct link between these meetings and North Korea's Africa strategy.[83] Upon visiting the AAPSO conference held in Moshi, Tanzania, in 1963, North Korean diplomats travelled to Dar es Salaam to request permission to establish a diplomatic mission.[84] Already in the 1960s, North Korea's AAPSO committee supported anticolonial events of liberation movements in Angola and Zimbabwe.[85] When Pyongyang hosted an AAPSO conference on peace and security issues in the Asia-Pacific Region in 1987,[86] the conference was addressed by Zimbabwe's President Mugabe, who applauded North Korea's anti-American plans.[87]

In its charm offensive aimed at African delegates, North Korea was helped by the fact that it received full backing from the AAPSO Permanent Secretariat. Official statements from the organisation heralded 'the amazing development in every field of North Korean life' and denounced 'the puppet government of South Korea'.[88] These statements found their way to African liberation movements and governments.[89] Moreover, the AAPSO regularly organised anti-South Korea events, such as the 'Day of Common Struggle for the Withdrawal of U. S. Forces from South Korea', or the 'Week of Common Struggle for the Withdrawal of American Aggressive

Forces from South Korea', or the 'Month of Joint Struggle for the Withdrawal of the U. S. Imperialist Aggressive Troops from South Korea'.[90] The presidium demanded that 'the US and ROK accept the peaceful proposals of the DPRK', which included the 'withdrawal of US troops'.[91] The removal of American forces from Seoul would have been a major foreign policy win for North Korea.

On the thirtieth anniversary of the North Korean state, the AAPSO's secretary-general, Abdel Rahman El-Sharkawi, sent a telegram to Kim, celebrating 'his brilliant achievements' so far. 'In the past Korea was a backward colonial society', wrote El-Sharkawi, 'but now it has become a dignified, independent and sovereign country in the international arena'. The secretary-general continued by saying that Kim 'brought the status of the Korean people to a high standard by adopting the immortal Juche idea'.[92] In the ears of African delegates, such praise was a clear endorsement of North Korea over South Korea.

Meanwhile, South Korea hit a brick wall in the arena of Afro-Asian diplomacy. The South Korean Ministry of Foreign Affairs used its network of African embassies to monitor North Korea's successes in the AAPSO. Diplomats in Africa were tasked with investigating the composition of North Korean delegations and obtaining draft resolutions and news reports.[93] Nevertheless, the battle for the AAPSO was a lost cause for Seoul—the presidium publicly backed Kim Il Sung's proposals for reunification of the Korean peninsula.[94]

* * *

The NAM offered another compelling opportunity for North Korea to influence the narrative on Korean affairs. Established in 1961, the NAM was 'arguably the most important institution for the Global South during the Cold War' and was envisaged as a practical outcome of the Bandung Conference.[95] Both Koreas lobbied the NAM for membership, but only North Korea was accepted, joining the organisation in 1975. South Korea's bid was denied because of the continued presence of American soldiers in Seoul.[96]

COMPETITION

Again, North Korea benefited from a platform where it could connect with African states. Newly independent African countries often proclaimed themselves as proud members of the NAM. Yet, non-alignment was 'not a matter of neutrality', said Tanzania's President Nyerere at a NAM event in 1970: 'By no-alignment we are saying to the Big Powers that we also belong on this planet. We are asserting the right of small nations to determine their own policies'.[97]

According to Nate Kerkhoff, North Korea envisioned two goals for its membership to the NAM: the hosting of summits where it could boost Kim Il Sung's status as a postcolonial leader, and the rallying of support of NAM members in the UN General Assembly. Similar to the AAPSO, Kim aimed to persuade the NAM leadership to adopt an anti-South Korea agenda. Initially, North Korea was quite successful in this regard and, in the 1970s, the NAM churned out strongly worded pro-DPRK resolutions.[98] The support of African allies was indispensable. For instance, President Kaunda of Zambia, who sang at Kim's birthday party, used a keynote speech at a 1976 NAM conference to call for the withdrawal of American troops from South Korea.[99] Machel did the same at a NAM conference in 1986, concluding that 'Mozambique agrees with the proposals of the DPRK' regarding reunification.[100]

An additional benefit of the NAM was that North Korea and African states could try out cooperation in different policy areas, thus strengthening their mutual trust. In the 1980s, as part of the NAM's Action Program for Economic Cooperation, North Korea coordinated the domain of scientific and technological development together with Zaire, and coordinated the domain of fisheries together with Mauritania.[101]

North Korea hosted several policy-specific summits for the NAM to which African countries were invited and which resulted in productive bilateral spin-offs. For instance, when a Tanzanian minister visited Pyongyang for a five-day NAM symposium on food and agriculture, he also signed a bilateral protocol for technical assistance between Tanzania and the DPRK.[102] For Tanzania, North Korea's participation in the NAM was a key argument to support North Korea's reunification proposals and to hold off diplomatic

COMRADES BEYOND THE COLD WAR

ties with South Korea. British diplomats concluded that the NAM connection was 'a theme well exploited' by the North Korean embassy in Dar es Salaam.[103]

Nevertheless, as South Korea ramped up its efforts via economic diplomacy, North Korea slowly 'lost control of the narrative on the Korean question' in the NAM.[104] From the end of the 1970s onwards, Seoul used its developing economy to lobby NAM members and halt Kim Il Sung's diplomatic progress. Kerkhoff thus concludes that North Korea's relevance within the NAM 'lasted only for a few short years'.[105] Ultimately, North Korea failed to bend the NAM to its will.[106] Even so, North Korea's initial success in the first years of the NAM allowed it to build up valuable political capital with African members.

The Pyongyang Conference

In 1987, the NAM met in Pyongyang to discuss the future of South–South cooperation. This Extraordinary Ministerial Conference ran for four days and became known as the Pyongyang Conference.[107] It was a major diplomatic victory for Kim Il Sung as it cast North Korea as a leading voice in the struggle to create a new world. In his opening speech, Kim gracefully expressed his 'deep gratitude' for Zimbabwe's help in organising the conference.[108]

The Pyongyang Conference had a strong African connection and is a revealing case study of how African and North Korean political elites engaged in worldmaking. Getachew describes worldmaking as 'a project of reordering the world', which aimed to 'create a domination-free and egalitarian international order'. Anticolonial nationalism, as professed by Africans and North Koreans alike, was an ideal that went beyond political self-determination: it demanded the reinvention of the global order.[109] African–North Korean cooperation was thus not only useful in the quest to obtain independence, but continued into the postcolonial era.

The decision to organise the NAM conference on South–South cooperation in Pyongyang was made a year earlier in Zimbabwe, at the 8th Non-Aligned Summit in Harare.[110] In fact, the Harare

50

COMPETITION

summit was the very first time that the NAM adopted the term 'South–South cooperation' into a final declaration.[111]

Any NAM summit was a site of contestation between the two Koreas. In preparation to push its anti-ROK agenda in Zimbabwe, North Korea extensively courted its African allies in advance. Kim Il Sung reportedly donated $500,000 to Zimbabwe to support the summit preparations.[112] A range of high-level African political leaders were invited to Pyongyang, in the hope that they would support North Korea at the Harare summit. Visitors included the president of Tanzania, a Mali government delegation and Robert Mugabe, the leader of Zimbabwe.[113]

In 1986, the North Koreans travelled to the NAM summit in Harare with three objectives: obtaining support to co-host the 1988 Olympics with South Korea, proposing Pyongyang as the location for the next foreign ministers meeting and persuading the summit to adopt anti-ROK proposals in the final declaration. Even though South Korea was not present at the summit—it was not a member, after all—it worked with moderate countries within the NAM to counter these demands.[114]

North Korea deemed the first objective (co-hosting the Olympics with Seoul) the most important.[115] To this end, North Korea pushed the NAM delegates in Harare to endorse a report from a NAM Sports Ministers meeting held earlier in Pyongyang, which recommended exactly this decision. The Zimbabwean hosts had drafted a final declaration urging the implementation of this recommendation, but resistance from Egypt (a ROK ally[116]) ultimately toned down the language. The second objective (hosting the next NAM summit) was equally opposed by South Korean allies, and the NAM chose Nicosia (Cyprus) as the next location. However, North Korea was compensated through the offer to organise a conference on South–South cooperation the next year. The third objective (including anti-South Korea clauses in the final summit declaration) was only mildly successful.[117]

Some historians allege that the outcome of the Harare summit can be interpreted as a prime example of North Korea's 'incompetence in diplomacy'.[118] After all, most of its objectives were not met, and South Korea was evidently satisfied with the proceedings.[119] However, even though the Pyongyang Conference was not the desired summit that North Korea set out to host, it was another opportunity to realise Kim's vision of Pyongyang as the centre of the non-aligned world.[120] It gave Kim Il Sung a stage to highlight his vision on cooperation in the Global South, at a conference organised around the concept of self-reliance, a theme that was entirely on-brand with North Korea's Juche ideology. Moreover, it was another opportunity to engage with African allies. A consolation prize is still a prize.

Numerous African delegates at the Pyongyang Conference used this platform as a call for help. Kim's comrade Mugabe delivered a powerful statement in which he warned the audience that the situation in Southern Africa was deteriorating. Another speech was provided by Andimba Toivo ya Toivo, the secretary-general of SWAPO, who appealed to the Ministers of the NAM to 'do everything in their power to increase political, diplomatic and material assistance to the national liberation movements'. The United Nations Council for Namibia, represented by the Zambian Peter Zuze, also lobbied for this cause.[121]

The outcome of the Pyongyang Conference, the 'Pyongyang Declaration and Plan of Action on South-South Co-operation', was a 22-page blueprint for a new international economic order.[122] The blueprint was centred around the idea of 'self-reliance', a popular term at the time in which we can hear echoes of North Korea's Juche Thought. Among other things, the Declaration strongly condemned the apartheid regime in South Africa and repeatedly affirmed its support for SWAPO and the ANC.[123]

Conclusion

When a delegation of the Zimbabwean parliament visited Kim Il Sung in 1987, Kim emphasised the mutual friendship of their peoples, even though both nations were 'far from each other geographically'.[124] How is it possible that African freedom fighters and North Korean ideologues forged such close bonds, despite their obvious differences and the enormous geographical distance between them?

COMPETITION

Ultimately, it was diplomatic competition for UN recognition that brought the inter-Korean rivalry to Africa. The *Zeitgeist* mattered, as the revolutionary ferment in Africa, the rise of Afro-Asian solidarity and non-aligned politics benefited Pyongyang. North Korea was no stranger to African liberation movements through international platforms such as AAPSO and NAM. African guerrilla fighters learned about the ins and outs of the Korean peninsula by virtue of extensive lobbying efforts from Pyongyang and Seoul. AAPSO bulletins and NAM conferences further defined the narrative on the Korean question—one that ostentatiously favoured North Korea.

As a result, the tensions of the Korean peninsula trickled down to Southern Africa and permeated the discourse of the liberation struggles that turned the politics in this region around. SWAPO declared its support for North Korea through resolutions at a party conference in exile.[125] FRELIMO and MPLA did the same at their own party conferences.[126] Korean reunification was debated in the Zambian parliament dominated by UNIP.[127] Bulletins from UNITA and MPLA discussed the Pueblo incident of 1968, when North Korea captured an American navy ship.[128] The magazine of MPLA's army, *Angola in Arms*, proudly mentioned that the *Pyongyang Times* and *Corée Populaire* carried articles about the Angolan struggle.[129] North Korea's messages of support were published in the magazine of ZAPU-PF.[130] ZANU published photos of the North Korean army in its exile bulletins.[131]

Yet, it would go too far to say that the odds were always stacked in North Korea's favour. In fact, the changing fortunes of both Koreas is a remarkable feature of their rivalry during the twentieth century. At the start, shortly after the Korean War, South Korea had everything going for it: support from the United Nations, aid from the United States and recognition from approximately 50 'Free World' countries.[132] North Korea was able to fight its way back from a highly disadvantaged position, despite charges of 'clumsy and ill-conceived' diplomacy from American diplomats.[133] The key to Pyongyang's success was Africa.

If we think of inter-Korean competition as a two-horse race, the outcome was never certain.[134] The 1970s and 1980s were the

53

high point of North Korea's standing in Africa. But Kim Il Sung operated as a one-trick pony who constantly battered on about his desire for reunification. It worked until it did not. South Korea, after it changed its tactics from a Hallstein Doctrine to a more flexible approach, offered African countries attractive commercial opportunities and skilfully countered North Korea's charm offensive.

The nature of inter-Korean competition changed soon thereafter. In 1991, both Koreas were simultaneously admitted to the United Nations as full members of the UN General Assembly— an achievement that set Korea apart from other divided countries that competed for international recognition during the Cold War, such as the two Chinas, the two Germanies, the two Vietnams and the two Yemens. While the UN continues to be important for shaping inter-Korean rivalry, for example through the issuing of sanctions against North Korea, the AAPSO and NAM have lost their relevancy in global politics—even though these organisations still exist.

Much of this chapter focused on foreign policy in relation to multilateral fora. Nevertheless, it was ultimately bilateral statecraft that proved to be decisive for the future of the African–North Korean friendship. The following chapters therefore illuminate the three tools that brought Africans and North Koreans closer together—diplomatic travel, doctrine and development aid.

3

DIPLOMACY

AFRICAN PRESIDENTS IN PYONGYANG

Contemporary visitors to North Korea are usually taken on a guided tour to admire the highlights of Pyongyang. Government minders will gently escort them to the Kim Il Sung Square, the Victorious Fatherland Liberation War Museum, the Kumsusan Palace of the Sun and more mundane destinations, such as the Pyongyang Metro. A standard item on any itinerary is a visit to the International Friendship Exhibition House, a massive structure built within Mount Myohyang.[1] The enormous exhibition spreads across 150 rooms and contains over 40,000 gifts from over 170 countries and organisations that were, at one time, presented to the Kim family.[2]

A significant part of the International Friendship Exhibition House is dedicated to Africa.[3] A wooden elephant from Zimbabwe, ivory carvings from Angola, a crystal owl from Gabon, a silver ostrich from Ethiopia, a table lamp made from a stuffed porcupine fish from Mauritius, spears from Burundi, a ceramic vase decorated with gemstones from Nigeria and much, much more.[4] These unique items were gifted by African leaders upon visiting Pyongyang and are tangible reminders of a key part of African–North Korean diplomacy during the Cold War. Julius Nyerere, the Tanzanian leader, presented Kim Il Sung with ivory walking sticks.[5] Robert Mugabe, the leader of Zimbabwe, presented Kim with a stuffed buck.[6]

As the previous chapter emphasised, the two Koreas developed different strategies towards Africa. The scholar Park Sang-Seek observed in 1978 that North Korea practised an 'invitation diplomacy' with a focus on cultural engagements, whereas South Korea utilised a 'visitation diplomacy' centred on trade.[7] When the president of the Seychelles, Albert-France René, decided that his first official trip abroad would be to North Korea, he was asked by the press why he would travel to a communist country. 'Because they invited me', he responded curtly. North Korea subsequently became a 'loyal ally and important aid donor' to René's country. Ten years later, the Seychelles would be one of a mere handful of countries in the world to boycott the Olympic Games in South Korea.[8]

'African visitors kept on pouring into Pyongyang', wrote the scholar Byung Chul Koh in 1969. 'North Korea's well-calculated campaign to woo the Third World has been both successful and productive'.[9] During the Cold War, a few hundred to a thousand foreign delegations visited Pyongyang every year. North Korean watchers were astounded by the 'extraordinarily high level of effort and resources' that Kim Il Sung spent on diplomacy.[10] North Korea targeted a wide range of leading figures in Africa and went a long way to deliver personal invitations: when North Korean diplomats visited Kinshasa in 1973 and realised that Mobutu Sese Seko was on holiday in Belgium, they travelled all the way to his holiday address to disturb the president for a mere two-hour audience. Mobutu subsequently accepted their invitation to come to Pyongyang.[11]

How did invitation diplomacy work in practice? Park's quantitative approach focused on tabulating UN General Assembly votes and glossed over the question of what exactly invitation diplomacy entailed.

Benefiting from novel archival sources and knowledge of the events that occurred after 1978, this chapter offers the first comprehensive assessment of North Korea's invitation diplomacy

DIPLOMACY

in the context of Southern Africa. Who was invited to Pyongyang, and why? What did these visits look like and what were their lasting effects? This chapter examines the significance of Pyongyang as a meeting space and Kim Il Sung's personal travel policy. At the heart of this chapter are five case studies of African presidents in Pyongyang. The conclusion reflects upon the question of what both sides gained from the invitation diplomacy and offers three additional remarks.

Welcome to Pyongyang

The capital city was the pride of North Korea, a socialist paradise on earth, a city like no other. This illustrious status was a result of the devastating Korean War (1950–53), when the American army bombed Pyongyang to utter ruin. During North Korea's post-war development, its urban planners had a *tabula rasa* to create a new city appropriate for a people destined for socialist greatness. The traumatic experience of the war allowed the DPRK to create a version of socialist realism that was distinctly different from that of China or the Soviet Union.[12]

Personal invitations to Pyongyang were a powerful tool in the goodwill campaign that North Korea utilised to impress African countries. In the first two decades after the Korean War, North Korea's economy performed better than South Korea. Pyongyang showcased the impressive post-war reconstruction and Juche ideals of the North Korean regime, which had risen from the ashes of war like a socialist phoenix. The scholar Cheehyung Harrison Kim described Pyongyang's rebuilding as an 'extraordinary undertaking', with striking utopian and utilitarian features.[13] For the sake of the argument, picture Pyongyang in the 1970s: the splendour of its monuments, the strong militarisation, the cosmopolitan feel from international visitors, the energy of the place. Pyongyang, its architecture and people, harboured a promise to the oppressed or recently liberated peoples across the globe. This experience greatly added to the anti-imperialist credentials of North Korea.

57

Over the years, Pyongyang became a hub of the non-aligned world.[14] To this end, North Korea hosted several multilateral summits that were often attended by African delegations. The Pyongyang Conference of 1987, as discussed in the previous chapter, was not the only NAM event organised by North Korea. The DPRK also hosted more specialised events such as the 2nd Meeting of the Non-Aligned Sports Ministers in Pyongyang, in 1986, and the NAM Film Festival, in 1987.[15] The latter event was opened by the Zimbabwean Nathan Shamuyarira, a high-ranking ZANU official.[16]

North Korea was able to organise large-scale conventions. The 1983 'World Conference of Journalists against Imperialism and for Friendship and Peace' conference was a five-day event in Pyongyang attended by nearly 3,000 delegates (including members of SWAPO, the Namibian liberation movement).[17] In 1989, Pyongyang hosted the 13th World Festival of Youth and Students, a seven-day gathering of 15,000 delegates from 180 countries.[18] A Swedish colonel who attended the events entrusted to a British diplomat that it 'was every bit as impressive in terms of numbers, organisation and facilities as the Seoul Olympics last year'. Mugabe was one of the honoured guests who addressed the festival.[19] Nyerere was another high-profile visitor.[20] Among the visiting students were exiled South Africans from the Solomon Mahlangu Freedom College, an ANC school in Tanzania.[21]

North Korea's skill in organising mass events was best visible in domestic celebrations. A prime example is the annual Day of the Sun (15 April), Kim Il Sung's birthday, which was regularly attended by African dignitaries.[22] Military parades, spectacular mass gymnastics and events such as the Arirang Mass Games and the April Spring Friendship Art Festival were designed to reaffirm the power of the North Korean state and impress both domestic and international audiences.[23]

Another reason why invitations to Pyongyang were important was because Kim Il Sung seldom left North Korea. Kim was presented as the architect of the new Korea, a man who physically and ideologically embodied the promise of postcolonial development that attracted visitors from all over Africa. Yet, he only

DIPLOMACY

travelled to the continent once. In 1975, Kim Il Sung undertook a 'world tour' that covered a few countries in Europe and Africa. Romania, Bulgaria and Yugoslavia were honoured with a visit, as well as Algeria and Mauritania.[24] Both African countries were one-party states with charismatic authoritarian and socialist leaders, not unlike North Korea. Furthermore, both were among the first non-communist nations to establish relations with Pyongyang.[25]

A defected diplomat of the North Korean Ministry of Foreign Affairs explained to me that the tour destinations were selected on the basis of comfort and security. The North Korean government was concerned about Kim's health and therefore favoured countries with an amenable climate and predictable political situation. At the time, Southern Africa was embroiled in numerous low-intensity guerrilla wars. Despite Kim's desire to visit sub-Saharan Africa, North Africa was deemed a better option.[26]

A propaganda video that was aired on North Korean television shows Kim being welcomed in Algeria by Chairman Houari Boumédiène and a roaring crowd of allegedly 600,000 citizens. Kim was received by a military guard at the airport and driven through Algiers by motorcade, while rows of spectators cheered him on. He received an honorary doctorate from the University of Algiers and honorary citizenship from the city of Algiers.[27] In his acceptance speech, Kim said that 'their exchange of valuable experience and mutual support' was important for 'strengthening the anti-imperialist revolutionary forces'.[28]

Mauritania was not in the original tour itinerary. The country was added last-minute at the request of the Mauritanian government, which was very keen to host Kim.[29] His visit was no less of a spectacle. Banners in French, Arabic and Korean welcomed 'Comrade Kim Il Sung, the Great Leader'. Kim was driven through the streets of Nouakchott in an open car, and the propaganda video shows thousands of people cheering and dancing. President Moktar Ould Daddah bestowed the 'Supreme National Declaration of the Grand State Order of Merit' on Kim, in recognition of his 'tremendous services to the building of an independent state' in Mauritania.[30]

59

In the 1980s, the British Foreign Office recorded rumours of a follow-up visit to Africa.[31] Indeed, the former North Korean diplomat confirmed that, in 1988, Kim planned to visit his long-time friend and ally Robert Mugabe in Zimbabwe. This plan went into the preparation phase but Kim's health eventually prevented him from following through. Kim Jong Il, his son and successor, only visited two countries in his tenure as leader (China and Russia) because he did not feel secure.[32] This meant, in general terms, that if African leaders wanted to meet the Kim family, they needed to book a flight to Pyongyang.

Case studies

While the multilateral conferences in Pyongyang were special occasions that caught the public eye, the more common bilateral visits of African leaders were arguably better suited to fostering strong African–North Korean relations. The entire first generation of Southern African presidents visited Pyongyang and maintained friendly, personal ties to the Kim regime throughout their tenure in government.

Across the region, interactions with North Korea share a number of similar characteristics. Importantly, North Korea received African delegations with the highest honours. Liberation movements in particular were welcomed as statesmen in waiting, at a time when they were regarded with suspicion by large parts of the Western world.[33] Moreover, bilateral ties were personal ties. Kim Il Sung was seen as a charismatic leader who fostered strong personal relations to African leaders. Finally, there appears to be a clear return on investment. Invitation diplomacy was the basis of African–North Korean interactions and, as this book shows, ultimately resulted in stronger diplomatic relations, military cooperation and the sale of North Korean monuments.

A focus on African visits to Pyongyang allows us to draw open the curtains of Cold War era statecraft and to showcase the choreography of Afro-Asian diplomacy, the effects of which still linger on today. 'Kim had the citizenry of the North line the streets of Pyongyang monthly to welcome some African chief or

DIPLOMACY

illustrious president of an obscure island they had never heard of', wrote his biographer Dae-Sook Suh.[34] To an important extent, these visits were performances, in which Kim and African heads of state were the protagonists.

Just as for contemporary tourists today, the bilateral visits from African elites followed a fixed routine. Foreign delegations participated in a photo opportunity with their Korean hosts at the Kumsusan Palace of the Sun, laid a wreath at the Revolutionary Martyrs' Cemetery and visited other heritage sites. Occasionally, field visits to schools and factories were part of the programme. The traditional highlight of any journey was a lavish banquet, with speeches, gifts and other ceremonial fuss.

The role of North Korean heritage in these visits deserves a special mention. Heonik Kwon and Byung-Ho Chung assert that these constructions were more than national monuments—they articulated global prestige.[35] For Kim Il Sung's birthday party in 1982 (where Kaunda sang *Tiyende Pamodzi*) 'two of the most iconic North Korean monuments' were unveiled, which coincidentally symbolise North Korea's appeal for African revolutionaries.[36] The Juche Tower (claimed to be the tallest stone monument in the world) represented North Korea's diplomatic strength, an anti-imperialist worldview. The Arc of Triumph (claimed to be larger than the victory gate in Paris) represented North Korea's military strength, as evidenced in the successful resistance against Japanese colonialism. Together, they displayed 'the global fame of the country's founding revolutionary leader', Kim Il Sung.[37] African leaders visited and admired these monuments. As the final part of this book will show, they later hired North Korean art studios to replicate similar structures at home.

By way of analysing the choreography of Afro-Asian diplomacy, the sections below present five historical vignettes of first-generation African leaders to North Korea: Kenneth Kaunda (president of Zambia), Seretse Khama (president of Botswana), Samora Machel (president of Mozambique), Robert Mugabe (president of Zimbabwe) and Sam Nujoma (president of Namibia). This selection covers the diversity of Southern Africa, but could have included virtually every first-generation president in the

61

region. Each case study briefly lifts the veil on how their visits elapsed and what this meant for the development of bilateral ties between their own country and the DPRK.

* * *

The introduction to this book began with Kenneth Kaunda's attendance at Kim Il Sung's birthday party in 1982. In addition to his eloquent rendition of *Tiyende Pamodzi*, his liberation song, Kaunda gifted Kim a bronze map of Zambia, supported by two elephant tusks. This is one of the many African gifts that ended up in the International Friendship Exhibition House.[38] Kim also received a Zambian honorary medal.[39] Kaunda was accompanied by his wife, Betty Kaunda, and she was so impressed with the hospitality of the North Koreans that she decided to stay on for an extra week and was flown back to Lusaka by special plane.[40]

Kaunda visited Pyongyang numerous times throughout the Cold War, including twice in 1980 and in 1987.[41] The British Foreign Office noted that 'Kaunda appears to be an admirer of the North Korean system'. While Zambia became disillusioned with the Soviet Union and the German Democratic Republic, they were 'genuinely impressed' with North Korea, as Kaunda's philosophy of Zambian humanism 'may after all be compatible on the North Korean model'. This ideological attraction resulted in cultural exchanges of radio and television material, the outsourcing of ten North Korean instructors for paramilitary training and agricultural assistance.[42]

* * *

Botswana is in some ways an outlier in Southern Africa. Although it was a founding member of the Frontline States, it did not allow African liberation movements to use its territory as a launch base for military excursions. Botswana was a strong United States ally and has been described as 'mainland Africa's most notable outlier' in terms of democratic governance and economic growth.[43] Nevertheless, Gaborone followed regional trends with regard to its ties to North Korea.

DIPLOMACY

Seretse Khama, the first president of Botswana, undertook a four-day visit to North Korea in 1976, much to the dismay of the United States.[44] He was accompanied by a large entourage, which included his wife, Lady Ruth Khama, and two future presidents: Festus Mogae (president between 1998 and 2008) and Khama's son, Ian Khama (president between 2008 and 2018).[45]

The Batswana delegation was picked up by a private Korean jet from Beijing. Upon arrival, the streets of Pyongyang were lined with the national flags of both countries and people holding portraits of Kim and Khama. The visitors were impressed by a mass performance of school children in the national stadium of Pyongyang, as they sang a Setswana song (*Dintlenyane tsa Botswana*, or 'The Beauty of Botswana').[46]

Khama, in turn, addressed a mass rally, where he publicly praised North Korean Juche Thought, which he believed to be compatible with indigenous Batswana development philosophy. Photos of the visit show Khama dancing, carefree, alongside a Korean music group during a visit to a cooperative farm.[47] When Khama returned home, he reflected in a private letter to Kim on the impressive sights he had witnessed. 'Not only have you rebuilt your cities out of the rubbles ... but you have also turned the whole country-side into an oasis'. The Korean people, Khama concluded, 'have gone a long way in proving what a determined nation can do to improve its lot'.[48]

Despite the friendly atmosphere, Khama's visit was a bit of a culture shock for both parties. Some Batswana regarded the North Koreans as 'stiff and humourless'. The North Koreans, on the other hand, were surprised by the 'free and easy relations' among their guests, especially when a Korean interpreter visited the small basement room of the Batswana guest house in Pyongyang. When the interpreter entered the room, the Batswana were playing a game of billiards, and he was 'horrified when Khama was allowed to lose the game to his juniors'.[49] This was unthinkable in North Korea.

Cultural differences notwithstanding, the invitation diplomacy had its intended effect. During the 1970s, Botswana sided with North Korea in the United Nations.[50] In the next decade, North

Korea trained Batswana police officers in unarmed combat and gifted military weapons to the young nation.[51] In 2005, a North Korean art studio constructed the Three Dikgosi Monument in the capital city of Gaborone. The monument is a bronze sculpture of three historical figures that are considered the 'Founders of the Nation', including Khama's grandfather, Khama III. The monument was inaugurated by Festus Mogae, who accompanied Seretse Khama to Pyongyang all those years ago.[52]

* * *

Samora Machel, the charismatic leader of FRELIMO, visited North Korea in 1971, four years before Mozambique became independent. According to his biographer, Iain Christie, this visit 'was very important in establishing lasting links of solidarity between FRELIMO and the North Korean leadership'.[53] In 1973, Machel thanked North Korea for 'performing their internationalist duty towards us in an exemplary manner'. He stressed that 'the political, moral, diplomatic and material support they give us is constantly increasing'.[54]

Kim Il Sung supported Machel's liberation movement during the Mozambican struggle for independence and provided, among other things, medical aid.[55] FRELIMO officials had been travelling to Pyongyang since 1964.[56] Mozambican guerrillas were sent to North Korea for military training as early as 1968, to learn 'new tactics and strategies' in warfare.[57] Machel visited Pyongyang again in his capacity as the first president of Mozambique, directly after his country obtained independence in 1975. During a banquet in Pyongyang, he endorsed Kim Il Sung's plan for the reunification of the Korean peninsula.[58] Kim replied by stating that he was indebted to Machel and other African revolutionaries and that he intended 'to repay this debt at some time in the future'.[59]

When Machel visited again in 1978, he brought along his wife Graça Machel.[60] Thousands of spectators cheered on the motorcade that brought them to the heart of Pyongyang. They received the most extensive tour: the inspection of a military guard, visits to factories and farms and impressive displays of mass

DIPLOMACY

gymnastics and traditional dances.[61] Samora, standing on a balcony, addressed a crowd of hundreds of thousands of people holding gigantic portraits of him and Kim (though some banners contained slogans in Spanish, rather than Portuguese). The two leaders were photographed holding hands, both smiling warmly.[62]

Machel would continue to visit North Korea fairly regularly during his tenure as president, including in 1982, 1984 and July 1986—up until his untimely death in a plane crash on South African soil, in October 1986 (widely thought to be orchestrated by the apartheid regime).[63] Cooperation between Mozambique and North Korea continued without him. Throughout the 1980s, high-ranking Mozambicans continued to travel to Pyongyang, including the president's special adviser and a number of army officers for 'special military training'.[64] As Chapter 10 describes in more detail, North Korea trained elite Mozambican forces in Maputo and provided weapons and repair services for tanks until recently.[65]

The friendship between Kim and Machel remains an important symbol of this bilateral relationship. One of the central streets in Maputo, Mozambique's capital city, is named after Kim Il Sung. It is a short walk from a bronze statue of Machel, which was erected by a North Korean art studio in 2011.

* * *

Robert Mugabe visited North Korea for the first time in 1978 as leader of ZANU, two years before Zimbabwe became independent. The DPRK supported ZANU in exiled bases in Tanzania and Mozambique and provided weapons and military training in Pyongyang. When Zimbabwe gained independence in 1980, Mugabe became the prime minister and later president, until he was ousted in a coup d'état in 2017.[66]

Shortly after the independence festivities, in October 1980, Mugabe again travelled to Pyongyang to attend the 35th anniversary of the Korean Workers' Party. During his speech at the customary banquet, Mugabe hailed Kim Il Sung's support during the difficult years of ZANU's operations against white minority rule: 'we defied our geographic apartness … and successfully blended our revolutions into one'. The result was a 'binding alliance' between the two nations. And now, Mugabe said, came the time for the consolidation of Zimbabwe as an independent state. 'A few acts of violence are unavoidable', he proclaimed to the North Korean delegates in the room, 'as the negative but insignificant features of an otherwise successful process'.[67] In a subsequent private meeting with Kim, Mugabe requested his assistance in forging a new army brigade.[68] As Chapter 9 explains in more detail, Kim Il Sung dispatched over a hundred military advisors to Harare to train and arm the Zimbabwean Fifth Brigade. In the early 1980s, Mugabe used this private army to wipe out his opposition in Matabeleland.[69]

During the first years of his rule, Mugabe frequently met with Kim and addressed multilateral gatherings in Pyongyang, such as the NAM conference or the World Youth Festival. Relations between the two men were cordial, and Mugabe considered Kim 'a great close friend and indispensable ally'.[70] As a token of friendship, Mugabe gifted Kim two rhinos for the zoo in Pyongyang, named Zimbo and Zimba.[71] North Korean artists were also commissioned to construct a national cemetery and a statue in Harare.[72] Today, Zimbabwe is one of the few countries in the world whose citizens do not require a visa for North Korea.[73]

* * *

During the Namibian liberation struggle, Sam Nujoma visited North Korea multiple times in his capacity as president of SWAPO. His first visit to Pyongyang was in 1965.[74] Guerrillas of SWAPO's armed wing, the People's Liberation Army of Namibia (PLAN), were trained by North Korea as early as 1967.[75] In 1983, 1986 and 1989, Nujoma and other SWAPO officials travelled to Pyongyang to strengthen diplomatic ties with Kim Il Sung. Photographs show Nujoma attending military displays and visiting the Kumsusan Palace. When Namibia finally became independent in 1990, Nujoma naturally ascended to the highest office of his country and became the first president of Namibia.[76]

DIPLOMACY

In recognition of their mutual affection, Kim Il Sung awarded Nujoma the Korean Order of Freedom and Independence in 1986. During an ensuing banquet, Kim Il Sung thanked Nujoma for being 'an intimate friend of our people' and said that his visit 'will be important in consolidating the friendship and solidarity between our Party and SWAPO'. Nujoma, in turn, thanked his host for 'the practical material assistance, political and diplomatic support' of the Koreans during the liberation struggle. Kim assured Nujoma that 'our Party and people will firmly stand by you in the future too'.[77]

Kim kept his word. Namibia became independent in 1990, SWAPO won the general elections and Nujoma ascended to the presidency. In 1991, Nujoma travelled to Pyongyang and signed a 'General Agreement' with North Korea to enhance cooperation between the two nations. The SWAPO government found that the North Koreans were, for example, 'keenly interested in erecting monuments in our country'.[78] In the next couple of years, North Korean art studios designed and constructed a range of public buildings and monuments, including a bronze statue of Nujoma.[79]

The Namibian government asked North Korea to train its Presidential Guard. The British Foreign Office privately lamented the 'embarrassment' of this decision, but explained that it was no surprise that the 'Neanderthal ex-PLAN element' in the Namibian government sought the help of their North Korean comrades: 'they place a high value on old friendships, and have little if any understanding of the world beyond SWAPO'.[80] While the British analysis is rather rude, it hit the nail on the head: the North Korean investments in solidarity with SWAPO paid off once independence was secured. Nujoma remained president for the first 15 years of Namibian independence, and SWAPO still holds power as the largest political party.[81]

Conclusion

North Korea's invitation diplomacy was a catalyst for the development of more intimate relations between Kim's regime and African liberation movements. It was a crucial first step in

67

establishing trust and building personal relations that remain relevant today, since the majority of Southern Africa continues to be ruled by the political elites that were invited to Pyongyang. Kim Il Sung was one of the original guerrillas, who combined his charismatic personality with impeccable struggle credentials that included partisan fighting and imprisonment.[82]

Kaunda's singing and Khama's dancing showed how at ease African visitors felt in the DPRK. The convivial atmosphere worked to their advantage. Travel to North Korea gave them a decisive edge over rival national liberation movements, and they used this opportunity to ask for political support, development aid and military cooperation, as the next chapters illustrate.

For North Korea, the African connection was important for boosting its image at home and abroad. African visits were extensively covered in North Korean newspapers and propaganda videos. Some visits, such as those by Mugabe in 1981 and France-Albert René (the president of the Seychelles) in 1983, were captured in full-length documentaries.[83] Domestic audiences were thus reminded of Kim Il Sung's glorious position on the world stage. The warm embraces between Kim and African leaders also contributed to North Korea's 'export track' of propaganda, which cultivated North Korea's position as a non-aligned power house.[84]

The previous case studies focused on Cold War-era visits of Africans to North Korea. I offer three additional remarks. Firstly, Kim Il Sung's reluctance to travel to Africa does not mean that North Koreans in general seldom travelled to Africa. On the contrary, over the past decades lower-status North Korean officials and diplomats have regularly visited African countries. In archival sources, these officials mostly remain anonymous and, unfortunately, little is known about their experiences. The African visits, however, were highly effective in fostering personal ties and concluding business. Important decisions, generally speaking, were taken in Pyongyang.

Secondly, these diplomatic exchanges continue to this day. North Korea's disastrous decade in the 1990s, with economic collapse following the end of the Cold War and the death of Kim Il Sung in 1994, did not spell the end of African visits to North

DIPLOMACY

Korea. Kim Il Sung was an important factor in forging the early connections with African regimes, but the continuation of the relationship was not entirely dependent on him. Chapter 14 describes in further detail how the succession of Kim Il Sung had already started in the 1970s.

In 2008, for example, the SWAPO government and North Korea again exchanged delegations. The North Koreans visited Windhoek in March with a 23-person delegation. The itinerary included a stay at the luxurious Safari Hotel, a lion feeding exercise, visits to the State House and the National Heroes' Acre (a presidential palace and cemetery built by North Korea) and a courtesy call to Nujoma, the retired president who was the basis of Namibian–North Korean friendship. In turn, a Namibian delegation travelled to Pyongyang in October of the same year and visited, among other places, the International Friendship Exhibition. As always, local North Korean newspapers covered this and other visits extensively.[85]

Essentially, Kim Il Sung's successors benefited from the goodwill he had amassed in Africa. Interestingly, this also worked the other way around. In 2013, the vice president of Zambia, Guy Scott, travelled to Pyongyang for a diplomatic visit. In his autobiography, Scott recalls the customary banquet, during which he was asked by a North Korean official: 'is your former president still alive and waving his handkerchief and dancing?' Kaunda was clearly remembered fondly in Pyongyang. 'I didn't know he was so famous in that neck of the woods', concluded Scott.[86]

Thirdly, there is a bias in the archival sources towards elite histories, and a question remains about how we can write African–North Korean histories from below. Throughout the second half of the twentieth century, a wide array of African intellectuals, guerrilla fighters, journalists and students travelled to Pyongyang.[87] Their experiences remain mostly undocumented, with the exception of the Guinean student Aliou Niane and the Equatorial Guinean Mónica Macías. Niane studied at the Wonsan Agricultural College between 1982 and 1987, his scholarship a direct result of Sékou Touré's attendance at one of Kim Il Sung's birthday parties. In North Korea, Niane encountered students from Madagascar,

69

Mali, Tanzania, Equatorial Guinea, Ethiopia, Lesotho, Zambia and Togo.[88]

Macías was the daughter of Francisco Macías Nguema, the first president of Equatorial Guinea. Before he was executed in a coup, he sent his three children to North Korea for study. Monica lived for 15 years in Pyongyang under the protection of the Kim family, where she met other African students (including the sons of Mathieu Kérékou, the president of Benin). She published her memoirs first in Korean in 2013 and then in English in 2023.[89] While the accounts of Niane and Macías fall outside the geographical focus of this study, they nonetheless offer fascinating insights. Unfortunately, to date, there are no accounts from the North Korean military advisors, cultural instructors and artists who travelled to Africa.[90]

4

DOCTRINE

JUCHE IDEOLOGY IN AFRICA

From the outset, ideology greased the wheels of African–North Korean diplomacy. It was a shared framework of political ideas that allowed the development of strong ties between African liberation fighters and Korean comrades. North Korea framed its charm offensive in Africa in terms of Juche Thought, an approach that was happily reciprocated by their African counterparts. Usually translated as self-reliance and understood through its main principle that 'man is the master of all things', Juche replaced Marxism–Leninism as the official ideology of the DPRK in 1970.[1] This decision was essentially 'a declaration of political independence' from its two main communist sponsors, China and the Soviet Union.[2]

Changing the state ideology from communism to Juche made North Korea more appealing to the non-aligned countries of the African continent, which gave it a diplomatic advantage over South Korea.[3] Precisely because Juche was vague and emphasised self-reliance, it was remarkably compatible with indigenous African development philosophies, such as Kenneth Kaunda's humanism, Kwame Nkrumah's consciencism, Julius Nyerere's *Ujamaa* and Seretse Khama's *boipelego* principle.[4] After decades of oppression

71

by capitalist colonisers, African nationalist elites took inspiration from socialism while their political programmes were built around ideas of political and economic independence. African desires for autonomy, anti-imperialism and postcolonial development were echoed in Juche Thought, which hinted at socialist principles and underlined the importance of self-determination.

While it is often assumed that Juche serves as North Korea's guiding principle for domestic policymaking, and is thus closely entangled with its iconic 'hermit kingdom' status, Brian Myers argues that Juche 'was never meant to work ideologically'. According to Myers, Juche is part of North Korea's multi-track discourse, which consists of the inner track (propaganda for domestic consumption only), the outer track (propaganda for domestic consumption but aware of outside monitors) and the export track (propaganda for outsiders). Juche was specifically designed for the export track.[5]

North Korea's main strategy for exporting Juche to Africa was the establishment of ideological institutes, or Juche Study Centres. Juche Study Centres offered ordinary Africans the opportunity to learn more about North Korea through discussions, the distribution of translated Korean literature and the organisation of film viewings and photo exhibitions. The centres were also a gateway for travel to North Korea.

Kim Il Sung's persona took centre stage in Juche Thought. On the surface, it may look as if comrade Kim drank deeply from the cup of vanity and envisioned the state ideology as an expression of his personality cult. The reality is more nuanced. Juche was originally designed as a way to define North Korea's independence from the Communist Bloc, but Kim Jong Il later used Juche to protect his own status as his father's successor. By elevating his father to the level of eternal leader, Kim Jong Il became the guardian of his father's legacy (this is discussed further in Chapter 14).[6]

In practice, the personal portraits of Kim Il Sung always loomed large over the meetings held in African Juche Study Centres, while the books containing his speeches ended up in virtually every library and archive in Southern Africa. In merging the personal with the political, the establishment of Juche Study Centres was a result of Kim Il Sung's invitation diplomacy that was discussed in Chapter 3, and a prerequisite of the development aid that is discussed in Chapter 5.

Today, Juche Study Centres are largely forgotten in Africa and beyond. Very little documentation and even less scholarship relating to this phenomenon exists. The analysis of this chapter is largely based on an archival treasure trove that I accidentally stumbled upon in Namibia. The archives of the former United Nations Institute for Namibia, a school in Zambia that offered training for exiled Namibians during the liberation struggle, contain an extensive collection of Cold War era editions of the *Study of the Juche Idea* journal.[7]

In addition to short texts by Kim Il Sung and Kim Jong Il, and information about the organisation of Juche Study Centres, *Study of the Juche Idea* features written contributions from foreign Juche followers. Many contributions were submitted by ordinary Africans and therefore provide a unique insight into how Juche was received and applied in Africa. The fact that an educational body in the heart of the Frontline States assembled such an extensive collection of Juche journals (with editions running from 1979 to 1990) reveals that many Africans were sympathetic to Juche Thought. I am grateful to the archivists of the University of Namibia, where this collection is housed, for access to the archives while the finding aids were not yet completed and publicly available.

This chapter offers a critical analysis of Juche Study Centres and seeks to understand why they were founded, how they operated and their impact on the African continent.[8] The subsequent section provides a basic introduction to Juche Study Centres, with an emphasis on Southern Africa. The next section examines how Juche Study Centres became a vehicle for the dissemination of North Korean soft power through literature, visual art and travel. The subsequent section considers how African elites used Juche as inspiration for postcolonial governance. The conclusion reviews the question of whether African–North Korean friendship was motivated by ideology or whether, in the end, pragmatist motives prevailed.

COMRADES BEYOND THE COLD WAR

Juche Study Centres

Juche Study Centres were ultimately established around the world, but the first one opened its doors in Africa—in Mali, to be precise. On 15 April 1969, the 'Study Group of the Works of Comrade Kim Il Sung' was founded on the occasion of the 57th birthday of Kim Il Sung.[9] Mali was one of the first African countries to establish full diplomatic relations with North Korea, in 1960.[10] 'Juche', wrote the editors of *Study of the Juche Idea*, 'like oasis, has been flowing into the hearts of the African people who recently liberated themselves from the colonial rule of imperialism and are on the way of building a new society'. The foundational meeting was attended by several Malian intellectuals.

Mali became a model for Juche Study Centres globally. Individual Juche Study Centres became part of a National Committee—in Mali, a National Committee was established in 1985—which, in turn, became part of a continental body. In Africa, this became the African Regional Committee for the Study of the Juche Idea. The international body that oversaw these activities was the International Institute of the Juche Idea.[11] Approximately 30 African states hosted Juche Study Centres during the Cold War.[12] In reality, this number might be higher, as my data set is incomplete (some editions of the *Study of the Juche Idea* were not covered in the Namibian archive and are difficult to find elsewhere).

The majority of Juche Study Centres in Africa were located in West Africa, whereas relatively few centres were located in Southern Africa. This makes sense, as West Africa was the first African region to be liberated from colonialism, and Southern Africa was the last. Political independence and formal diplomatic ties with North Korea were necessary requirements for the establishment and funding of Juche Study Centres—up until the end of the Cold War, when North Korea no longer had the money to fund these operations. This is why, for example, Namibia and South Africa never hosted Juche Study Centres. When these countries liberated in 1990 and 1994, it was, in a sense, too late.[13]

Exiled Southern African freedom fighters who were unable to join Juche Study Centres in their home countries frequented

DOCTRINE

study groups in the liberated parts of Africa. For example, MPLA members visited Sierra Leone to join the first Pan-African Seminar on Comrade Kim Il Sung's Juche Idea in 1972, a few years before Angolan independence. The meeting was attended by 50 delegates from 16 African countries.[14] Exiled Zimbabwean students in Sierra Leone joined the 'Group for the Study of the Immortal Juche Idea of the Supreme Leader Comrade Kim Il Sung', prior to Zimbabwean independence in 1980.[15] SWAPO members participated in study groups in Tanzania, prior to Namibian independence in 1990.[16]

The distinctions between Juche Study Centres, North Korean embassies and friendship societies were often blurred: the embassies provided funding and reading materials for the study groups, and meetings were often held on embassy premises.[17] Editions of the *Study of the Juche Idea* contain lavish descriptions of such meetings, which took place according to a set protocol. A portrait of Kim Il Sung was symbolically placed in the room (this is also a significant custom in North Korea), sometimes joined by Kim's translated books and photographs of the Dear Leader. A meeting sometimes consisted of a speech, sometimes a lecture, and would usually adopt a number of proposals, working plans and letters for Kim Il Sung or Kim Jong Il (and sometimes for both). The attendance of high-ranking African officials was always highlighted in official reports.

Some meetings took the form of conferences and lasted for several days, such as the 'National Meeting on Socialist Revolutionary Charter of Madagascar-Juche Idea', held in Antananarivo, Madagascar, from 31 August to 2 September 1988. Organised under the auspices of the National Committee for the Study of the Socialist Revolutionary Charter of Madagascar and the Juche Idea of the Malagasy Vanguard of Revolution (short titles were never North Korea's forte), this event was apparently visited by some 200 persons, 'including senior officials of the party and government'.[18] Such gatherings were given special attention in North Korean propaganda: descriptions boasted about the number of participants and reported glowing well-wishes from foreign dignitaries for Kim Il Sung.

75

Soft power

Juche Study Centres became the primary vehicle for the dissemination of North Korean soft power in Africa. While South Korea concentrated on trade diplomacy, North Korea relied 'heavily' on cultural diplomacy.[19] Juche Study Centres were ideological spaces accessible to the wider public. From the perspective of African populations that were preoccupied with defying colonial rule and rebuilding newly independent societies, the Korean peninsula was far away. But Juche Study Centres brought North Korea much closer to home. Through the organisation of meetings, the distribution of literature and visual art and the opportunity for travel, Juche Study Centres became the catalyst for deeper relations between Africans and North Koreans.

* * *

Literature was perhaps the most important form of North Korean propaganda. The Pyongyang Foreign Languages House, an organisation that falls under the Propaganda and Agitation Department of the Workers' Party of Korea (WPK), translated and produced North Korean books for global export. The majority of titles were works ostensibly written by the North Korean leadership, which often concerned the subject of Juche.[20] The apartheid regime in South Africa and Namibia banned such books through the Suppression of Communism Act.

Kim Il Sung's speeches were translated from Korean into numerous languages, including Afrikaans, Kirundi and Swahili and were disseminated as bound books.[21] North Korean diplomatic personnel were extensively trained in African languages, both at home and abroad. In the 1970s, 32 North Koreans undertook a five-year course in Swahili and English at Tanzania's College of National Education.[22] North Korea also distributed newspapers (such as the *Pyongyang Times*) that informed African readers about day-to-day events.[23] In Tanzania, North Korean newspaper articles were translated into Swahili by the local journalist Peter Msungu, who was a member of a local Juche Study Centre and had visited

DOCTRINE

North Korea. It is alleged, however, that Msungu 'pretended to do the work himself' and instead delegated the work to a friend, all the while cashing in on North Korea's remuneration.[24] Another tactic was the placement of North Korean supplements in local African newspapers, such as *The People's Weekly* of Zimbabwe.[25] In Tanzanian newspapers, some North Korean columns were 'more than twice the length of the actual newspaper', and local publications became financially dependent on the advertising income from Pyongyang.[26]

In addition to books and newspapers, North Korea disseminated (trade) magazines in Africa, such as *Korea Today* or *Foreign Trade of the Democratic People's Republic*. The latter, for example, explained the rules and regulations of the DPRK on joint ventures and featured successful North Korean businesses.[27] This illustrates North Korea's interest in monetising their fraternal ties with newly or soon-to-be independent nations in Africa.

Such literature found its way into African hands via Juche Study Centres, which stimulated the establishment of North Korean bookshops and libraries in Africa. In 1970s Mauritius, the Kim Il Sung Works' Library distributed all sorts of North Korean texts to the local population.[28] In 1980s Zimbabwe, the Kim Il Sung Bookshop in Harare did the same. Eager customers could not only obtain copies of the *Study of the Juche Idea* but also North Korean bulletins such as *Age of Juche* and the *Banner of Independence*. This was not exceptional. In 1989, the International Institute of the Juche Idea had distributed North Korean propaganda to 80 countries across the world.[29]

In addition to Juche Study Centres, bookshops and embassies, North Korean literature was routinely gifted to African leaders during the visits of North Korean delegations. A 1973 meeting of North Korean officials with the cabinet of Botswana resulted, in the words of the British High Commission in Gaborone, in 'a fully mounted propaganda exercise'. The North Koreans brought 'books and brochures and photographs of the illustrious (almost deified) Kim Il-Sung'. Books about Juche 'were dished out by the hundredweight to all Ministers and Senior Civil Servants and to anyone else who fancied a set of the red-covered publicity material'. In addition, the cabinet of Botswana received beautiful

Korean porcelain and *hongsam* (Korean red *ginseng*), which was described as 'pieces of fabulous Korean dried root with alleged aphrodisiacal qualities'. The British diplomats gleefully added that they did not know if there 'were any private requests from Ministers for second helpings'.[30]

A British diplomat in 1982 was 'struck how frequently the works of Kim Il-sung appeared on officials' desks' in East Africa. This development worried the British Foreign Office, which called for a 'comprehensive study of the North Korean role' in Africa.[31] Juche literature penetrated the bookshelves of many key figures of Africa's liberation struggle. Through these texts, African political elites were directly exposed to North Korean doctrine. A useful illustration is the personal papers of Mose Penaani Tjitendero, a Namibian freedom fighter who went into exile in Tanzania in 1964 and steadily climbed SWAPO's ranks. His private library included numerous North Korean books, journals and magazines such as *Korea Today* and *Pyongyang Review*.[32]

* * *

The written word was complemented by visual art.[33] Juche Study Centres across the continent organised public film screenings and photo exhibitions.[34] A Zimbabwean Juche enthusiast wrote in the *Study of the Juche Idea* that 'since all the people cannot visit Korea to see the realities there, film shows were frequently arranged to show the realities of Korea where the Juche idea has been materialised and realise the correctness of the Juche idea'.[35] The earlier-mentioned visit of North Korean officials to the cabinet of Botswana was accompanied by a film show, which was held in the Capitol Cinema in Gaborone and publicised through Radio Botswana.[36] To celebrate Kim Il Sung's 56th birthday, the North Korean embassy in Mali showed a film about his life in the Librairie Populaire. The event was open to all Malians and accompanied by photographs of Kim. American diplomats at the time were extremely sarcastic about the event, noting that the film, which was 3 hours and 45 minutes long, 'bored the unboreable'. Irked by the 'verbose repetition of the party line and paucity of action', they

DOCTRINE

wished that Kim 'had remained an unsung hero'. This unsolicited cinematographic review, however, is entirely beside the point. The event was successful in strengthening Malian–North Korean ties, especially as the film was accompanied by a speech from the Malian minister of justice, who praised Kim Il Sung.[37] North Korean films were also screened in other parts of Africa, including in Burundi, Guinea, Liberia, Mali, Niger, Somalia and Uganda.[38]

The North Korean leadership, and in particular Kim Jong Il, loved film.[39] The medium was 'the preferred genre of the state' and played a vital role in the propaganda machine that churned out stories of the regime's heroic exploits.[40] North Korean films highlighted the amazing qualities of Kim Il Sung and were famously anti-American.[41] The first ever NAM Film Festival was held in Pyongyang, in 1987, and was organised around the theme of 'The Role of the Film Industry in the Anti-Imperialist Struggles'.[42] As highlighted in Chapter 3, the visits of African leaders to Pyongyang were captured in documentaries.

In some cases, North Korean teams produced films in Africa. In Tanzania, for example, a North Korean camera crew shot the Swahili documentary *Tanzania Yasonga Mbele* ('Tanzania Forges Ahead').[43] The film featured Saba Saba celebrations, life in *Ujamaa* villages and milestones of 'the ever advancing revolution in Tanzania'.[44] British diplomats called it 'an effective piece of propaganda' because it showed 'Tanzanians parading in the North Korean way'. Tanzania's film industry was relatively young, and the documentary was seen as a pioneering step in an upcoming industry.[45]

* * *

For selected devotees, Juche Study Centres offered the opportunity for ideological training in Pyongyang. In the 1980s alone, at least 200 students from various African countries (including Madagascar, Tanzania and Zambia) travelled to Pyongyang to attend Juche courses.[46] Some of them stayed in North Korea for up to three months at a time.[47] The *Study of the Juche Idea* journal occasionally featured travel reports from African visitors, which reveals that visitors were mostly well-established men in high-ranking positions in society: journalists, ruling party officials, members of parliament and university employees.

North Korean propaganda can be dull and monotonous, but the descriptions in the *Study of the Juche Idea* are written by real people who were excited about travelling to distant destinations. The director of a Togolese research institute, Sossa Kounoutcho, attended the International Seminar of the Juche Idea in 1977 and enthusiastically described how he was able to shake hands with Kim Il Sung. E. S. Mushi, an Inspector of Schools for the Ministry of Education in Tanzania, visited North Korea twice to learn about Juche education in the 1980s and was 'deeply impressed' by what he saw.[48]

O. T. Mupawaenda, a librarian at the University of Zimbabwe, visited North Korea for a month in 1986 together with two other Zimbabweans (a lecturer in law and an officer of the Ministry of Justice).[49] Mupawaenda wrote about his experiences in the *Study of the Juche Idea*, but also in an American journal under the title 'A Zimbabwean Librarian Visits North Korea'. 'The Korean experience', according to Mupawaenda, 'was far more rewarding, gratifying and interesting than previous visits to other countries, socialist, capitalist or non-aligned'.[50]

Inspiration for postcolonial rule

Juche stimulated African ideas about postcolonial rule. In the *Study of the Juche Idea*, African contributions applied Juche to domestic policymaking, for example in the fields of education, agriculture and industry. Importantly, Juche also influenced ideas about political power. In Southern Africa, the majority of independent states were ruled by former liberation movements that believed that they were destined to rule. To this end, African elites found inspiration in Juche Thought. Juche emphasised the importance of a glorious revolution and the importance of a single, united organisation that remained in charge of this revolutionary heritage.[51] North Korea embodied this ideal—despite tremendous internal and external pressure, the WPK had governed North Korea since its inception

DOCTRINE

in 1948, on the basis of the heroic exploits of the struggle against Japanese colonisation and American imperialism.[52]

Kim Jong Il famously said that for a revolution to succeed, the masses 'must be united into one organisation ... under the guidance of the party and the leader'.[53] Newly independent African states were often ruled by a single powerful regime. Zambia, for example, became a one-party state in 1972 when Kaunda's UNIP banned rival political parties.[54] In a 1988 edition of *Study of the Juche Idea*, lecturers at a UNIP school underlined the similarities between Zambian humanism and Kim Jong Il's teachings. The dean of the UNIP school wrote that the 'principle of revolutionary duty and comradeship' revolves around unity and 'the cohesion of the leader, the party and the masses'. A colleague argued that the University of Zambia should award Kim an honorary degree.[55]

Similar proceedings can be observed in the case of Zimbabwe, where Mugabe's ZANU sought to sideline its political competition, particularly the rivalling ZAPU. ZANU officials had intimate knowledge of Juche Thought. Seminars of local Juche Study Centres were sponsored by the Zimbabwean Ministry of Education and the Department of Information of ZANU and were visited by high-ranking government officials and party members. 'In the coming years, under the guidance of the ZANU (PF)', the deputy chairman of the National Committee for the Study of the Juche Idea promised in Zimbabwe, 'we will further deepen our study of the Juche idea'.[56]

One example of a dedicated ZANU member with an interest in Juche was Edson Shirihuru, a member of parliament in the 1980s who later became the deputy director of the Central Intelligence Organisation. He had attended Juche seminars in Nigeria before establishing the National Committee in Zimbabwe.[57] Echoing the blood-related discourse of this era, Shirihuru advocated for 'the building of a new society by enhancing the function and role of state won at the cost of blood'. In a 1981 edition of the *Study of the Juche Idea*, Shirihuru praised the ideas of Kim Il Sung and concluded that it was 'very important to use state power as a powerful weapon' to consolidate national independence—a telling statement by the man who would lead the Zimbabwean secret services.[58]

A professor at the University of Zimbabwe argued that Juche 'provides us with powerful theoretical and practical weapons capable of building up the firm independent subject of the revolution'.[59] Shirihuru's Juche-inspired argument that state power is a powerful weapon for the consolidation of independence eerily foreshadows the establishment of the Fifth Brigade that is discussed in Chapter 9. During the Zimbabwean liberation struggle, Shirihuru was part of the 'Crocodile Gang' together with Emmerson Mnangagwa, who played a vital role in the training of the Fifth Brigade.[60]

Conclusion

A question that pervades this book is whether African–North Korean cooperation was motivated by ideology or pragmatism. Ideology, as Christopher Clapham argues, 'is not merely an alien imposition on willing Africans. It also strikes a local resonance, and serves to build moral linkages that extend beyond mere economic interests'.[61] This chapter showed that numerous African elites were receptive to the ideas of Juche Thought as it resonated with domestic issues, most notably the challenges of postcolonial rule.

Juche was thus instrumental in creating a shared ideological framework that brought the distant political struggles of African liberation movements and North Korea closer together. This, in turn, allowed the development of practical connections that benefited all sides. As subsequent chapters demonstrate, African elites benefited from all sorts of material and military support that would have been difficult to materialise without Juche. North Korea, on the other hand, reaped the propaganda benefits of the numerous Juche Study Centres that existed in the African continent.

Yet, the reach of Juche certainly had its limits. There is no evidence of genuine collaboration between North Korean and African followers of Juche Thought. African citizens travelled to North Korea for ideological education, but regular North Korean citizens were never allowed to travel the other way around. There are no examples of articles or books jointly written by African

DOCTRINE

and Korean authors. The appeal of Juche was apparently limited to certain African elites who were closely intertwined with the prevailing regimes of their countries and did not reach the masses.

Moreover, North Korea abandoned its African Juche Study Centres when it faced economic hardship at the end of the Cold War. Kim Jong Il no longer had the money to bankroll such elaborate displays of soft power. As a result, Juche Study Centres largely disappeared in Africa. Today, no party or government official in Southern Africa is involved in the development of Juche Thought, and references to North Korea have largely vanished from public discourse.

Nevertheless, a few local Juche chapters continue to exist in Africa. Despite the odds, in recent years, loyal followers of the Kim family have organised meetings in the Democratic Republic of Congo, Ethiopia, Guinea, Nigeria, South Africa, Tanzania and Uganda.[62] It can be difficult to appreciate the wisdom of a philosophy that is often defined through indecipherable statements, such as Kim Jong Un's dictum that 'even an egg, charged with ideology, can break a rock'.[63] At the same time its impact should not be underestimated. Juche has proven to be an effective tool for the North Korean brand.

Although the Juche Idea has become a niche phenomenon in the world, it remains alive in certain parts of Africa. In 2023, for example, the Congolese professor of philosophy Jean Mallaud Mbongo Pasi Udumbula Pambi published a treatise on how Juche could be applied to ideas about African sovereignty. Pambi compares Juche to African philosophies such as Senghor's ideas about African socialism and *Ujamaa*. Titled *L'imaginaire politique Nord-Coréen*, the book highlights a continuing African interest in North Korean political thought. The book is dedicated to *Mzee* Laurent Désiré Kabila, the former president of Congo, who is now immortalised via a grandiose personal statue—naturally designed by a North Korean art studio.[64]

5

DEVELOPMENT

SOUTH–SOUTH COOPERATION

A largely unexplored area of diplomatic engagements between African states and North Korea is development aid. Numerous African leaders had already marvelled at the wonders of a socialist paradise in Pyongyang, while the proliferation of Juche Study Centres allowed the population at home to learn about North Korean ideology. Development aid was the logical next step in putting these ideas into practice, and, as a result, North Korean technical advisors were sent to newly independent African states to pave the way for postcolonial development. This chapter considers the questions of why African states were sympathetic to North Korean ideas about development, what both parties gained from cooperation and how aid projects evolved in practice.[1]

During the Cold War, the newly elected leaders of Africa looked east for ideological inspiration. Walter Rodney hailed North Korea as a development model for Africa in the postscript of his seminal work *How Europe Underdeveloped Africa*.[2] North Korea was equally praised in an edition of the *Third World Forum*, which argued that its rapid development presented 'major lessons' for African countries such as Tanzania.[3]

85

There were two main reasons for Africa's interest in North Korean development aid: its miraculous post-war reconstruction and its emphasis on independence from external actors, especially from major powers. After the devastating Korean War of the 1950s, North Korea recovered much faster than its southern rival.[4] Already in 1965, the Cambridge economist Joan Robinson admired North Korea's economic growth by commenting that 'all the economic miracles of the post-war world are put in the shade by these achievements'.[5]

Moreover, North Korea's independent image was attractive to countries that were hostile to foreign investment.[6] Although the transfer of North Korean expertise to Africa was part of a larger trend of socialist aid, it would be a mistake to view the DPRK as a Soviet or Chinese surrogate.[7] The Sino-Soviet split presented an opportunity for North Korea to chart its own foreign policy course.[8] A British diplomat keenly observed that, at the time, 'the North Koreans have pitched their appeal, in the eyes of recipients of their aid, very much as a small, unthreatening country, seeking and promoting independence of great power influence'.[9]

Development aid as foreign policy

For North Korea, development aid was a central part of its foreign policy in Africa, especially with regards to agriculture. In the twentieth century, most African countries were predominantly rural, and agriculture—especially subsistence farming—was vital for the survival of millions of people. The political economist Lynn Krieger Mytelka argues that 'the limited scope and scale of African industrialisation was widely regarded as an opportunity' for the nationalisation and modernisation of industries in newly independent states.[10] In other words, the field of agriculture presented an ideal opportunity for cooperation between African states and the DPRK.

North Korea ascribed its own agricultural success in terms of Juche Thought. Juche agriculture was 'the poster child' for the successful socialist modernisation of the DPRK. Chong-Ae Yu argues that soon after North Korea was established, the state 'embarked on a modernisation project that fundamentally transformed its society from agrarian to industrial, with the aim of achieving food self-sufficiency'. The key to this project was the perception of agriculture as a matter of national security. In practice, Juche agriculture consisted of rescaling the land through collectivisation and heavy technological intervention. The use of capital-intensive, mechanised production, the heavy application of agrochemicals, an extensive system of irrigation and mono-cropping were essential.[11]

In the 1950s, North Korean agricultural production was, in the words of the historian Balázs Szalontai, 'very low' and techniques were 'quite primitive'. Severe food scarcity led to a crisis in 1955.[12] In 1978, however, the CIA reported that North Korean 'grain production may have grown at a more rapid pace' than South Korea, due to its advances in agriculture.[13] A few years later, in 1984, the DPRK celebrated a record grain production that exceeded the consumption requirements of its population. Its ability to supply the daily caloric requirements to its population was 'consistently higher' than that of China.[14]

The high point of North Korea's development aid in Africa was during the 1980s, a period marked by two important conferences in Pyongyang. These meetings—held in 1981 and 1987—were ideal opportunities for North Korea to market its experience to African states.

In 1981, Kim Il Sung invited several African agriculture ministers to the 'Symposium of the Non-Aligned and Other Developing Countries on Increasing Food and Agricultural Production', which can be viewed as the kick-off for the North Korean agricultural campaign on the African continent. Kim treated his African audience to an eloquent speech, titled 'For the Development of Agriculture in African Countries', in which he argued that symposia and declarations were not enough—action was necessary. Kim vowed to increase agricultural production in East and West Africa by providing farm machinery, irrigation projects and experts.[15]

The North Korean aid crusade was framed as 'South–South cooperation', a phrase coined for the 'building of independent economies based on self-reliance' that implies the central role of Juche ideology in North Korean development aid. Kim believed that African countries had won political independence but were yet to gain economic independence. The North Koreans were convinced that South–South cooperation would ultimately lead to the establishment of a New International Economic Order.[16] Their African allies offered vocal support. Ultimately, the North Korean strategy aimed to rally support within the NAM, with the ultimate objective being to diminish South Korea's standing in the world.[17]

African enthusiasm for Juche agriculture is also evident in issues of the journal *Study of the Juche Idea*, which contain several submissions from African writers on this subject. A school principal from Madagascar argued that North Korea 'is giving vital assistance towards solving the food problem in many African countries'. African states were instructed in 'Juche farming methods created by President Kim Il Sung', through the secondment of North Korean 'agricultural scientists, technicians, and irrigation experts'.[18] A contributor from Tanzania, who had also joined the 1981 conference in Pyongyang, celebrated 'the great successes achieved in the agricultural field through the cooperation between Korean and Tanzanian agricultural scientists and experts'. The North Korean–Tanzanian development experiences and techniques were a 'shining example of south-south cooperation'.[19]

The orchestrated campaign to woo African allies through agriculture reached its pinnacle in 1987 in Pyongyang with the Extraordinary Ministerial Conference of the NAM on South–South Cooperation, which I already touched upon in Chapter 2. Kim Il Sung's keynote speech summarised his views on North Korean development aid in Africa. 'The developing countries must advance agriculture', said Kim. As non-aligned countries, he believed they should undertake joint ventures for 'the construction of irrigation works, the improvement of farming methods, research on agricultural science and the production of farm machinery'. The aim should be 'complete self-sufficiency in food as soon as possible'.[20] North Korea considered it 'a sacred duty to fight for ... the success of South-South cooperation'. Kim proudly announced that 'we have set up institutes of agricultural science

DEVELOPMENT

and experimental farms in some African countries' and promised to 'expand cooperation with African countries' in the future.[21]

Kim's ambitious agenda notwithstanding, North Korea's dream of leading the developing world in the quest for South–South cooperation would disappear in a few years' time. The end of the Cold War and North Korea's subsequent economic crisis resulted in the discontinuation of many North Korean aid projects.[22] Kim Il Sung simply no longer had the money to spend on technical advisors, and it was no longer considered a priority by his son, Kim Jong Il.

The pinnacle of North Korean aid in Africa thus came to an end in the 1980s. Approximately 20 African states benefited from North Korean aid, and I suspect this number will even be higher if more research is dedicated to this history.[23] A careful reading of the archival record reveals a flurry of different projects in Southern Africa alone. In Lesotho, a North Korean team rebuilt the national stadium, ran vegetable farms and experimented with maize production and irrigation, although frustration arose due to the North Koreans' language difficulties and their failure to submit reports to the Ministry of Agriculture.[24] The Seychelles benefited from the donation of thousands of tons of cement for housing projects, tractors for agricultural development and the supply of rice for a reduced price.[25] In Angola, the North Koreans ran an irrigation project and were involved in the production of cotton and the construction of a dam. The Angolans turned down the offer to establish state farms.[26] Mozambique and North Korea cooperated in the fields of irrigation and agriculture.[27] During a visit to Zimbabwe in 1981, North Korea promised 'total assistance' in the agricultural development of Zimbabwe when a government delegation toured a farm.[28] The Zambian government asked for North Korea's help with a rural development programme, which included manpower and cash. A Zambian official commented upon the news by saying that 'we value our friendship because we share common ideals'. In turn, a North Korean official praised the 'identical views' of both parties.[29] Zambia expressed gratitude for North Korean assistance in paddy rice growing.[30]

89

COMRADES BEYOND THE COLD WAR

Two case studies of strategic hubs

In order to analyse the success and failure of North Korean development aid in Africa, this book presents two detailed case studies of aid projects in Tanzania and Ghana. North Korea invested considerable energy in these places because of their strategic importance. Although Tanzania is located in East Africa and Ghana is located in West Africa, both states were crucial for the liberation of Southern Africa. As mentioned before, Tanzania hosted the OAU Liberation Committee while Ghana was home to the Bureau of African Affairs—two organisations that provided financial assistance and military training to Southern African liberation movements.[31] Ghana and Tanzania thus were strategic hubs, not just in a practical sense, but also in ideological terms: Julius Nyerere and Kwame Nkrumah were influential thinkers on African decolonisation.

As the names already reveal, the establishment of a Chollima Agricultural Science Institute in Tanzania and the Ghana Juche Farm were highly symbolic places of cooperation that were meant to advertise the benefits of North Korean-style development. *Ch'ŏllima* refers to a mythical winged horse that became a symbol of socialist transformation in North Korea, and Juche naturally references Kim's ideology of self-reliance.

Tanzanian and Ghanaian politicians encountered their North Korean colleagues at multilateral fora where they discussed postcolonial politics. A prime example is AAPSO, which, as Chapter 2 highlights, considered the struggle in Southern Africa to be one of its main priorities and, at the same time, was an avid supporter of the North Korean regime.[32] North Korean delegations attended the AAPSO conferences that were held in Tanzania in 1960 and 1963, and in Ghana in 1965.[33] Years later, in 1987, African diplomats attended an AAPSO conference in Pyongyang.[34]

In addition, North Korea invested heavily in fraternal bilateral relations with both states. As a result, large numbers of local elites were exposed to North Korean notions of development. Tanzanian politicians were schooled in the wonders of North Korean

DEVELOPMENT

ideas through regular invitations to study party organisation in Pyongyang. In the 1970s, North Korea even established a political school in Zanzibar that offered three-month ideological courses.[35] North Koreans who visited Tanzania received 'the red carpet treatment'.[36] The Tanzania–Korea Friendship Society ('*Chama cha urafiki kati ya Tanzania na Korea*') organised monthly meetings in the North Korean embassy in Dar es Salaam.[37] The opening of the Society attracted high-ranking Tanzanian officials, including the speaker of the national assembly, the minister of foreign affairs and the commissioner of culture.[38] Ghanaian newspaper editors were similarly invited to stay in Pyongyang, sometimes for months at a time, in exchange for positive coverage back home.[39] Ghanaian citizens learned about Korea through the Ghana–DPRK Friendship Society and events such as the 'month of solidarity with Korean people'.[40]

North Korea used the political capital that resulted from these long-term engagements to propose aid projects in the 1980s. The ensuing programmes were meant to showcase South–South cooperation to the wider world.

* * *

In 1967, Nyerere announced the Arusha Declaration and TANU's Policy on Socialism and Self-Reliance. This policy was Tanzania's philosophy of self-reliant development and one of multiple examples where African postcolonial political ideologies aligned very well with Juche. The seminal declaration stated that 'agriculture is the basis of development' and stressed that 'Tanzanians can live well without depending on help from outside if they use their land properly'.[41]

Agricultural aid from North Korea was thus a logical way to strengthen the ties between both countries. One year after the Arusha Declaration, in 1968, Nyerere visited Kim Il Sung in Pyongyang.[42] In subsequent years, North Korea proposed ambitious plans for irrigated farmlands, promised machinery and technical support, developed plans for brick and tile production, medical training and a national irrigation programme, and offered 700 technical

COMRADES BEYOND THE COLD WAR

drawings for parks, gardens and playgrounds.[43] Tanzania received hundreds of thousands of dollars' worth of building material as a gift from North Korea, such as cement, iron bars and glass sheets.[44] As a way to showcase its own development, North Korea organised a trade show in Dar es Salaam. The goods on display featured machine tools, textiles, liquor, one large orange farm tractor and other products. In his opening speech, the Tanzanian minister for commerce and industry 'praised North Korea's industrial progress' and advocated for closer relations with Pyongyang.[45]

The first North Korean agricultural project in Tanzania was the Chollima Agricultural Science Institute, otherwise known as the Dakawa Rice Irrigation Project. Located 200 km from Dar es Salaam, this 260-million-shilling project comprised 2,000 hectares of rice fields and facilities to process paddy cultivation and store 10,000 tonnes of rice.[46] The project commenced in 1975. While it was funded primarily by the African Development Bank and the Tanzania Development Bank, North Korean experts supported the practical day-to-day execution.[47] The Tanzanian government paid for the accommodation, international transport, leave and salaries of the North Korean advisors. However, disagreements between the North Korean team and other labourers resulted in significant delays to the work. The Chollima Agricultural Science Institute was dissolved in 1982.

Despite this obvious setback, cooperation between the two nations deepened throughout the 1980s. The Chollima Agricultural Science Institute was, in a way, succeeded by the Agro-Scientific Research Centre, a place that would showcase Juche agriculture in the whole of East and Central Africa.[48] The construction began in 1982 and took two years. Valued at approximately 2.4 million British pounds, the project was financed and executed by North Korea.[49]

Frequent exchanges between Tanzanian and North Korean delegations resulted in dozens of other projects. Around the time of the problems at the Chollima Institute, another 105 North Korean advisors were dispatched to eight regions in Tanzania. They worked on maize production, vegetable gardens and mini-hydroelectric power stations. More and more would follow over time.[50] Some teams stayed in Tanzania for multiple years, for example on a farm

DEVELOPMENT

in the Iringa region, where North Korean advisors supervised farm work and established a weather forecasting station.[51] Even President Nyerere's home village became a hotspot for North Korean agricultural experts and town planners, who were naturally attracted to the symbolism of this location.[52] In 1970, the village was toured by a North Korean minister of culture, who was greeted by Nyerere's brother. Wangazi Nyerere asked the minister to convey the villagers' 'warm greetings' to Kim Il Sung.[53]

While archival evidence suggests that the aid projects were hindered by practical problems, as was the case with the Chollima Institute, the Tanzanian elites continued to publicly praise North Korea's help. In 1973, Prime Minister Rashidi Kawawa celebrated the 'exemplary' work of the Koreans in his country, which he said was an example of 'that spirit of hard work and dedication which has made Korea a strong and prosperous nation'.[54] Kawawa also 'reiterated CCM's firm support to efforts by the DPRK to bring about the re-unification of Korea'.[55] Over the years, the Tanzanian politician had developed close relations with his North Korean counterparts, whom he had visited in Pyongyang as early as 1965.[56]

When Nyerere attended a banquet in Pyongyang in 1985, he took the opportunity to thank the Great Leader in person: 'We greatly appreciate the work which Korean citizens have done, and are doing, to help in our agricultural development'. He continued by saying that the North Koreans 'encourage by example and practical action the development of our self-reliance. I can only say thank you'.[57] A similar disconnection between practical realities and political objectives can be identified in the Ghanaian case study.

* * *

In the early 1980s, North Korea provided technical aid and expertise to develop 13,200 hectares of farmland in Ghana. Three agricultural research stations were established in the vicinity of the capital city of Accra to train Ghanaian farmers. In return, Ghana promised to export farm produce to North Korea as payment.[58] The flagship Ghanaian–North Korean cooperation was the Ghana Juche Farm.

A North Korean team of agricultural experts developed the Ghana Juche Farm in Akatsi, near the Ghana–Togo border, between 1982 and 1983. The team consisted of a rice specialist, a mechanical engineer, an irrigation engineer, an interpreter and a group leader. They brought fertiliser, a bulldozer, four 'Chollima tractors', a plough and ambitious plans to revolutionise the Ghanaian agricultural industry.[59] The 50-hectare farm was designed to produce rice, corn and other vegetables. In subsequent years, the farm would be enlarged to about one hundred hectares, and the lessons learned would, in time, be applied to other projects across Ghana.[60] However, poor results led to the decision to move the North Korean team to Aveyime, a rice farm some 90 km from Accra. They arrived there in 1984.[61]

The Aveyime Rice Project was run by the Ghanaian Development Authority. The decision to transfer the North Korean team was not requested by the Ghanaian Development Authority, nor were they informed about the details of the cooperation.[62] Instead, the project was discussed during a visit of a high-level Ghanaian minister to Pyongyang for Kim Il Sung's birthday.[63] Despite the Ghanaian Development Authority's opposition, the Ghanaian government keenly accepted North Korean aid. The administration provided air transportation (including an annual holiday trip to the DPRK), local transportation, accommodation, food and a living allowance. The South Korean embassy in Accra cynically remarked that costs were 'bigger than the aid itself, and their purpose is to advertise their propaganda rather than to help'.[64]

At Aveyime, the North Koreans executed a field survey and repaired an irrigation pump, but their agricultural yields were disappointing. The North Koreans requested 20 hectares to conduct rice-growing trials but were only granted one by the suspicious Ghanaian staff. Despite their heavier use of fertiliser, the yield on this hectare was half the usual average yield of the rest of the farm. It is fair to say that despite the high expectations of the Ghanaian and North Korean governments, the practical results were dismal. The local Ghanaian staff did not want North Korean assistance, and contact between the two groups was limited because of the language barrier. Social relations between the two

DEVELOPMENT

groups 'were poor, and at times appeared overtly hostile'.[65] The Korean equipment broke down on the unfamiliar terrain and was difficult to repair because spare parts were unavailable.[66]

It was difficult for the political elites to deny this reality. During a 1986 visit of North Korean Vice Premier Jong Jun Gi (Chŏng Chunki) to the farm, Ghanaian officials explained the need to reappraise the project.[67] Nevertheless, political will prevailed. Three years later, in 1989, another team of North Koreans—consisting of seven irrigation experts—arrived in Ghana and worked at the Aveyime Rice Project. Again, Ghana paid the accommodation, food and logistical costs of the team, which stayed in the country for 15 months.[68]

Conclusion: failure and success

The examples of Tanzania and Ghana offer a number of observations that are relevant to DPRK development assistance in Africa. North Korea was keen to offer aid and tried to push their expertise on their African allies. Even if the envisaged host countries were initially reluctant to accept help, North Korea persisted and repeated their offers multiple times.[69] The invitation diplomacy of North Korea often resulted in the signing of large and vague friendship treaties that covered technical assistance and agriculture. Local Juche Study Centres in Africa had already laid the groundwork for the ideological underpinnings of North Korean aid.

The ensuing projects were framed as South–South cooperation, but as the stories of the Tanzanian Chollima Institute and the Ghana Juche Farm illustrate, North Korean aid projects were not particularly successful venues for promoting Juche Thought. Perhaps Juche is the reason for these failures—it was, after all, a one-size-fits-all ideology that cared little for local nuances. North Korea saw all African countries as more or less the same: anti-imperialist nations with a desire for self-reliance. In truth, the North Korean experience could not easily be replicated in Africa.

The South–South cooperation between African states and North Korea was characterised by top-down decisions made in Pyongyang, with little consideration for local realities. The

Tanzanian and Ghanaian case studies show that language barriers, cultural differences, and other practical problems disrupted genuine cooperation. As a result, exchanges between North Korean advisors and African staff were limited at best.

Yet, despite evidence of practical failure, African countries continued to accept new offers of North Korean aid and even offered to occasionally pay their salaries and other costs. The deployment of North Korean experts across a wide range of projects produced the image of success. In Tanzania, the British embassy reported that North Korea was able to maintain 'a high profile at little cost'.[70] In terms of diplomacy, the outsourcing of North Korean experts, the establishment of Juche farms in Africa and the public praise from African leaders constituted major victories for the North Korean regime.

North Korean development aid must be seen in the light of the ideals of South–South cooperation. Agricultural aid benefited African efforts to transform colonial economies and become self-reliant, and it enhanced North Korea's efforts to gain diplomatic prestige. Unfortunately, many idealistic projects of the 1980s became obsolete in the following decade, when African countries were hit by structural adjustment programmes and North Korea was plunged into an economic crisis following the end of the Cold War.[71] This meant that many programmes could no longer be continued and Juche agriculture fell out of fashion.

Nevertheless, one should not disregard the legacy of African–North Korean development aid too hastily. Despite the tumultuous geopolitical shifts that obstructed the realisation of the Juche revolution, agricultural ties continued at a slower pace after the Cold War. In 2022, North Korea sent 30 technicians to Guinea, in West Africa, to support agricultural research at the Kim Il Sung Agricultural Research Centre in Kilissi.[72] This Research Centre was founded in the same year that the Chollima Institute in Tanzania was concluded and that the Ghana Juche Farm was established. It is a clear, albeit barely noticed, sign that joint African–North Korean projects in the field of agriculture continue into the present.

EPILOGUE

MICROPHONE REVOLUTION

At a meeting of the Organisation of African Unity in Dar es Salaam (Tanzania) in 1975, the Zambian politician Vernon Mwaanga underlined Zambia's solidarity with the anticolonial movements in neighbouring countries. He explained that his fellow freedom fighters had written the story of their struggle in blood and that 'Zambian blood is part of the ink'. As one of the principal Frontline States, Zambia was at the heart of the various revolutions that engulfed Southern Africa. At the end of his speech, Mwaanga turned to Nyerere and said that 'a very strange form of revolution seems to be emerging in our ranks—and that is [a] "Microphone Revolution"'.[1]

The term 'Microphone Revolution' is a useful metaphor for analysing the diplomatic dimension of the era of decolonisation.[2] The metaphor of a microphone is not only effective to determine who speaks, but also to detect who listens. Words mattered during the liberation of Africa because it was diplomacy that permitted African liberation movements to rally support for their cause from individual governments, multilateral fora such as the NAM and the OAU Liberation Committee, and international solidarity movements. The struggle was often fought through a microphone.

Mwaanga emphasised that non-African socialist countries were 'the backbone' of the struggle. While we tend to think of the

97

Soviet Union and China in this regard, the important role of North Korea must not be overlooked. African liberation movements depended upon North Korean support, but this was also true the other way around. Both sides desired international recognition and acknowledged each other's anti-imperialist credentials. Africans and North Koreans framed their diplomatic relations as a form of solidarity, or in slightly different phrasing, as South–South cooperation.

A key message in this microphone revolution was the gospel of Juche Thought. A tool specifically designed to boost North Korea's global image, Juche was instrumental in strengthening the ties between North Korea and African liberation movements. Juche was, as Myers argues, part and parcel of the 'export track' of North Korean propaganda.[3] At the same time, the resulting connections were valuable for the 'inner track' of North Korean propaganda, as domestic audiences in North Korea were constantly reminded that Kim Il Sung was a leading figure in the anti-imperialist movement and envied across Africa.

The freedom fighters of Africa were particularly receptive to the message of Juche as it branded the DPRK as an example of a successful party state based on the mythology of a liberation struggle. Juche made North Korea distinct from mainstream Communist powers and thus an attractive ally for non-aligned countries. The emphasis on self-reliance resonated with anticolonial movements seeking independence.

Moreover, Juche opened the doors to tangible rewards for African movements. The invitations to Pyongyang provided a stage for African leaders to advertise their campaigns for independence and request support. Juche Study Centres presented the opportunity to meet people, read literature, watch films and travel. They were both physical and ideological spaces that offered ideological scaffolding at a time when African elites were imagining and exercising their newly found power. North Korean development aid was most welcome at a time when postcolonial African governments were rebuilding their states.

We must not forget that the process of decolonisation was often long and the outcome uncertain. Mwaanga was speaking at a time

EPILOGUE

when the Portuguese colonial empire was not yet dissolved, when the white minority government in Rhodesia had issued a unilateral declaration of independence and when the South African apartheid regime was still going strong.[4] 'The Southern African crisis for us is a matter of life and death', Mwaanga said. 'Freedom fighters have needs we must meet', he continued, 'the manpower, time energy and material resources demanded of us is incalculable'.[5]

And here Mwaanga brings us to a key point of the struggle: 'Africa's success cannot depend on words, however revolutionary. Our success depends on the material contribution to the struggle'.[6] The Microphone Revolution has its limits. Several—though not all—liberation movements became convinced that diplomacy would take them a long way, but not far enough. In the end, action speaks louder than words. As the second part of this book shows, microphones were not always sufficient—sometimes bullets and guns were deemed necessary.

PART TWO

BULLETS

MILITARY COOPERATION

Mother.
I have an iron rifle
your son,
the one you saw chained
one day
(when you cried as if
The chains bound and battered
Your hands and feet)
Your boy is free now
Mother.
Your boy has an iron rifle,
My rifle
will break the chains
will open the prisons
will kill the tyrants
will win back our land
Mother,
Beauty is to fight for freedom,
Justice rings in my every shot
and ancient dreams awaken like birds.
Fighting, on the front,
Your image descends.
I fight for you,
Mother
to dry the tears
of your eyes.

– 'Poem for a Militant', by Jorge Rebelo,
Mozambique

PROLOGUE

THE BARREL OF A GUN

Blood, the first theme of this book, not only symbolises comradeship, but it also signifies the willingness to fight, to shed blood on the battlefield. The decision to pick up arms set certain African anticolonial movements apart from those—often domestic rivals—that stuck with non-violent resistance. The Chinese revolutionary Mao Zedong famously said that 'political power grows out of the barrel of a gun'—a statement that widely resonated in Southern Africa and North Korea.

The gun appeared in ANC propaganda, SWAPO speeches, and ZANU education, and was repeated by FRELIMO and UNIP officials, among other examples.[1] The signature tune of Radio Freedom, the exiled radio station of the ANC, included the sound of an AK-47 rifle. The tune 'was intended to inspire defiance and insurgency' and signalled 'the ANC's determination to employ violent means to end apartheid'.[2] The South African musician Abdullah Ibrahim (Dollar Brand) sang the words 'freedom comes from the barrel of a gun' at the funeral of Ruth First, an anti-apartheid activist who was murdered by the South African secret police.[3] Jorge Rebelo's poem captured the feelings of many when he wrote that 'My rifle / will break the chains ... Beauty is to fight for freedom / Justice rings in my every shot'.[4]

COMRADES BEYOND THE COLD WAR

Guns, and the AK-47 in particular, featured prominently in the aesthetics of liberation propaganda.[5] The ANC periodicals and ZANU posters often displayed guns in their designs, and the logo of the exiled Namibia Press Agency combined a Kalashnikov with a pen. Its motto, 'Fighting for Truth' underlined the importance of the information war alongside the actual war. There is not much difference between a bullet and a bulletin.

North Korea similarly believed that 'armed struggle was the supreme form of struggle for national independence'. According to North Korean mythology, Kim Il Sung received two pistols from his father when he was just 14 years old—'the gift of the gun' would become a major theme in Kim's transformation from exiled guerrilla fighter to esteemed state leader. Many years later, Kim Il Sung would gift his ten-year-old son, Kim Jong Il, a gun to symbolically designate him as his successor. The gun, according to North Korean propaganda, embodies 'the destiny of the nation and the revolution'. As this book will discuss in further detail, the country became guided by the 'philosophy of the barrel of a gun' (ch'ongdae), which seeks to create unity between the military and society.[6]

The gun holds a sacred place in North Korean political culture. Many North Korean education materials include the guns of the Kim family to exemplify their moral leadership in the revolutionary struggle.[7] When the poet Jang Jin Sung composed the epic poem 'Spring Rests on the Gun Barrel of the Lord' in 1999, Kim Jong Il (the lord in question) was so delighted that he made Jang part of the 'Admitted', the inner circle of North Korea's elite. Jang, who later defected to South Korea, said this honour changed his life 'in the way that winning the lottery might do in a capitalist nation'.[8]

Most of the victorious liberation governments that are in power today in Southern Africa resorted to violent resistance. They fought against minority rule and established guerrilla armies in the process. The armed wings of these liberation movements were in dire need of military hardware and training. North Korea offered exactly this and gradually became 'an exceptional player' in Africa, the continent 'that witnessed the DPRK's greatest overall success and involvement' in terms of military support.[9] Several liberation movements, including FNLA, FRELIMO, MPLA, SWAPO,

104

PROLOGUE

TANU, ZANU and ZAPU, benefited from North Korean military training.[10]

'Bullets', the second theme of this book, symbolise the military cooperation between African liberation governments and North Korea. Kim Il Sung had listened to Mao's advice and supplied African liberation armies with cheap reverse-engineered guns and copious quantities of bullets.[11] With hardware came the goose-stepping: North Korean military advisors travelled to Africa or invited African guerrilla fighters to North Korea for extensive training in the art of war.[12]

The military mindsets of African liberation governments that were shaped during the wars of liberation continue to influence contemporary political culture in Southern Africa. Again, North Korea is never far away—illicit military cooperation between African states and North Korea is ongoing despite United Nations sanctions.

Today, the Kalashnikov features proudly on the flag of Mozambique's and Zimbabwe's coat of arms. Harare, the capital city of Zimbabwe, accommodates a cemetery shaped in the form of two AK-47s lying back-to-back, where each grave represents a bullet. The monument was designed by a North Korean art studio and is a copy of a cemetery in Pyongyang.

This second part of the book provides a brief account of why African liberation governments depended, in part, upon North Korean military support. Chapters 6 and 7 explain how some African nationalists came to view the armed struggle as inevitable and looked to Pyongyang for arms and training. The final chapters, 8 through 10, cover the three eras during which liberation movements and subsequent governments profited from relations with North Korea: the eras of achieving power (1960–1980); consolidating power (1980–2000); and maintaining power (2000–present).

6

WAR

THE BATTLEFIELDS OF AFRICA

In 1960, the British prime minister, Harold Macmillan, gave a historic speech in the parliament of South Africa. 'The wind of change is blowing through this continent', Macmillan remarked on the rise of African national consciousness. 'The great issue in this second half of the twentieth century', according to the British leader, was 'whether the uncommitted peoples of Asia and Africa will swing to the East or the West'. In front of the South African political class, he described this issue as 'a struggle for the minds of men'. Macmillan was convinced that 'what is now on trial is much more than our military strength or our diplomatic skill. It is our way of life'.[1]

For the South African apartheid government, these winds of change were experienced as an 'impending storm'. South Africa was 'virtually isolated and alone' and responded to this challenge with 'a vast increase in military preparedness'.[2] While most of the African continent had been liberated by the 1960s, large parts of Southern Africa were embroiled in a struggle without a clear outcome. The African liberation movements that advocated for self-governance were 'like a pale flame that at any moment could become a devastating fire'.[3] As their attempts to find legal or political solutions proved to be futile, only the gun was left.

Understanding the ebbs and flows of violence that spilled across the continent is crucial for any analysis of African liberation governments. This chapter is therefore centred around the Southern African battlefields of the second half of the twentieth century. The first section describes the shift in African political thought that caused anticolonial leaders to abandon the negotiation table and embrace the armed struggle. For a man like Kenneth Kaunda, the shift from his humanist ideas to supporting war was 'painful'.[4] However, a number of events made African nationalists realise that fighting for freedom was inevitable—a gradual transformation in belief that was captured in a succession of political declarations.

The second section provides an overview of the different wars that occurred in Southern Africa between the 1960s and the 1990s. As South Africa became the 'final major obstacle to Africa's march to liberation', a confusing mix of low-intensity guerrilla warfare ensued.[5] The third section highlights an existential problem for African nationalists: a lack of weapons. As Julius Nyerere said, 'a police state cannot be fought with bows and arrows'.[6] However, the assistance from the Liberation Committee was inadequate in terms of meeting the expectations of African freedom fighters. The Communist Bloc therefore emerged as a major benefactor of African decolonisation.

Embracing the armed struggle

African liberation movements contemplated two different paths to power, summarised by Nyerere as the 'conference' and the 'battlefield'. Between the 1950s and 1960s, optimistic nationalists organised political platforms, staged protests and appealed to the world community for change.

One important tool was petitioning. Africans in, for example, Namibia and Zimbabwe brought their nationalist claims to the UN and other international bodies—sometimes through Western advocates, oftentimes with great difficulty.[7] A former British representative to the UN Trusteeship Council spitefully remarked

WAR

that petitioning had become 'a national sport in tropic Africa'.[8] Nevertheless, the UN had limited capabilities to change the political landscape in Southern Africa.

Legal challenges proved to be equally ineffective. In 1960, Ethiopia and Liberia challenged South Africa's mandate over Namibia at the International Court of Justice in The Hague (the Netherlands). SWAPO and fellow revolutionaries across the continent were hopeful that the illegal occupation of Namibia would soon be over. However, the Court ultimately rejected Ethiopia's and Liberia's claim and ruled that both states had no legal right or interest in the matter.[9] This moment was a huge blow for African decolonisation. The UN African Group expressed its 'dismay and indignation at the incredible decision' in a press conference. For Africans, the court ruling was evidence of the unfair and unequal world in which they were living. It demonstrated that they were stuck in a 'white man's world with a white man's court'.[10]

In the years following the end of World War II, several tragic events darkened the dreams of liberation in Southern Africa. The crushing of the Mau Mau rebellion in Kenya between 1952 and 1960, the Sharpeville massacre in 1960 when South African police killed dozens of protestors, the assassination of Patrice Lumumba and the betrayal of Congolese independence in 1961—it all boiled down to the idea that African people were not allowed to determine their own destiny.

For large parts of Southern Africa, attempts to reach a peaceful transition to independence proved to be futile. Once African revolutionaries felt that they had exhausted all of their diplomatic options, only the battlefield was left. This progression in thinking is captured in a succession of political declarations by leading African states. These documents are revealing examples of African political thought that guided the actions of liberation movements. The following paragraphs describe the Lusaka Manifesto of 1969, the Mogadishu Declaration of 1971 and the Dar es Salaam Declaration of 1975.

* * *

The Lusaka Manifesto of 1969 confirmed African commitment to the total liberation of the continent. It was prepared by Zambia and Tanzania and adopted by several states in East and Central Africa. Crucially, the manifesto declared that 'we would prefer to negotiate rather than destroy, to talk rather than kill'. Nathan Shamuyarira observed that diplomacy and war were presented as two sides of the same coin. 'Negotiating whenever and wherever possible, and fighting only when all else has failed'.[11] It encouraged the Western world to engage with Africa.

The Lusaka Manifesto was a 'rallying point' for moderate and radical African states and was adopted by the Organisation of African Unity and the United Nations as an important policy document. However, several liberation movements were 'quietly dismayed' about this strategy as they feared that the emphasis on negotiation would lead to the abandonment of the armed struggle. 'Their attempts to win freedom by peaceful means had been suppressed ruthlessly', said Julius Nyerere at a meeting of the Liberation Committee. 'The only choice left to them was surrender, or armed struggle. And everywhere surrender had been rejected'.[12]

The ANC, in many ways the blueprint for liberation movements across the region, led the way in asserting the inevitability of violent resistance.[13] 'The sixty years of struggle led by the ANC is sufficient proof that dialogue is not possible', said a Zambian cabinet member in 1972. 'We should now talk through the barrel of a gun'.[14] The ANC itself believed that their propaganda gave the South African people confidence to complete the transition from information warfare to actual warfare: 'They know it is leaflets today; but they know too it will be the bark of our guns soon'.[15]

A coalition of more radical African states and liberation movements lobbied for the abandonment of the Lusaka Manifesto. Their efforts led to the Mogadishu Declaration of 1971, a document adopted during a meeting of Eastern and Central African States. The Mogadishu Declaration stipulated that 'there is no way left for the liberation of Southern Africa except armed struggle'. In response, the guerrilla fighting across the region became more intensified.[16]

WAR

In 1974, a military coup in Lisbon marked the end of the violent conflict between Portugal and its African colonies.[17] The collapse of the Portuguese Empire was bad news for the minority regimes of South Africa and Rhodesia. The subsequent independence of Mozambique and Angola resulted in a significant crack in the 'security umbrella that shielded minority regimes from the pressures of African nationalism'.[18] Again, the violence across the region intensified.

From the perspective of African nationalists, 1974 was a major success. Julius Nyerere viewed this event as a 'clear and unmistakable result of the armed struggles' in Angola and Mozambique. He congratulated their populations and announced that the members of the Liberation Committee can give themselves 'a little pat on the back'.[19] Yet, the battle for freedom was not over. Samora Machel said that 'talks are an important factor for victory, but they are not the decisive factor. Mozambique regards the armed struggle as the decisive factor for victory'.[20] This lesson was clearly understood in the headquarters of the liberation movements that remained oppressed.

In 1975, the Liberation Committee adopted the Dar es Salaam Declaration. Its members called for a new strategy for the liberation of Southern Africa, in particular for Namibia and Zimbabwe. It was decided that there was no need for dialogue with South Africa.[21] Nyerere believed that the regional dynamics of the struggle were 'completely transformed' by the end of Portuguese colonialism. Namibia and Zimbabwe were now prioritised by the Liberation Committee. The Dar es Salaam Declaration reaffirmed the call for an intensified armed struggle.[22]

The battlefields of Africa

Generally speaking, the drive for African decolonisation was at odds with colonial powers that were based abroad. African nationalists thus opposed centres of power in Britain, France or other European countries. Southern Africa differed from this convention. After the fall of the Portuguese Empire, settler regimes were the last barrier to majority rule. Thus, Nyerere concluded in 1975 that

'Africa's confrontation in Southern Africa now is basically with South Africa'.[23] The influence of the apartheid regime extended far beyond the borders of South Africa. Pretoria had incorporated Namibia as a fifth province and supported the regime of Ian Smith in Zimbabwe. As such, the final phase in the liberation of Southern Africa took on a different character than in other parts of the continent.

'The forces of darkness have transformed the whole of Southern Africa into a zone of war and death', said the Secretary-General of the ANC, Alfred Nzo, in 1982. 'Daily, from Angola through to Mozambique and from Zambia to South Africa, they murder, rape and pillage. Everyday their manhating system spews out corpses that are riddled with bullets'. For Nzo and many other liberation movements, the forces of darkness were the apartheid regime in Pretoria in all its shapes and forms, described as a dangerous beast with 'merciless talons dripping with blood'.[24]

Even though the objective of African nationalists seemed clear—defeat South Africa, gain independence—the ensuing military state of affairs was far from simple. From the 1960s onwards, liberation movements 'fought different sorts of wars', often at the same time. They fought against settler colonialism and against each other, resulting in various interrelated conflicts that were turbocharged by the Cold War.[25] Despite Nzo's belief that that South Africa was engaged in a 'desperate rear-guard fight', several key military campaigns against Pretoria dragged on for years, even decades.[26]

In essence, there were four different battlefields in Southern Africa: the Zimbabwean War of Independence (1966–79, also known as the Rhodesian Bush War); the Namibian War of Independence (1966–90, also known as the South African Border War); the Mozambican War of Independence and subsequent Mozambican Civil War (respectively 1964–74 and 1976–92); and the Angolan War of Independence and subsequent Angolan Civil War (respectively, 1961–75 and 1975–2002). For historical context, each battlefield will be briefly discussed below.

The Zimbabwean War of Independence started in 1966. Originally a British colony, Zimbabwe briefly became part of the

WAR

Central African Federation, together with Zambia and Malawi. A failed political experiment, the federation lasted only from 1953 to 1963.[27] While Zambia and Malawi were granted independence soon thereafter, the white minority regime in Zimbabwe issued a Unilateral Declaration of Independence in 1965. Led by Ian Smith, the country (now known as Rhodesia) broke off its relation to Britain but withstood black majority rule. Rhodesian security forces were opposed by the guerrillas of ZANU and ZAPU in a low-intensity guerrilla conflict that also became known as the Second *Chimurenga*. The conflict finally ended in 1980, with the Lancaster House Agreement that introduced a cease-fire and elections.[28]

The Namibian War of Independence commenced in 1966 when SWAPO fighters clashed with South African Defence Force soldiers for the first time. South Africa was desperate to hold on to its colony and the ensuing conflict was long, costly and traumatic.[29] Also known as the 'Border War' or 'Bush War', the fighting spilled over into Zambia and Angola as the South African Defence Force—in cooperation with Rhodesian soldiers—sought to destroy SWAPO bases in exile.[30] The war came to an end with the removal of South African and Cuban troops from Angola, with Namibian independence in 1990.[31]

The Mozambican Civil War erupted in 1976, when the insurgent group RENAMO challenged FRELIMO's rule. RENAMO opposed FRELIMO's one-party state and authoritarian politics. The insurgents were backed by Rhodesia and South Africa, who had vested interests in putting a halt to FRELIMO's support of ZANU and the ANC.[32] The war wrought havoc across Mozambique and ended in 1992 when 'a return to war was impossible' because of external factors, including the collapse of the Soviet Union and the impending end of apartheid.[33]

Angola's transition to independence was 'markedly different' than Mozambique's, even though both states were part of the same Portuguese Empire.[34] In 1975, a 'ferocious civil war' ensued between the MPLA, the FNLA and UNITA, three movements that all claimed to be the legitimate power in Angola. The MPLA was backed by the Soviet Union and Cuba, while the latter two organisations received support from China, Congo, the United

States and South Africa.[35] South Africa perceived the presence of thousands of Cuban troops as a security threat and therefore funnelled money and weapons to the fighters that countered the 'communists' of the MPLA.[36] The Cuban intervention coincidentally also influenced the Namibian War of Independence, as the US linked the removal of Castro's forces to Namibian independence.[37] In 2002 the MPLA achieved a military victory that ended the civil war.

In all four cases it is evident that war cannot be fully understood in isolation. The regional violence reached a peak in the 1980s, when South Africa was convinced that the communist world directed a 'Total Onslaught' against their minority rule. Pretoria introduced a 'Total Strategy' to withstand the pressures against apartheid.[38] In addition to the aforementioned cases of subversion, South Africa deployed counterinsurgency operations in Botswana, Lesotho and Swaziland. It created and funded non-state groups to destabilise neighbouring countries. Clandestine commando units and death squads were given 'free reign to infiltrate, destabilise and hunt down' any person or organisation that opposed Pretoria.[39] As such, the various national uprisings in Southern Africa became closely intertwined.

Tangible solidarity

The decision to take up arms against the apartheid military machine was not taken lightly by African anticolonial activists. Andreas Shipanga recalled that 'it was grim to have to accept the inevitability of armed struggle. Grim for myself and for many others ... we knew it would be terrible'.[40] Julius Nyerere believed that 'no African people enjoy fighting for the sake of fighting'. But the people of Southern Africa yearned for freedom, and it was clear that a peaceful resolution was impossible. There was 'no alternative but to take up arms'. Nyerere emphasised that Africans 'will then be prepared to kill, and to die, for their independence'.[41]

But even as the SWAPO leadership made the firm decision to wage armed struggle, Shipanga realised that they were still a long way from launching a convincing military offensive. 'We had no

WAR

weapons', was the bottom line of SWAPO's problem—a problem shared by virtually all liberation movements that decided to take up arms.[42] 'Even if we wished', announced ZANU in 1972, 'we cannot supply every adult Zimbabwean with a rifle—at least for now'. The liberation movement urged their fellow compatriots to 'fight with bare hands and feet, with stones and half-bricks, and with paraffin and matches'.[43]

In short, African revolutionaries were in need of modern military hardware and professional training in order to stand a chance on the battlefield. They primarily relied on African solidarity to acquire such expertise. 'Africa has no choice but to side with the freedom struggle of Southern Africa', proclaimed Nyerere.[44] To this end, the Liberation Committee of the Organisation of African Unity was designed to supply African revolutionaries with the means to win liberation through the barrel of a gun. But as was already mentioned in Chapter 1, the Committee's aid was insufficient. Shortly after its creation in 1963, the Committee 'lost a good deal of its revolutionary ferment' when the influential leaders Ben Bella in Algeria and Kwame Nkrumah in Ghana were removed from power via coup d'états.[45]

Political tensions were followed by economic difficulties, and in 1966 the budget of the Liberation Committee was rejected by its members. One delegate said that 'we have no desire to empty our coffers so that a handful of second-rate politicians can travel all over the world'. This deadlock was resolved through the intervention of Julius Nyerere. Mwalimu Nyerere threatened to expel the Committee from Dar es Salaam if the OAU did not cough up the necessary funds.[46] Nevertheless, the Liberation Committee could never meet the needs of all African guerrilla movements.

Those that were dependent on the Liberation Committee often despaired about its inability to provide sufficient material aid. In a speech delivered on behalf of multiple liberation movements, Agostinho Neto stated that 'pious resolutions, sympathetic declarations and repeated promises cannot solve the problems of war ... what we essentially need are weapons and money'. Neto reminded the outside world that 'solidarity is a duty'.[47] Joshua Nkomo echoed this sentiment a few years later, when he asked the world not to send 'big bundles of resolutions, but big bundles of guns'. He coined this 'tangible solidarity'.[48]

Nonetheless, it proved impossible for the Frontline States and other African states to offer adequate tangible solidarity. This was not because of ill will—they were simply limited for practical reasons. Nyerere admitted that Africa had in effect 'very little power to affect the outcome' of the struggle. 'We are all poor nations. We have no effective economic power to use. Further, we do not even manufacture arms'.[49] The last point was the sum and substance of the dilemma that haunted African guerrillas: relying on African solidarity was not enough to win a war. The readiness of forces outside Africa to supply weapons thus became a factor of importance.

Conclusion

The start of the armed struggle is a watershed moment in the mythology of any liberation movement. It was the proverbial crossing of the Rubicon; moving beyond the negotiating tables of the diplomatic arena into the fields of war. In the case of Namibia, SWAPO believed that 'the first bullets fired by Namibian compatriots signalled the tide and direction of the Namibian history'. The first clash between SWAPO guerrilla fighters and the South African Defence Force on 26 August 1966, the drawing of first blood, 'marked a new era' in Namibian history. It was a symbolic point of no return, as SWAPO devoted itself to pursuing its 'political goal through the barrel of a gun'.[50]

In practice, the process to establish military wings, decide on strategies and train and arm a sufficient number of fighters was slow and difficult. Support from abroad was deemed a crucial factor for success.[51] In anticipation of its own armed wing, ZAPU, for example, sent over 100 members to the Soviet Union, China, Cuba, Egypt and North Korea for military training.[52] After months of training, the group reconvened in Zambia and were instructed to agree on the establishment of a formal liberation army. Dumiso Dabengwa recalled how he and his comrades engaged 'in daily, highly charged debates' about what strategy to pursue. It would still

WAR

take years before ZAPU could execute proper military operations. Dabengwa—nicknamed the 'Black Russian' on account of his own exile experience in the Soviet Union—ultimately became the Chief of Intelligence of ZAPU's armed wing.[53]

The communist support for African liberation worried the Western world. However, Dabengwa explained that ZAPU did not cooperate with countries like North Korea because they were socialist, but simply because 'they were willing to help'.[54] While the West refused to provide arms and training to Zimbabwean nationalists, North Korea vowed to give them 'full support and encouragement'.[55] Kim Il Sung believed that 'it is inevitable that oppressed people should fight for their emancipation ... the oppressed people can liberate themselves only through struggle'.[56] African revolutionaries refused to accept the 'white man's world with a white man's court' any longer.[57]

African revolutionaries were therefore primarily motivated by pragmatic reasons to accept non-Western aid. This does not detract from the fact that China and the Eastern Bloc did their utmost best to convert African freedom fighters to card-carrying communists. As the next chapter shows, African freedom fighters were not always keen on socialist literature, but they were impressed by anti-imperialist revolutions. The Korean War in particular was an example of a battle that inspired African liberation movements— not least because North Korea actively exported its war experience to the African continent.

7

WEAPONS

NORTH KOREAN WAR EXPERIENCE

'When we speak of Communism in Africa', an American government official said in 1979, 'we are speaking almost exclusively of the Soviet Union, Eastern Europe, Cuba, and China'. The US worried about the 'extensive flow of weaponry from Communist countries to Africa' but overlooked North Korea as a possible player with influence. For many years, North Korea was able to gradually build up its military relations with African guerrilla groups and states without being noticed, up until the point it became impossible for the West to ignore.[1]

Why did African freedom fighters connect with the Korean People's Army? The armed struggle for African decolonisation and the stalemate after the Korean War inspired the friendship between two sets of very different anti-imperial fighters, from Southern Africa and East Asia. The Korean War was the 'first major military conflict of the Cold War', one that would have reverberating effects across the entire world.[2] This chapter argues that the Korean War was crucial for kickstarting the networks between Pyongyang and African capitals. Some African countries fought on behalf of South Korea, while other countries took inspiration from North Korea's legacy of the war.

The first section considers the African–Korean connections that existed prior to the start of Korean diplomatic competition in the 1960s. Ethiopia and South Africa participated in the UN Command that defended South Korea during the Korean War. The second section describes how the arms industry was a key component in North Korea's post-war reconstruction. Importantly, North Korea did not just export weapons to Africa, but also war experience. The latter in particular resonated with anti-imperial activists across the continent. The third section explores African motivations for cooperation with North Korea. Were they motivated by ideology or pragmatism? While Western actors were convinced that all Africans were communists, this chapter argues that it is imperative to move beyond the East–West binary as predicted by Harold Macmillan in his 'winds of change' speech.[3]

The Korean War

At the end of World War II, the Korean peninsula was the site of 'intense great power competition'. Scholars have therefore highlighted the international dimensions of the Korean War, though this often entails geopolitical giants such as the United States, the Soviet Union and China.[4] The focus on great power competition obscures the fact that the Korean War had a distinct African dimension, years before both Koreas launched their diplomatic campaigns in the continent. Two of the 16 members of the UN coalition that defended South Korea were African: a South African air squadron and the Ethiopian Kagnew Battalion.

Both South Africa and Ethiopia were motivated to join the coalition by a desire to enhance their status within the UN system. South Africa aimed to 'bolster its standing' after it received widespread criticism of introducing apartheid legislation, while Ethiopia sought UN permission to incorporate neighbouring Eritrea.[5] The Ethiopian contingent were the only Black troops in the war and were therefore met with suspicion by American troops, but they fought with distinction and quickly 'earned the respect of their comrades after countless bloody, often hand-to hand battles'.[6]

120

WEAPONS

After the Korean War ended in a stalemate, relations between both African states and the UN remained relevant. The Ethiopian army continued to serve in the UN Command that defended South Korea. This command—the first in the history of the UN—was tasked with defending the Korean armistice.[7] The Ethiopian army questioned the usefulness of its continued presence in the command, but the Americans were determined to keep them in. Internally, the State Department agreed that the Ethiopian involvement was militarily insignificant. It did, however, contribute significantly to the multinational character of the mission. If the Ethiopians withdrew, others might be tempted to do so as well. Therefore, participation 'even of a token nature' was an 'important symbol'.[8]

South Africa's participation, however, was more of a headache for the Washington–Seoul axis. The South African government was 'justifiably proud' of its participation in the Korean War and used it as diplomatic currency. When, in 1961, an American government official criticised the apartheid policies of South Africa, the South African minister of foreign affairs met with the American ambassador to remind him that both countries 'share the common aim of opposition to Communism'. As an example, the minister reiterated that South Africa 'although having no political or economic interests in the Far East, was one [of the few countries worldwide] to fight side by side with the American airmen in Korea'. And the critique on apartheid was simply based on 'distorted and often false press reports'.[9]

However, South Korea's connection to South Africa became an obstacle for its diplomatic standing in the UN. In 1963, South Korean diplomats hoped that South Africa's co-sponsorship of pro-South Korea resolutions could be avoided 'in light of their recent difficulties with Africans'. As apartheid came under increasing international scrutiny, South African appreciation of the UN also 'declined markedly', and Pretoria questioned why they would contribute to an organisation that might take action against them.[10]

The early African involvement in the Korean War on the side of South Korea is an interesting precursor to the events that are described in this book. It illustrates that before the eruption of

121

COMRADES BEYOND THE COLD WAR

diplomatic Korean competition in Africa, there were already diplomatic and military links between African countries and the peninsula.

Post-war reconstruction

It is hard to overstate how utterly destructive the Korean War was. North Korea lost 8,700 industrial plants, 600,000 homes were destroyed and 10% of its population was killed, wounded or went missing. The Korean War utterly changed the fabric of society and became a foundational myth of the North Korean state, just as the African wars of independence became the origin myths of African liberation governments (see Chapter 11). The North Korean leadership internalised 'the bitter lessons of national ruin' and turned this into an advantage.[11] The miraculous post-war reconstruction inspired awe in the African continent and beyond.[12] The North Korean state believed that 'history shows that national sovereignty and independence is guaranteed by the strength of arms, military strength'.[13] A key aspect of the reconstruction of North Korea was the development of a military industry.

The basis for the North Korean arms industry was established in the early Cold War, when China and the Soviet Union granted licence agreements to North Korea for the production of small arms, light weapons and munitions. Both communist states were also involved in the establishment of arms factories in North Korea. Around the late 1960s or early 1970s, North Korea's arms industry entered a new phase when it began to modify and update existing communist weapons technologies. Around the same time, the export of weapons and training services to foreign allies began.[14]

North Korea modified, updated and reverse-engineered military technology until it maintained a 'vast catalogue' of hardware and services. The analyst Andrea Berger estimates that this catalogue included:

> complete off-the-shelf weapons systems and so-called 'knock-down kits'; spare parts for those systems and for supporting infrastructure; weapons designs and technology; whole arms

122

WEAPONS

manufacturing lines and complexes; repair, maintenance and upgrade services; military training in a wide variety of disciplines; and brokering, procurement and logistical services.[15]

Military exports became a key component of North Korea's foreign policy during the Cold War. In a bid to improve its standing in the NAM and to marginalise South Korea, it offered military instructors and weapons to trusted partners.[16] As such, Pyongyang emerged as an 'important player' in the global arms market. More than 60 state and non-state actors across the world benefited from this form of assistance between 1960 and 1990.[17] The majority of its customers were located in Africa.[18] A CIA report from 1984 estimated that North Korea earned around $300 million per year through the sale of arms.[19] Increasingly, military exports became a means to earn hard foreign currency.[20]

North Korea's value to African liberation movements went beyond the export of reverse-engineered Kalashnikovs or instructions for goose-stepping: it shared an experience of anti-imperial revolution. North Korean political thought is infused with references to anticolonial partisan fighting against Japanese colonisation and the Korean War, which was envisaged as an anti-imperial struggle against the United States. Kim Il Sung received two guns from his father and became the liberator of the North Korean people—years later, Kim Il Sung allegedly gifted his own gun to Kim Jong Il to ordain him as his successor, another symbolic moment that 'took place in the fog of the Korean War'.[21]

The Korean struggle credentials resonated with African liberation movements under siege. When Andreas Shipanga visited Pyongyang for the first time in 1965, one year before the start of SWAPO's armed struggle, he recalled that 'North Korea was a country permanently prepared for war'. It was his first official foreign mission for the liberation movement. He admired the monuments dedicated to Kim Il Sung and saw glimpses of whole factories hidden away inside mountains. It made a deep impression on him.[22]

Indeed, North Koreans experienced the Korean War as 'total war' and internalised this mentality in the post-war development

123

of their state.[23] In an impeccable case of the invention of tradition, the North Korean state would turn historical exploits of guerrilla warfare into political concepts that sustain the incumbent leadership.[24] *Ch'ongdae* ('barrel of the gun philosophy') advocates 'an absolute moral unity between the army and the gun ... a practical and spiritual unity between the person and the gun'. As discussed further in Chapter 13, Kim Jong Il would use *ch'ongdae* to introduce a 'military first' policy that privileges the army (*sŏn'gun*). In both concepts, the revolutionary past plays an important role.[25]

For Africans looking to defeat colonial states and Western interests, the North Korean war experience was appealing. In the conclusion of the previous chapter, I mentioned that North Korea served as an example in ZAPU's discussions about the formation of its armed wing. Dumiso Dabengwa remembered that during those heated arguments in 1964, his comrades gave presentations about the strategies and ideologies used by the Chinese, Cuban and North Korean revolutions, 'based on the experiences of Mao Zedong, Che Guevara and Kim Il Sung'.[26] The next chapter will provide more examples of how the Korean War inspired African soldiers.

Moving beyond the East–West binary

African interest in North Korea's war experience fell within a broader framework of Afro-Asian solidarity. Many believed that 'the progressive African states regard the socialist countries as their natural allies'.[27] As already highlighted in Chapter 1, the ever-closer fraternity between African liberation movements and their socialist sponsors raised the alarm in Western capitals. 'As soon as they run short of argument and force, the colonialists call our movement a communist movement', grumbled the steering committee of the MPLA. The Angolan organisation was adamant about its own position: they were not communist, and 'never pretended to be'.[28]

Julius Nyerere feared that the freedom struggles in Africa would 'become confused by a power conflict which is irrelevant to it'.[29] Nyerere was tired of the inevitable question about whether

WEAPONS

African states were pro-East or pro-West. 'Every possible attempt is made to squeeze African events into the framework of the Cold War'. According to him, these were 'the wrong questions for anyone who wishes to understand what is happening in Africa'. The fundamental mistake that outsiders have always made is that they assume that 'Africa has no ideas of its own and no interests of its own'.[30]

For this reason, African politicians often embraced a non-aligned foreign policy. 'We are not interested in Cold War rivalries and quarrels', stated a Batswana minister in Tanzania in 1970. This was 'the primary reason for our decision to be non-aligned'. Like many African states, the minister stated that 'we wish to be free to seek aid from any quarter which will serve to sustain our independence'.[31] Non-alignment opened the door for relations with North Korea and other communist states, which African elites viewed through a practical rather than an ideological lens.

Nevertheless, the communist label was effective in depicting African liberation movements as a danger to world peace and a threat to global stability.[32] For instance, the South African apartheid government warned the world that the ANC would introduce a communist regime. Alfred Nzo called this 'noisy propaganda distorting the aims of our peoples', pointing at the Freedom Charter that was adopted in 1955.[33] Nelson Mandela ridiculed the 'communist bogey', which he called 'an American stunt'. Such accusations were only meant 'to distract the attention of the people of Africa from the real issues facing them, namely American imperialism'.[34]

Western insistence on communist 'indoctrination' irked African nationalists, who were motivated by a domestic agenda. Joshua Nkomo questioned why the West believed that simple exposure to the East would turn Africans into communists. He recalled his education by the British colonial authorities, where he had to memorise Shakespeare and read Adam Smith. 'But we never became British! So why do the people who for years drilled us in their doctrine believe that two days in Moscow will make us communists?'[35] Kaunda lamented that 'four trips to the West were not sufficient to make me a capitalist! Only one trip to Peking will make me a communist! What reasoning is this?'[36]

When Andreas Shipanga appeared in front of the US Senate, he noted that SWAPO's leadership 'never had time [for] or real interest' in reading the socialist literature that was gifted to them upon their visits to the East.[37] Indeed, a UN official who was intimately involved in Namibia's decolonisation process later remarked in his autobiography that he 'doubted if Nujoma would know a Marxist-Leninist idea if he met one in the street'.[38] During Shipanga's testimony, he criticised the hypocrisy of American politicians, asking if they really believed that 'the bushes and sand dunes of Namibia to be teeming with red blacks, all indoctrinated with Soviet ideology? I can testify here truthfully that in Namibia I have never come across a single communist black person'. Shipanga turned the question around: 'Instead of investigating Reds in our bushes, you could easily have caught them by their hundreds in the concrete and glass forests across the whole of the USA'.[39]

What many Western politicians missed at the time was the fact that exposure to communist ideology could sometimes be counterproductive. A case study from South Africa is illustrative of this point. All exiled ANC students in the Soviet Union received extensive lessons in Marxist–Leninist philosophy and scientific communism. In a note from 1988, the students voiced their concerns to the ANC leadership: they felt that the Soviets were 'trying to indoctrinate' them, as the work had 'nothing to do with their specialities', and, in any case, the lessons contained 'too much repetition'. There was little appetite for Soviet ideological publications either. 'The females usually do not read them. They rather read a novel'. But the main problem was that young people liked to have fun. 'If there is a party somewhere, everyone will leave what they are doing and go to party'. The results of the exposure to the Soviet Union were sobering, as 'some comrades have made it clear in private discussions that they don't want socialism in our country'.[40]

In 1979, a report from the Bureau of African Affairs of the US State Department rightfully concluded that 'nationalism is a powerful force in Africa, and no African leaders or peoples

WEAPONS

wish to come under the lasting influence of any foreign power'. However, their warning that 'Africa is a continent of moving, not still, pictures' did not reach American politicians.[41] It is important to note that the Africans who sought cooperation with Pyongyang never understood this relationship through the lens of communism. Rather, they were motivated by a practical need to bring their own revolution to a successful conclusion. Subsequently, the main goals were consolidating and maintaining power.

The *Journal of African Marxists* concluded bitterly that 'the re-colonisation of Africa does not require the use of guns, the cheque book is sufficient'. It was a striking comment on the ideological route that most liberation governments took when they finally got a hold on power: 'Most African states have consciously or unconsciously taken the capitalist road'.[42] Despite the sometimes overt communist rhetoric of the Cold War, most liberation movements were not truly socialist—they simply desired independence.

Conclusion

'If the door to freedom is locked and bolted, and the present guardians of the door have refused to turn the key or pull the bolts, the choice is very straightforward', Nyerere said in 1969. 'Either you accept the lack of freedom or you break down the door'. African nationalists across the continent envisioned the armed struggle as inevitable. However, for the revolution to succeed, arms were necessary. 'Not even the most skilled guerrilla movement can fight machine guns with bows and arrows', he added. There was one downside to this strategy: 'Africa cannot supply these arms; we do not make them, and we have no money to buy them'. For Nyerere and other revolutionaries, there was only one viable alternative. 'So we accept arms from communist states, and say "thank you" to them'.[43]

Among a number of other nations, North Korea became a principal supporter of African nationalists who desired self-governance. Pyongyang's timely intervention in the struggle for freedom was not forgotten in African capitals. In a speech aptly titled 'The Weapons That Brought Us Victory', Samora Machel celebrated the 'natural alliance' between socialist countries and Mozambique. It was the tenth anniversary of the start of the Mozambican war of independence and Machel emphasised that FRELIMO would 'never forget the exemplary solidarity extended by North Korea'.[44]

While these events were shaped by the Cold War, African guerrillas and North Korean instructors were not Cold Warriors, as they were fighting for independence. Nationalism mattered most, not ideology. Nyerere was confident that external aid would not corrupt the quest for African freedom. 'We know our own motives ... We are not communists; we are nationalists desiring freedom'.[45] This sentiment was also captured in the military doctrine of the ANC, which envisaged nationalism as the driving force for revolution, not internationalism. The military vision of MK stipulated that 'the national character of the struggle must dominate our approach ... The national sense of grievance is the most potent revolutionary force'. The ANC believed that to blunt this revolutionary force 'in the interest of abstract concepts of internationalism, is, in the long run, doing a service neither to revolution nor to internationalism'.[46]

North Korea's military experience, a virtue closely associated with Pyongyang's idiosyncratic recovery from the ruins of the Korean War, caught the attention of African liberation movements. For them, North Korea's appeal did not come from its communist background, but rather from its successful resistance against imperialism—a revolution that, during the decades of African decolonisation, was still within recent memory. The next three chapters in this part of the book will explain how North Korea moved from being a theoretical inspiration to a practical partner for exiled liberation movements that wanted to achieve, consolidate and maintain power.

8

TRAINING

ACHIEVING POWER, 1960–1980

In his autobiography, the SWAPO leader and Namibian president Sam Nujoma described his strenuous efforts to acquire the first weapons for the armed struggle in Namibia.[1] In 1963, Nujoma and his SWAPO aides travelled to Algeria to pick up two 'pepesha' (PPSh-41) sub-machine guns and two 'TT' pistols. They smuggled the weapons in four black bags from Algiers to Cairo (Egypt), then to Nairobi (Kenya) and then to Dar es Salaam (Tanzania), travelling by plane. At the airport in Tanzania, Nujoma was 'extremely worried' that custom officials would discover the firearms. Much to his relief, he was waved through by the airport staff 'with my heart still pounding'. From Tanzania, the weapons were driven to Lusaka by car with the help of friendly UNIP members from Zambia.[2]

Nujoma's clandestine mission illustrates the ordeal that African freedom fighters faced when trying to acquire weaponry in the early days of the armed struggles in Southern Africa. It was not easy to get your hands on a rifle in those days. A single ZANU guerrilla unit could simultaneously use a Soviet sniper rifle, a NATO bazooka, a Romanian AK-47 and a World War II-era machine gun from Germany.[3] And weapons were just one piece of

129

COMRADES BEYOND THE COLD WAR

the puzzle: the cadres of African liberation movements were also in need of military training. In addition, Nujoma's story highlights the transnational dimension of the armed struggle: his dependency on friendly African governments was common among liberation movements. Again, exile was key.[4]

African liberation was never an entirely African affair. As decolonisation occurred in parallel with the Cold War, powerful external forces sought to influence events in Africa. This provided opportunities for African nationalists, such as Nujoma and his comrades, who desired arms and training. China and the Soviet Union were well-known benefactors of liberation movements, but not the only ones. North Korea emerged as another major player in the armed struggles of Southern Africa. A Korean version of Nujoma's autobiography is also available in North Korea.[5]

The first section of this chapter discusses exile. In the early years of African decolonisation, liberation movements flocked to places such as Algeria and Ghana for military support. These were precisely the states North Korea targeted in its African foreign policy programmes. The second section describes the rise of military mindsets within African liberation movements. The armies of liberation movements were impressed by North Korea's achievements during the Korean War. In the decades to come, these military mindsets would determine political culture in Southern Africa. The third section uncovers the military training that North Korea provided to Southern African liberation movements. African freedom fighters received training in North Korean embassies and camps in the Frontline States, and advanced training in North Korea.

African revolutionaries

The Algerian Revolution occupies a special place in history. Algeria was an inspiring model for most African liberation movements and the key to North Korea's diplomatic offensive in Africa. The Algerian War for Independence lasted from 1954 to 1962 and resulted in a victory over colonial France. Led by the FLN, the war became a symbol of African decolonisation. Both Koreas competed

TRAINING

for the support of Ahmed Ben Bella, the leader of the FLN and first president of Algeria.

The United States saw it as 'a major victory' for North Korea when Algeria accepted a North Korean ambassador in 1963.[6] Ahmed Ben Bella's government did not recognise South Korea. In 1965, Algeria was set to host the Afro-Asian Conference, which was effectively 'Bandung II', the successor of the Bandung Conference in 1955. Evidence of North Korea's impending attendance came in the form of a Mercedes 600 'Pullman' limousine, which was ready to transport Kim Il Sung across Algiers. It was dubbed the 'People's Democratic Socialist limousine' by jealous American diplomats, who secretly commented that the American ambassador drove a mere second-rate Checker Sedan.[7] South Korea lobbied for a formal invitation, but was apparently not invited to participate.[8] Even though the conference was ultimately called off (because of the coup against Ben Bella), the interest of the Koreas illustrates how they both vied for influence in Algiers.

The US found it 'difficult to believe' that Algeria would champion North Korea's cause at the United Nations and warned that this would 'seriously jeopardise' Ben Bella's chance to visit America. Nevertheless, Algeria became an essential part of North Korea's success in the UN General Assembly.[9] Within the OAU, North Korea was also 'dependent on Algeria to sponsor its cause in corridor discussions'.[10] It is no surprise, therefore, that Algeria is one of the only two African countries ever visited by Kim Il Sung (in 1975), as highlighted in Chapter 3.

An important reason why North Korea invested so much political capital in Algeria was its status among African revolutionaries. Nelson Mandela, the illustrious leader of the South African struggle, was inspired by the Algerian Revolution, like many other African nationalists. He saw it as 'the closest model' to South Africa.[11] In 1962, he travelled to the Algerian Liberation training camps to learn how to wage an armed struggle. Later, Mandela would say that the military training he received there 'made me a man'.[12]

One of the lessons Mandela internalised from the FLN was the importance of discipline and unity. After meetings with Algerian

COMRADES BEYOND THE COLD WAR

revolutionaries, Mandela recorded in his notebook that: 'A revolution cannot move with two heads ... One bad head is better than two good ones'.[13] This quest for unity would be a recurring theme in the organisation of all victorious African liberation movements.

Mandela not only sought training for himself, but also support for the ANC. The FLN promised him weapons, money and training.[14] In subsequent years, MK combatants were trained in FLN camps.[15] The ANC was not the only liberation movement that modelled itself on Algeria. Other influential visitors to the FLN training camps were Agostinho Neto (MPLA), Eduardo Mondlane (FRELIMO) and Samora Machel (FRELIMO).[16] ZAPU's military cadres began training in Algeria in 1965, the year that the Zimbabwean armed struggle began in earnest with small-scale bush operations. To acquire weapons, Joshua Nkomo made a journey that was as tedious as the one undertaken by Nujoma: the arms he picked up in Egypt were brought to Tanzania and then driven by car to Zimbabwe.[17]

Algeria was important, but naturally there were more places and institutions that mattered in the armed struggle for African liberation—Ghana, for example, organised the All-African Peoples' Conference in 1958.[18] One of the speakers was Frantz Fanon, who called for the armed struggle on behalf of Algeria's FLN.[19] His book *The Wretched of the Earth* would have a striking impact on African revolutionaries across the continent.[20] Ghana's Bureau of African Affairs and the OAU Liberation Committee in Tanzania were discussed in Chapter 5. The main takeaway from these displays of African solidarity was the profound impact of exile on the development of liberation movements.

The former SWAPO ambassador Andreas Shipanga provided a moving account of finding refuge in exile. When he arrived in Congo in the 1960s, a 'cloud of sadness settled over' him as he remembered the fate of one of Africa's greatest freedom fighters: 'the memory of Lumumba haunted me like a ghost'. In Congo, Shipanga was tasked with finding training opportunities for SWAPO's liberation army, PLAN. Visiting Western embassies 'was like knocking your head against a brick wall', but the Algerian

TRAINING

ambassador 'became a real friend'. Soon thereafter, Namibian revolutionaries were trained in various spots around Africa, including Ghana, Egypt and Tanzania.[21]

Exile equalled opportunities, but also anguish—being removed from home, the constant travelling and bartering for support, the despair that kicked in when victory seemed far away. 'The years of exile had taken a heavy toll', confessed Shipanga. Chapter 1 described his participation in the 1965 AAPSO conference in Cuba. On New Year's Eve, Fidel Castro threw a party for all delegates and invited SWAPO. There was plenty of rum and cheerfulness. But while the delegates were dancing, Shipanga and his comrades 'sat in the subdued light and cried ... homesickness swept over us at once'. Havana was one large party, but Namibia seemed far away. 'It was the first time that the reality of exile had hit me'.[22] The experience of exile, good and bad, became hardwired into the DNA of African liberation movements.

Military mindsets

In training camps across Africa, the armed wings of liberation movements launched revolutionary programmes to transform their rank and file into proper soldiers. In the fight for independence, political and military struggles were essentially the same. 'Our trained cadres must be imbued with political theories and ideas', wrote the ANC revolutionary Ronnie Kasrils. 'They must understand that politics guides the gun'.[23] SWAPO's political programme was designed around the principle that 'it is politics which leads the gun'.[24] ZANU also believed that 'the struggle we are waging is primarily a political struggle'. Hence, 'the Party should direct the gun'.[25] This sentiment was widely shared among political elites in Southern Africa and led to the formation of military mindsets that came to define the political culture of much of the region, past and present.[26]

The key to these military mindsets was the idea that the struggle in itself was a transformative experience. In 1972, Agostinho Neto, the leader of the Angolan MPLA, said that armed action is not only a sacrifice, but also 'a school'. One of the lessons was

133

that 'the party must control the life of the country during every moment'. For Neto, it was necessary that the party constituted 'the backbone, the base and the principal element' of the nation.[27] For this reason, the liberation movements and their armed wings were closely intertwined.

ZANU echoed the idea that the liberation war was a 'school for the masses'. The first task of the revolution was to 'establish the people's army as a central organ of the party'. Hence, all ZANU members became automatic members of its liberation army, ZANLA. It was strongly believed that ZANLA was not 'a militarist organisation like the regular national armies of nation states'. Rather, it was a 'politico-military organisation' that emphasised the political dimension of the struggle.[28]

However, becoming a successful guerrilla fighter requires skill and therefore training. Across Southern Africa and beyond, liberation movements established new or joined existing training camps. Here, students were educated in the art of war.

In 1964, the Angolan MPLA launched the Centre of Revolutionary Instruction, a politico-military school. From the perspective of the MPLA, the guerrilla was 'an essentially political person'. Cadres were trained in all aspects of the struggle, from agricultural work to military training. The MPLA stated that its 'concept of warfare embraces every aspect of the struggle'. Education was thus vital in forming the new 'man' that MPLA desired.[29] The rivalling FNLA also designed a Revolutionary Educational Programme that combined standard military courses (military history, weaponry, cartography, radio) with courses in health, agriculture and industry. After examinations, the students received the title 'scientist of the revolution'.[30]

SWAPO saw its freedom fighters 'first and foremost [as] armed political militants'. The party proudly announced that every fighting unit had a political instructor who educated the guerrillas before and after battle.[31] Upon graduation, soldiers from MK who were trained in Angola were inaugurated with the words: 'You are soldiers of our revolution. You are political soldiers'.[32] An MK soldier reminisced in 1978 about the impact of guerrilla training. As a civilian, S. Mokoena did not fully understand what it meant

TRAINING

to be a freedom fighter. 'To my surprise I realised that a guerrilla is in fact a politician who fights with gun in hand'. The lesson from MK was that politics comes first, and the gun is a tool for political liberation. 'I found myself with a gun in my hand, politics in mind and the enemy in the correct perspective'.[33] The 'Organisation Plan for the preparation of Armed Revolution' of MK quoted Kim Il Sung's ideas about revolutionary warfare, as did Mandela.[34]

The art of war is best taught through examples. Exiled African guerrilla fighters learned about past revolutions that were inspiring. In 1973, on the 25th anniversary of the founding of the Korean People's Army, the North Korean Embassy in the Republic of Congo organised a meeting for exiled MPLA soldiers. The Angolan nationalists were taught the history of the Korean People's Army: the long struggle against Japanese imperialism and American aggression, the wise leadership of Kim Il Sung and its 'decisive contribution to the revolutionary struggle of the peoples of the world'.[35] A special booklet, titled 'Victory or Death' was produced and included photos of Kim and Neto.

SWAPO's political programme for its military cadres borrowed heavily from materials produced by countries that supported their struggle: 'a strong internationalist flavour permeates these classes'.[36] A political commissar from the Zimbabwe People's Army said in 1976 that 'in the history of revolutionary struggles we find examples that closely approximate our own situation'.[37] Occasionally, North Korea would feature as a model for success. Indeed, the political commissar highlighted Korea. Two years later, in a published version of the Political Commissariat Lecture Series that outlined the Zimbabwean revolutionary education, ZANU included a photograph of the North Korean army. The Korean War was seen as the 'first victory of the people' after World War II, an example of how Koreans successfully 'smashed imperialism'.[38]

In the years that followed, North Korea would become more than a theoretical example of a successful military revolution—it would offer practical aid for African revolutionaries that wanted to replicate North Korea's achievements as an independent state that withstood Western imperialism. Aid was made available on the African continent via outsourced military advisors and in North

COMRADES BEYOND THE COLD WAR

Korea through targeted invitations to promising soldiers. It was a chance for Kim Il Sung to show that the political and military struggle in North Korea was essentially the same.

North Korean training

From the 1960s onwards, North Korea became militarily involved in the low-intensity guerrilla warfare that spilled across Southern Africa. A crucial aspect of Pyongyang's military programme was the support for (exiled) liberation movements. The Frontline States played a key role in facilitating interactions between African nationalists and North Korea.

Initially, North Korea dispensed military aid through ad hoc operations that were executed via North Korean embassies in the Frontline States. For example, the North Korean embassy in Lusaka (Zambia) organised military training for ZANU forces that fought for a liberated Zimbabwe.[39] In 1966, North Korea had denounced Rhodesia's unilateral declaration of independence as a 'robberish act', a mere attempt by 'the imperialists to trample down the national sovereignty of Zimbabweans ... The Korean people stand foursquare behind the African people'.[40] North Korean training activities for ZANU were later moved to Mozambique, after tensions arose between ZANU and ZAPU members in Zambia (the resulting altercations had offended their host, Kenneth Kaunda).[41]

The North Korean embassy in Tanzania similarly provided training for ZANU members, but also helped FRELIMO, the Union of the Peoples of Cameroon, and the Eritrean Liberation Front.[42] As already discussed in Chapter 5, the North Koreans invested heavily in Tanzania as they recognised that Dar es Salaam was an important hub for African liberation. The North Korean embassy, established in 1965, was the largest in Africa and the only one actually built by North Korea.[43] Around half a dozen North Korean intelligence officers were stationed in the country.[44] Tanzania is recognised as the place where North Korea enjoyed one of its 'greatest successes' in terms of military aid.[45]

In addition to ad hoc training operations through embassies in African capitals, North Korea offered training programmes at

136

TRAINING

camps that were established in the Frontline States. In the early 1970s, a North Korean training camp was established in Tanzania (in Tabora, a place 740 km from Dar es Salaam). It is estimated that 1,000 African soldiers were trained by North Korean advisors at Tabora—although this number is impossible to verify.[46] There must have been a high level of trust between Tanzanian political elites (TANU/CCM) and the North Korean regime to make this happen. Several high-ranking members of TANU and the Tanzanian People's Defence Force received military training in North Korea during the 1970s.[47] North Korean advisors were active in the TANU Youth League and allegedly wielded 'considerable potential political influence', while senior Tanzanian politicians visited Pyongyang to study the intricacies of party organisation.[48]

In the early 1980s, another North Korean training camp was located in Angola. Like Tanzania, Angola was a Frontline State and therefore a strategic location for North Korean investment. Moreover, the ongoing civil war in Angola—a conflict inflamed by foreign powers—was critical for the stability of Southern Africa and thus closely connected to the Namibian liberation struggle. In 1983, the MPLA government signed a military agreement with North Korea for military support. An estimated 1,000 to 3,000 North Korean military advisors were subsequently stationed in Quibaxi (a place 150 km from the capital Luanda) until at least 1988. MPLA forces were trained in sniper skills, hit-and-run techniques and combat operations.[49] The North Korean advisors in Angola also trained fighters from PLAN, the military wing of SWAPO.[50] Pyongyang gave 'substantial military assistance' to the Namibian nationalist cause.[51] Nujoma, the SWAPO leader, publicly praised North Korea's military support during a banquet in Pyongyang, in June 1986.[52] In front of Kim Il Sung, he cited the 'material assistance' of North Korea as the reason why SWAPO was able 'to maintain the banner of the struggle higher and inflict casualties on the South African racist troops'.[53]

The North Korean operations in Africa—either through embassies or camps—were focused on basic training. Advanced training, on the other hand, was offered within North Korea.[54] Promising African soldiers travelled to Pyongyang for this purpose as early as the 1960s.[55] For example, American diplomatic files indicate that, between April and August 1965, 15 Zimbabwean revolutionaries were trained in the use of explosives and arms in a camp close to Pyongyang.[56]

Towards the end of the Cold War, North Korea was reported to maintain 10 training facilities in and around Pyongyang.[57] Short-term courses lasted three to six months, but long-term courses could run up to 12–24 months. African nationalists were trained in a variety of skills by North Korean special forces, ranging from marksmanship, map reading, ambush and counter-ambush, explosives, communications, intelligence and medical training. It is estimated that 10,000–15,000 foreign nationals profited from this training, including trainees from Latin America and other parts of Asia, although this number is impossible to verify.[58]

What is certain, is that several contemporary ruling parties in Southern Africa benefited from military training in North Korea before independence. Among them are MPLA (ruling Angola since 1975), FRELIMO (ruling Mozambique since 1975), ZANU (ruling Zimbabwe since 1980) and SWAPO (ruling Namibia since 1990).

Conclusion

When, in 1985, a North Korean delegation arrived in Zambia, they were met with immense gratitude. Alexander Grey Zulu, an eminent Zambian politician who was involved in the liberation struggle, 'lauded the Korean government for its invaluable aid to the oppressed people in Southern Africa'. Zulu (who had already met Kim Il Sung in 1975) thanked North Korea for its help 'during times of need when the country provided a rear base to freedom fighters'.[59]

The provision of weaponry and military instructors was a 'key feature' of North Korean assistance to African liberation movements, and this first occurred in places of exile on the African continent.[60] In several cases, liberation movements received arms and training for free, or at reduced prices, as this was a cornerstone of North Korean foreign policy during the Cold War.[61] From

TRAINING

the perspective of Pyongyang, military strategy and diplomatic strategy were closely intertwined.

Helped by North Korea, national liberation movements defeated white settler regimes and colonial governments. But liberation came at a price. The lesson that African revolutionaries learned from their experiences in exile was the importance of control. Liberation movements were guided by military mindsets that would have lasting legacies on the political culture in Southern Africa, something that is explored in more detail in the third part of this book.

The roots of authoritarian or anti-democratic behaviour that characterise so much of contemporary politics in Southern Africa can be traced to this era. Within the exile camps of numerous liberation movements, party leaders forged unity with all means necessary—even if this included violence. Paranoia quickly led to repression, as critical party members became dissidents. When, in the 1970s, Andreas Shipanga, the 'roving ambassador of SWAPO', criticised his party's leadership and called for more internal democracy, he was branded a spy by Nujoma. Shipanga and his allies were arrested by the Zambian government and jailed for two years in Tanzania.[62]

Nujoma used this incident to strengthen his control over the party, a pattern commonly adopted by other African liberation movements. Human rights violations also occurred in ANC camps in Angola, where dissident members were detained, tortured and executed.[63] These dark pages in the history of African decolonisation are taboo in Southern Africa today, not least because, in many cases, the perpetrators remain in power. They are the excesses of a mindset that valued unity above all else—a mentality that also informed the desire to consolidate newly found political power, as is covered in the next chapter.

9

VICTORY

CONSOLIDATING POWER, 1980–2000

During the liberation wars in Southern Africa, national liberation movements benefited from North Korean training programmes in counterinsurgency and guerrilla warfare. But what happened when victory was achieved? 'The attainment of political independence', according to Kim Il Sung, 'is no more than the initial step towards the ultimate victory of the national-liberation revolution'.[1] In 1982, the Great Leader proclaimed that 'the most important problem confronting the peoples who have won their national independence today is how to consolidate the political independence of their countries'. African revolutionaries should therefore consider the question: 'how to defend independence'.[2]

Defending independence became a key priority for newly installed African governments. They were anxious not to succumb to the internal and external pressures that marked postcolonial politics and lose power as a result. African leaders struggled with domestic opposition to their authority and faced South Africa as a mighty adversary that sought to destabilise the entire region. Again, North Korea proved to be a reliable partner during these difficult times. North Korea took on a new role by offering internal regime support to African states.[3] More specifically, the

141

provision of presidential security became a key theme in African–North Korean relations in the last decade of the Cold War.[4]

North Korea provided training that was compatible with equipment gifted by the Soviet Union or China, two major suppliers of arms in Africa. Nonetheless, its independent foreign policy, underlined by its membership of the NAM, was a significant advantage in convincing African liberation governments to work together.[5] 'The DPRK does offer an attractive option to governments that are not too keen to accept a large Soviet or Cuban presence', stressed a British report from 1984. 'They can certainly improve the effectiveness of host nation armed forces'.[6]

The best-known example of a North Korean training mission in Africa is the Fifth Brigade in Zimbabwe, which wreaked havoc in Matabeleland in the 1980s. As the historian Stuart Doran points out, this episode is fairly well-known today because of a report from the Catholic Commission for Justice and Peace in Zimbabwe, which exposed the 'savage killings' to a wide audience in 1997.[7] Largely unexplored, however, is the fact that North Korea also trained military divisions of other countries in Southern Africa—and that the Zimbabwean example was a factor in the diplomatic negotiations with African countries concerning North Korean aid.

Newly elected African governments faced a rapidly deteriorating security situation in Southern Africa, a region marked by civil war, assassinations and other forms of instability. The widespread presence of North Korean bodyguards was not a sign of African paranoia, but the result of an objective need for protection. African states had the freedom to organise their own security the way they saw fit and deliberately chose to trust North Korea with this important task.

This chapter seeks to illuminate the proliferation of North Korean training missions in 1980s Southern Africa. The first part provides a detailed account of the military cooperation between ZANU and North Korea in the first years of Zimbabwean independence. The second part consciously moves beyond Zimbabwe and uncovers a wide range of North Korean training missions in neighbouring states in Southern Africa. The third

VICTORY

section analyses the impact of these collaborations on African–North Korean relationships.

The Fifth Brigade of ZANU

When Zimbabwe gained full independence on 18 April 1980, large crowds gathered in Harare to celebrate the victory over the Rhodesian settler regime. One of the highlights of the festivities was a performance by Bob Marley, the Rastafarian singer who was incredibly popular across Africa. For this special occasion, Marley performed a song called 'Zimbabwe'. Thousands of people cheered when Marley sang the words 'no more internal power struggle', a line that eerily foreshadowed the tensions that would follow in the years to come.

The two main liberation movements of Zimbabwe, ZANU and ZAPU, had a 'strained relationship' that would define much of Zimbabwe's postcolonial future. In the meantime, South Africa sought to destabilise Zimbabwe through a range of covert actions. Shortly after independence, South African agents sabotaged 'key sites' in Zimbabwe, spread rumours that ZAPU would overthrow the ZANU-dominated government and destroyed large quantities of ammunition in an attack on military barracks just outside Harare. Moreover, in 1981, South African operatives bombed the ZANU headquarters in Harare and 'almost killed many senior leaders' from the party, including Robert Mugabe.[8]

Power struggles were at the heart of the newly independent nation of Zimbabwe. In a quest to consolidate his power, ZANU leader and prime minister Robert Mugabe approached Kim Il Sung, the man who had already supported ZANU during the liberation struggle. In October 1980, six months after the festive independence celebrations in Harare, Mugabe travelled to Pyongyang to discuss a possible North Korean training mission for the Zimbabwean military. He 'spoke in warm terms about his talks with Kim Il Sung' during a press conference in the capital and said that Zimbabwe had much to learn from North Korea. The two nations subsequently signed a treaty that underlined their mutual friendship and cooperation.[9]

COMRADES BEYOND THE COLD WAR

The North Korean minister of foreign affairs, Ho Dam (Hŏ Tam), characterised the ties between both countries as that of 'intimate comrades-in-arms and brothers' during a return visit to Harare in 1980.[10] Another agreement between Zimbabwe and North Korea was signed in May 1981 during a visit of North Korean prime minister Li Jong Ok (Ri Chong'ok). Li visited Zimbabwe again in June 1981.[11] During a banquet to honour his esteemed guest, Mugabe embraced North Korea's foreign policy agenda by professing his 'fullest support' for the WPK and denouncing the 'military occupation' of South Korea by the United States.[12]

* * *

Shortly after Mugabe's visit to Pyongyang, rumours about the impending North Korean training mission were quickly spreading within Zimbabwe. The new Zimbabwean army was originally designed as a merger of former ZANU and ZAPU fighters, and the British military had deployed a training mission in 1980 to help shape four brigades. The North Korean security assistance would instead focus on a so-called Fifth Brigade (or 5 Brigade) that was almost entirely composed of ZANU fighters.[13] It was evident that this would be a powerful tool for Mugabe to exercise control. In the run-up to the arrival of the North Koreans, tensions were already building in Zimbabwean politics. Two thousand members of ZANU's youth movement took to the streets to call for the installation of a one-party state and the Fifth Brigade. The crowd was addressed by Mugabe, who encouraged the youths to help ZANU succeed. Naturally, this terrified the ZAPU base. In response, ZAPU organised a counter march, with some members carrying banners displaying the text 'Koreans go home'.[14]

By then, it had also become clear to the outside world that North Korea would train a Zimbabwean military brigade. Mugabe's decision to approach Kim Il Sung for this kind of mission raised widespread international concern. The ZANU government defied extensive diplomatic pressure to stop its cooperation with North Korea, which underlined the strong bonds between Harare and Pyongyang.

VICTORY

The United Kingdom was deeply concerned about the North Korean arrival. Yet, the influence of the former colonisers in Harare had waned. In a meeting with Mugabe, the British Major-General Palmer—the commander of the British military training team in Harare—argued that accepting North Korean aid would result in a confusing mix of different army systems. Mugabe countered this argument by pointing to the example of Tanzania, a country that had done exactly the same (and had equally firm ties with Pyongyang). Palmer's response that Tanzania was hardly an example for Zimbabwe 'was not well received' by Mugabe. Instead, the prime minister reiterated that North Koreans had helped Zimbabwe during the struggle for independence and 'had to be given an opportunity to help Zimbabwe now'. The British counteroffer of help was rejected.[15]

Several other states added their voices to the chorus of disapproval. Diplomatic opposition against ZANU's military policy came from all corners of the world. An obvious contestant was South Korea, which realised it was losing the inter-Korean diplomatic competition in Southern Africa. South Korea's offer of unconditional aid was made in vain, as Harare chose to support North Korea.[16] South Africa, Zimbabwe's antagonist, and Japan, which had a strained relationship with North Korea, both voiced concern about Zimbabwean–North Korean cooperation. Australia offered alternative military training, to no avail.[17] The United States, which had fought North Korea during the Korean War, threatened the ZANU government that their move could jeopardise an American aid package with a value of $250 million.[18] Mugabe was steadfast in his decision.

This episode not only illustrates that Harare was independent in its foreign policy—Pyongyang was equally capable of making sovereign decisions. North Korea's military strategy was not dependent on the Communist Bloc. Following the failed diplomatic campaign to prevent the Fifth Brigade from coming into existence, British and Japanese diplomats concluded that the offer of aid was 'North Korea's independent action and could not be seen as a derivative of the Soviet strategy'.[19]

* * *

In August 1981, 103 military instructors from North Korea arrived in Zimbabwe to train the Fifth Brigade. Designed as a counter-insurgency force consisting of 5,000 men, the soldiers were mainly derived from former ZANLA forces, the military wing of ZANU during the liberation struggle.[20] The brigade was trained in a military base in Nyanga, close to the Mozambican border. The brigade later moved to Gweru.[21] The North Koreans specifically requested an isolated area for the training exercises and refused a location near Harare.[22]

The brigade's equipment (T59 tanks, AK-47 rifles, armoured cars, artillery and trucks) was imported from Pyongyang by rail, through the port of Beira, Mozambique. The material was a gift from Kim Il Sung, with a total worth of $12 million.[23] However, the salaries and in-country costs of the North Korean instructors were paid by the Zimbabwean government.[24]

At the end of 1982, the number of North Korean military advisors in Zimbabwe was 'higher than in any other developing country'.[25] As was generally the case with North Koreans in Africa, their presence was shrouded in mystery, and they seldom blended with the local population. The instructors could occasionally be spotted at public displays of the Fifth Brigade, where the soldiers displayed their newly acquired martial art skills, impressing the public by smashing logs of wood and blocks of concrete with their bare hands.[26]

It was rumoured that the brigade started each day with a salute to 'MUGABE!'.[27] A Zimbabwean officer later recalled that the training also included the teachings of Juche.[28] The emphasis on ideology was not a coincidence, but deliberate. Mugabe explained that the Fifth Brigade 'were trained by the Koreans because we wanted one arm of the army to have a political orientation which stems from our philosophy as ZANU ... their approach was not just to use the gun. It was also political'.[29] Mugabe's approach was thus a continuation of the military mindsets that were developed in exile.

Joshua Nkomo, the leader of ZAPU and long-time rival of Mugabe, feared that the Fifth Brigade would effectively become a private ZANU brigade and was part of a plan to establish a one-

VICTORY

party state in Zimbabwe.[30] His fears came true in 1982, when the Fifth Brigade invaded Matabeleland, the traditional ZAPU stronghold, and murdered an estimated 20,000 people. At least one operation was 'furthered by on-the-ground assistance from Korean officers'.[31]

In the early 1980s, for several years on end, the Fifth Brigade spread its terror across Matabeleland in a genocidal campaign that came to be known as *Gukurahundi*. Mugabe had already named the Fifth Brigade *Gukurahundi*, a Shona word that can be roughly translated as 'the rain that comes before the spring rains and washes away the chaff', or the 'first rains of the season that sweep away the rubbish'.[32] In 1979, shortly before Zimbabwean independence, Mugabe had called this year *Gore re Gukurahundi*, or Year of the People's Storm. 'Let the people's fury break into a revolutionary storm that will engulf and sweep the enemy completely from our land', Mugabe proclaimed in a New Year's message. 'The People's Storm must come with thunder, heavy rain and irresistible blasting gusts that will ransack the enemy strongholds'.[33] The sinister symbolism of the Fifth Brigade's nickname can hardly be missed. For Mugabe and his allies, the Fifth Brigade represented an opportunity to cleanse the nation of ZAPU's opposition and achieve unity through violence.

The exploits of the Fifth Brigade were extremely violent and gruesome. The violence was not 'simply a matter of soldiers running wild', but was meticulously planned and organised.[34] There was a method to the madness, as the historian Blessing-Miles Tendi notes. The Fifth Brigade was not designed to function as a regular army force, it was destined to spread terror. In addition to the thousands and thousands of killings, Mugabe's army division carried out widespread torture and rape in Matabeleland. Civilians were forced to chant ZANU slogans and Shona songs.[35] Victims were stuffed with mines and thrown in the water, their bodies only revealed by a long drought ten years later.[36]

The terrible events of the 1980s 'indelibly marked the foundational years of the Zimbabwean nation'.[37] Through mass killings, the Fifth Brigade effectively destroyed 'the backbone of ZAPU's party structure in Matabeleland, present and future'.[38]

147

Mugabe had foreshadowed the violence that would unfold in a 1981 newspaper interview, describing the militia as a 'crack unit'. Regular Zimbabweans should not fear the Fifth Brigade, Mugabe said. But 'if you plan to be a dissident, watch out'.[39] Joshua Nkomo, who had warned of violence against his political base from the onset, escaped execution by only 'the narrowest of margins' when he fled to Botswana in the dead of night.[40]

The Fifth Brigade wreaked havoc in Matabeleland from 1982 until 1987, when Mugabe and Nkomo signed the Unity Accord. ZAPU and ZANU were subsequently merged into ZANU-PF, a political organisation dominated by ZANU that remains in power today. In the same year, Mugabe was declared president instead of prime minister. The constitution was amended, giving him more extensive powers than before. Zimbabwe became a 'de facto one-party state'.[41] ZAPU has subsequently been largely erased from the historical record in Zimbabwe.[42] The archives of ZAPU's armed wing, ZIPRA, were confiscated by the Zimbabwean government during the genocide and are not accessible to the public, if they even still exist.[43]

Gukurahundi continues to loom over Zimbabwean politics, as the perpetrators remain in power today.[44] Mugabe remained in power for three decades. In 2006, one of his former ministers, Nathan Shamuyarira (the ZANU politician who visited Pyongyang) called the genocide 'not regrettable' as the Fifth Brigade 'were doing a job to protect the people'.[45] In 2017, Mugabe was ousted from the presidency by Emmerson Mnangagwa following a military coup, but even the new regime had personal ties to the Fifth Brigade. Mnangagwa acted as minister of state security during *Gukurahundi* and can be seen as one of its architects.[46] Furthermore, one of his ministers was Perrance Shiri, the former commander of the Fifth Brigade, who called himself 'Black Jesus' because 'he could say if you live or not'.[47]

In 2010, the Zimbabwean government planned to invite the North Korean football team to establish a training camp for the World Cup in South Africa. In an event reminiscent of the protest march of 1980, a large demonstration by Ndebele speakers voiced their grievances against ZANU's ambition.[48] In both cases, they

VICTORY

were largely ignored by the authorities. Moreover, attempts by the Gukurahundi Memorial Centre to honour the victims were met with violence. Part of a wider rise in 'popular counter-memorialism in Southern Africa', an attempt to erect a tombstone commemorating the victims in 2021 proved futile—the memorial was destroyed the very next day.[49]

Spill-over effects in Southern Africa

The massacres of *Gukurahundi* are commonly understood as a domestic event, a Zimbabwean tragedy, and existing scholarship largely overlooks the transnational dimensions of the Fifth Brigade. There are indications, as Doran argues, that the Fifth Brigade partly consisted of Tanzanian and Mozambican soldiers. Nyerere had supported ZANU when it competed with ZAPU prior to Zimbabwean independence. Nyerere's involvement in the Fifth Brigade might have been motivated by his willingness 'to help Mugabe deal with unfinished business'. Machel's involvement could have been a 'quid pro quo' for Mugabe's support in FRELIMO's civil war against RENAMO. In that sense, writes Doran, 'Machel was beholden to Mugabe'.[50]

Moreover, the ZANU–North Korean training mission reverberated throughout Southern Africa during the 1980s. As North Korea propped up the young ruling parties in other countries in the region, the Fifth Brigade was regularly discussed during diplomatic negotiations between African states and the British government, which, as a former colonising power, had a vested interest in the stability of the region. From the British perspective, the Fifth Brigade was a symbol of disaster, but many African liberation governments viewed this differently. For them, the Fifth Brigade symbolised the necessity of regime consolidation during the uncertain first years of independence.

As such, the Fifth Brigade was both a model for African states surrounding Zimbabwe, and a factor in the negotiations between these states and the United Kingdom. In the 1980s, North Korea excelled in providing presidential security for African regimes. The next sections examine military cooperation between North Korea

COMRADES BEYOND THE COLD WAR

and African ruling parties in the wake of *Gukurahundi* including those of FRELIMO (Mozambique), AREMA (Madagascar), SPUP (Seychelles), BNP (Lesotho) and SWAPO (Namibia).

* * *

In 1975, the year of Mozambican independence, Machel lauded the 'unsparing efforts' of North Korea to help FRELIMO win victory. 'Knowing our present needs', Machel continued, 'they are also willing and ready to support us in the consolidation of our power'.[51] Mozambique subsequently followed a similar trajectory as Zimbabwe.

In 1982, North Korean military advisors travelled to Mozambique to support the FRELIMO government during a deteriorating security situation: shortly after Mozambican independence in 1975, a civil war broke out with RENAMO, which was partly funded by South Africa. The North Koreans helped to establish the Clean Brigade, an elite counterinsurgency force led by Fernando Honwana. Honwana was a special advisor to Machel and held high-ranking positions in the military and security branches of the Mozambican government. He had developed 'close ties' with Zimbabwean leaders in the 1970s.[52] Moreover, Honwana had received 'special military training' in Pyongyang, together with other FRELIMO officials.[53] The South Korean government reported that, in 1976, North Korea offered to train Mozambican special forces, a mission with a value of $100,000.[54]

In the early 1980s, between 100 and 130 North Korean instructors resided at Chiduachine, in the Gaza province of Mozambique.[55] They trained soldiers of the Clean Brigade. In 1982, the Clean Brigade and the Fifth Brigade executed a failed joint operation against RENAMO guerrillas along the Umtali– Beira railway. Interestingly, this operation was the first combat action for the Fifth Brigade, occurring before the larger-scale *Gukurahundi* genocide in Matabeleland.[56] Zimbabwean soldiers remained in Mozambique for a number of years in order to support the weakened FRELIMO government in their fight against

150

VICTORY

RENAMO.[57] Critics have described the Zimbabwean forces as 'a pack of wild dogs looking for a fight'.[58]

The North Korean advisors left Mozambique in 1983. The Clean Brigade remained active for several years and then slowly sunk into oblivion, except for 1987, when it was reported to have massacred 380 people during a battle in southeast Mozambique.[59]

* * *

In 1975, Didier Ratsiraka came to power in Madagascar, the island nation east of Mozambique. The 'Red Admiral' introduced a socialist system and established firm control. In 1976, he founded AREMA and reached out to North Korea for help. Ratsiraka feared the South African apartheid regime, especially the prospect of assassination. In 1976, North Korean advisors arrived in Madagascar to train Ratsiraka's presidential guard and counterinsurgency forces.[60] Just outside of Antananarivo, North Korean labourers built a fortified bunker for him. In subsequent years, AREMA and North Korea concluded several military assistance agreements. Pyongyang provided arms and training for the Malagasy defence forces.[61] In the late 1970s, for example, Malagasy pilots practiced with four MiG-17 aircrafts and four naval patrol boats that were borrowed from North Korea, before the arrival of Soviet MiG-21 aircrafts.[62] A decade later, the North Koreans built a munitions factory in Madagascar.[63]

* * *

The case of the Seychelles, north of Madagascar, fits within the broader pattern of African–North Korean relations.[64] SPUP was the sole party from 1979 to 1991, when France-Albert René was president. In 1981, the regime of René survived a South African-backed military coup d'état by a mercenary force.[65] This was a sharp reminder of the perilous security situation that was emanating from Pretoria. Similar to the case of Madagascar, René requested Kim Il Sung's help with the training of his presidential guard.

The first North Korean training mission arrived in 1982.[66] For several years, the Seychelles Peoples' Defence Forces were supported by 110 North Korean instructors, who stayed for one year before they were rotated with new instructors. They kept a low profile and remained 'largely isolated from the people' but conducted a satisfactory job in the eyes of René.[67] The instructors were integrated into the Seychelles army at junior officer ranks and were outfitted in Seychelles uniforms.[68]

Outsiders viewed the close SPUP–North Korea relationship with curiosity. When a journalist asked a SPUP official why the Seychelles had opted for North Korean instead of Western assistance, the party member replied that the West 'would sit on their hands if mercenaries attacked us again. We know the North Koreans would fight to defend us'.[69] The trust that SPUP placed in North Korea is illustrative of a broader sentiment shared among African governing elites at the time, who saw North Korea as an ally.

* * *

Lesotho is a case study that reveals how the British government used the Fifth Brigade in diplomatic negotiations with African governments to illustrate North Korean failure, without success. Leabua Jonathan rose to power with the BNP in 1966, but when it appeared that he had lost the elections in 1970, Jonathan declared a state of emergency and nullified the vote. In addition to domestic turmoil, the prime minister was sensitive to Lesotho's precarious security situation: the nation is encircled by South Africa.

Jonathan visited Pyongyang in 1983 and signed extensive agreements with North Korea.[70] In that same year, North Korea opened an embassy in Maseru.[71] The British embassy discovered the developing military relationship between the BNP and North Korea by accident: one of their receptionists was married to a Basotho army sergeant who travelled to Pyongyang. This was crucial information for the British government, as Lesotho hosted a British military training mission. London feared a repetition of the Zimbabwean saga.[72]

VICTORY

British diplomats warned the Basotho authorities about the 'problems and dangers' of North Korean aid by referencing the Fifth Brigade. As was the case in Zimbabwe, it was argued that the presence of two different military training missions (one North Korean, one Western) would cause confusion for the Lesotho Paramilitary Forces. Instead, the British government offered to augment their existing mission. Jonathan followed the same reasoning as Mugabe and declined the offer.[73]

In 1983, a few months after the establishment of a North Korean embassy in Maseru, several North Korean military instructors arrived to train the LPF.[74] Senior army staff were sent to North Korea for military training, sometimes for as long as two and a half years.[75] Jonathan's decision to break off diplomatic ties with South Korea was the icing on the cake.[76]

This case study illustrates the pragmatic considerations that informed the decisions of African leaders. Before 1970, Jonathan 'identified communism as the major threat to Southern Africa'.[77] However, when the BNP was on the brink of losing power, with South Africa looming in the background as a threat, he was persuaded to accept North Korean aid.[78] While British diplomats called Jonathan 'disingenuous', the prime minister defended his policy by emphasising Lesotho's non-aligned status.[79]

* * *

The Zimbabwean Fifth Brigade also cast its shadows on the formation of the presidential guard of Sam Nujoma, the first president of Namibia. The SWAPO leader was elected as president in 1990 and was guarded by soldiers from SWAPO's liberation army. After decades of guerrilla fighting, these PLAN fighters struggled to adjust to their new role. Incidents occurred when guards fired at unarmed members of the public, and the newly established Namibian government decided to approach North Korea for training. Perhaps Nujoma remembered the banquet he had attended in Pyongyang, a few years earlier, when Kim Il Sung promised him future support.

Similar to Lesotho, Zimbabwe and other parts of Africa, the British government already trained certain parts of the Namibian national army.[80] They were deeply concerned by Nujoma's move. The Foreign and Commonwealth Office described it internally as a 'serious mistake ... naïve and staggeringly inept'. In a meeting with Prime Minister Hage Geingob, British diplomats emphasised the 'very unfortunate experience of North Korean training in Zimbabwe'. But this was an ineffective deterrent. The British objective to 'keep the North Koreans out', as they put it, ultimately failed as the Namibian government formally requested North Korean military aid in January 1991.[81]

Analysis

When Mugabe was pressed about why he chose North Korea to take care of his security, he hinted at the historical friendship between Zimbabwe and North Korea: 'It is those who come to you when you are in greatest need who are your friends indeed'.[82]

Nevertheless, North Korea's anti-imperialist struggle credentials do not adequately explain why African states desired North Korean security assistance in the 1980s. There was also a practical reason. Newly elected liberation governments in Africa faced internal opposition as well as external security threats. The civil wars in Angola and Mozambique were a nightmare scenario for anyone who had recently acquired power, such as ZANU in Zimbabwe. There was a real fear among African elites that independence was under threat. Such sentiments were deliberately fuelled by South Africa.

The South African apartheid regime experienced a 'sense of siege' as the countries surrounding its border became independent. The fall of the Portuguese Empire and the subsequent liberation of Angola and Mozambique in 1975 was a shock to the system, as was the liberation of Zimbabwe in 1980. South Africa saw itself as 'the only domino left standing' in the fight against Black majority rule and communism. As such, the apartheid government channelled its energies into creating 'division and instability' across the region.[83]

VICTORY

A wave of assassinations engulfed the continent: Patrice Lumumba, Eduardo Mondlane, Herbert Chitepo, Steve Biko, Clemens Kapuuo, Ruth First, Samora Machel, Anton Lubowski and Chris Hani—it was dangerous to be a high-ranking African nationalist or president. In a region rife with conflict, security assistance from the North Koreans—and, in particular, presidential security—was a welcome gift. Regime consolidation was the key concept.

As Mugabe explained to the public, the North Koreans 'assist us to consolidate our independence and strengthen our defence forces'.[84] For several neighbouring African states, the Fifth Brigade was not understood through the lens of genocide. Rather, it was understood through the lens of unity and control.

It should be noted that not all African governments accepted North Korean aid. Between 1983–84, the North Korean ambassador in Gaborone repeatedly offered to send 100 military instructors to support the army of Botswana, but despite the existing cordial bilateral ties between both nations the offer was declined by the Batswana.[85] However, Botswana is an outlier in the region.

Even though North Korea was able to penetrate the heart of African political and military nerve centres that governed much of Southern Africa, the impact of Pyongyang on African affairs was limited. In this case, too, African agency mattered. Mugabe and his presidential colleagues were not beholden to Kim Il Sung, and North Korea did not influence African domestic policies. The following three points should be kept in mind when discussing North Korean–African military cooperation.

Firstly, African leaders accepted North Korean aid with a healthy degree of suspicion. While publicly Mugabe expressed gratitude towards North Korea, in fact he remained distrustful of the actual instructors and 'tracked every move of the Koreans in the country' using wiretaps and intelligence officers.[86] Despite the fraternal relations between Kaunda and Kim Il Sung, the Zambian government sometimes refused North Korean appeals for visas if they thought that it was not 'the proper time' to grant such a request.[87]

COMRADES BEYOND THE COLD WAR

Another interesting example comes from Tanzania. When the North Korean embassy in Dar es Salaam held a reception to celebrate 'The Victory of the Korean People of the Imperialists' (imperialists meaning Americans), Nyerere forbade Tanzanian government officials from attending the festivities. Nyerere clearly did not condone the strong language of the North Koreans. When the North Korean chargé d'affaires gave a press conference later that day in which he condemned 'American aggression', he was summoned to the Tanzanian Ministry of Foreign Affairs, on Nyerere's instruction, and warned that further 'violation of Tanzanian hospitality' would result in him 'being declared persona non grata'.[88] A few days later, the Tanzanian newspaper *The Standard* wanted to criticise the North Korean embassy by recalling this incident. Before printing, the editor informally asked Nyerere's office if he would object to such an attack. His office responded that 'the President wanted him to publish the editorial'.[89] This goes to show that even Kim's strongest allies, such as Mugabe, Kaunda and Nyerere were guarded about North Korea's activities.

Secondly, North Korea's omnipresence in the region was partly the result of clever branding. North Korea allegedly assigned higher ranks to outsourced military advisors than they actually possessed back home. This way, Pyongyang could charge higher salaries to the host countries (resulting in more income) and simultaneously give the impression to their African hosts that they were 'getting first-class personnel'.[90] This was reported in several instances, including the case of the North Korean instructors of the Fifth Brigade.[91] The North Koreans were said to be 'extracting their pound of flesh from the Zimbabweans'. The ranks of the North Korean officers were 'artificially inflated', and they were seen 'spending lavishly in the most expensive hotels, demanding huge quantities of diesel and insisting on brand new staff cars'.[92] North Korea's military programme in Africa thus followed a similar pattern as its development programme, which was discussed in Chapter 5. North Korea was able to project an image of success at relatively little cost. The public praise from African leaders for North Korea's help was very valuable to Kim Il Sung.

156

VICTORY

Thirdly, the continuation of bilateral relationships depended on the survival of African regimes. This point is best illustrated through UNIP, the political party that governed Zambia from its independence in 1964 until 1991. UNIP ensured that Zambia followed the same pattern of military cooperation as its neighbours. In the early 1980s, the Zambian government sent a delegation of 'very senior military men' to Pyongyang to discuss cooperation.[93] North Korea, in turn, offered to train members of the Zambian army.[94]

As Chapter 3 revealed, Kenneth Kaunda, the Zambian president, maintained a personal relationship with Kim Il Sung. A high-ranking official of the Freedom House, UNIP's headquarters in Lusaka, entrusted to a British diplomat the secret of this relationship. While in other socialist countries 'the people serve the party', Kaunda believed that in North Korea 'the party serves the people'. The British government had 'no doubt' that 'Kaunda will be picking Mugabe's brains on his experience with them', which was another sign that the Fifth Brigade loomed in the background as an example.[95] This did not have the effect that the British intended. In 1982, North Korean instructors were reportedly based in Kabwe, in the Central Province of Zambia. While British sources spoke of ten advisors, South Korean sources assumed that there were 45 North Koreans present.[96] Their aim was to train Zambian soldiers, most likely paramilitary forces.[97] The former Zambian vice president Guy Scott remembered how they came to Zambia 'to show us to perform the goose step and other tricks'.[98]

However, when the Zambian people voted UNIP out of power in 1991, North Korea lost a valuable ally in which it had invested heavily. As a result, there is no evidence of post-1991 military ties between Zambia and North Korea. This book's emphasis on parties instead of countries is deliberate, as this seems to be a major factor for the success of North Korean aid. Currently, the majority of Southern Africa continues to be ruled by former liberation governments, but it is likely that if these parties lose power in the future, North Korea could lose allies.

Conclusion

The historian Basil Davidson wrote in *The Black Man's Burden* that the 'transfer of power' that African independence entailed was effectively 'a transfer of crisis'. With the attainment of state power came an incredible combination of political challenges that plunged newly elected African politicians into uncharted territory.[99] Although Davidson mainly focused on the inherited failures of colonialism, the sense of crisis can also be applied to the security system in which young African governments operated.

Southern Africa's deteriorating security situation was a major factor in the decision of African governments to accept North Korean help. During the 1980s, African governments were not deterred by Western warnings of the North Korean danger. Neither offers of aid nor direct threats could dissuade them from accepting Kim Il Sung's military consultants. In this sense, there is an interesting parallel between yesterday's North Korean military advisors and the contemporary Russian mercenaries of the Wagner Group. While the Western world fears it will lose influence in Africa, Wagner met a particular demand for African regime consolidation. Graham Harrison shows that the 'Liberalism 101' mantra of free elections and open economies fails to understand the 'lived-in crisis' that characterises many African governments. Both in the cases of Wagner and North Korea, 'Western circles share a deep and significant misreading of African politics'.[100]

With the end of the Cold War and the subsequent collapse of the North Korean economy, North Korea could no longer sustain its military programmes in Africa. In that sense, the military programmes faced the same fate as the Juche Study Centres (Chapter 4) and development aid projects (Chapter 5) that were hosted by African states. North Korea's decision to invest heavily in these areas was part of a foreign policy agenda that aimed to promote Kim Il Sung's standing in the world. The events of the 1990s severely disrupted these operations.

The turmoil of the 1990s could also be the reason why there is little evidence of extensive military relations between North Korea and South Africa. When the latter became independent, in

VICTORY

1994, it was arguably too late for the kind of regime consolidation programmes that had been executed in the 1980s. Nevertheless, it would be wrong to equate the diminishing of these military programmes with the end of the African–North Korean military alliance. As the next chapter shows, the end of the Cold War did not mean the end of North Korea's military adventures in Africa.

10

SURVIVAL

MAINTAINING POWER, 2000–2020

A luta continua became the rallying cry of FRELIMO during the Mozambican fight for independence, a slogan that was widely adopted among other liberation movements in the region. The idea that 'the struggle continues' can also be applied as a concept for contemporary Southern African politics. From the perspective of the liberation governments that are in power today, the struggle does continue—now with the aim to remain in power indefinitely. It is a desire that causes these once idealistic organisations to become increasingly authoritarian.[1]

The idea of a continued struggle is best observed in practice in Zimbabwe. In the nationalist myth-making of Zimbabwean liberation, the nineteenth-century revolt of indigenous peoples against British colonisation is known as the First *Chimurenga*, a Shona word that means uprising. In the twentieth century, ZANU and ZAPU nationalists framed their opposition against white minority rule as the Second *Chimurenga*. This was effectively the Rhodesian Bush War from 1966–79 that put Mugabe and his ZANU colleagues in power. But when their government came under internal and external pressure to leave office, ZANU officials framed their reforms as the Third *Chimurenga*: 'the *Chimurenga* became

161

a permanent institution'.[2] In this sense, liberation discourse is recycled by political elites to fit contemporary political purposes.[3]

ZANU's authoritarian turn is a sinister development that does not bode well for the future of Southern African politics.[4] Across the region, the question of what will happen when liberation governments lose power is one with grave consequences. In Angola, Mozambique, Namibia and South Africa, the prevailing governments are gradually losing popular support in consecutive election cycles.[5] How will these liberation governments respond when it appears that they will lose their parliamentary majority for the first time?

In their appetite to maintain power, African liberation governments are again finding a reliable partner in North Korea. While the previous phase of consolidating power (1980–2000) was marked by the protection of newly inaugurated African regimes, most prominently through presidential security, the current phase is defined by political survival. Southern African governments are facing unprecedented levels of opposition while North Korea is becoming increasingly isolated.[6] Today, some African governments continue to rely on North Korean military expertise, while the resulting hard foreign currency is a lifeline for the North Korean regime. 'Although the precise income it earned from this trade is subject to debate', observes the United Nations, 'there is no question that it is one of the country's most profitable revenue sources'.[7] Maintaining power thus has a double meaning: political survival is a motivation for both African states and North Korea.

This chapter considers African–North Korean military cooperation in the time of United Nations sanctions. The first section illustrates how African states continue their military relationships with North Korea through a number of case studies. The second section offers an analysis of North Korea's sanctions evasion in the African continent. The final section considers the reasons for African states to trade with North Korea despite international condemnation.[8]

162

SURVIVAL

Sanctions evasion

International pressure on North Korea's deviant behaviour, most notably the launch of a highly controversial nuclear programme, resulted in the most extensive sanctions regime in world history. In 2006, the United Nations Security Council (UNSC) passed resolution 1718, which condemned North Korea's nuclear and missile programmes and forbade the international community from dealing with North Korea's conventional weapons, missiles and nuclear industries.

The 2006 arms embargo was broadened in 2009 by UNSC resolution 1874, which included 'all arms and related materiel, as well as financial transactions, technical training, advice, services or assistance related to the provision, manufacture, maintenance or use of such arms or materiel'.[9] Individual countries, such as the United States and Japan, but also the European Union, have implemented additional sanctions regimes.[10]

Despite these efforts, several Southern African countries continued to engage with North Korea. In 2008, two years after the first UN sanctions, the highest-ranking North Korean delegation in years travelled to Africa 'in an apparent bid to expand economic and trade cooperation as well as to break [the] country's diplomatic isolation'. Angola and Namibia were among the visited countries. The 23-member delegation, led by Kim Yong Nam (Kim Yŏng-nam), was met by the respective presidents (Eduardo dos Santos and Hifikepunye Pohamba) and agreements were signed, which were rumoured to contain pledges of arms export and manpower.[11]

The political scientist Bruce Bechtol concludes that 'when it comes to proliferation of arms to other nations, North Korea has turned this into an art form'.[12] North Korea is an 'adaptable marketer' and uses a mixture of state-owned companies, high-level political visits and locally based embassy staff to push its military exports in Africa.[13] While North Korean military activities are generally secretive and difficult to track, they are not indecipherable. The internet offers access to many things, including English-language catalogues of North Korean arms companies.[14]

163

The reports of the UN Panel of Experts are an underrated source for the study of African–North Korean ties. The Panel was established in 2009 to monitor the UN sanctions regime against North Korea and produces annual reports that include fascinating details about North Korea's criminal exploits. Ten years after the first UN sanctions against North Korea, the Panel noted that the country 'continues to exploit long-standing military relationships in Africa'.[15] These relationships span the entire continent. This section illustrates the ongoing clandestine military alliance between Southern Africa and North Korea through case studies from Tanzania, Mozambique, Angola and Namibia.

* * *

The UN has implicated Tanzania, the former Frontline State and key ally of Kim Il Sung in his diplomatic offensive in Southern Africa, in several North Korean arms deals. In 2013, it was discovered that 18 North Korean technicians resided at the Mwanza Air Force Base to lend their services to the Tanzanian People's Defence Force Air Wing.[16] North Korea was hired to refurbish several F-7 fighter jets. A few years later, in 2017, Tanzania reportedly made a deal with the North Korean Haegeumgang Trading Corporation for the repairing and upgrading of surface-to-air missile Pechora (S-125) systems and a P-12 air defence radar. This deal was valued at €10.49 million. Again, the North Korean advisors that were outsourced for this job resided at a Tanzanian military facility. Haegeumgang Trading Corporation was also active in neighbouring Mozambique, where it upgraded the same type of air defence systems.[17] As is common in many African countries, Tanzania failed to respond to critical enquiries from the United Nations.[18]

* * *

Mozambique acknowledged that, between 2012–17, six North Korean nationals travelled to 'remote civil-military airfields with nearby military bases'. The precise reason for their journey remains unclear, but it is not unthinkable that they were selling

SURVIVAL

their expertise. They were working for two North Korean arms companies that were designated by the UN for breaking the sanctions regime. It was also discovered that a North Korean representative of Haegeumgang Trading Corporation, another sanctioned arms corporation, was stationed in Mozambique, although he was formally accredited to the North Korean embassy in South Africa.[19]

In 2018, the UN investigated a $6 million contract between Haegeumgang Trading Corporation and the Mozambican company Monte Binga for 'surface-to-air missiles, P-12 air defence radar, tank refurbishment and man-portable air defence systems'.[20] Although the UN is in the possession of the military contract and photographs of technicians of the Korean People's Army standing in front of refurbished tanks in Mozambique,[21] Mozambique did not respond to a request for information from the UN in 2019.[22]

* * *

In 2011, Angola was reported to have imported spare parts and equipment for submarines and military boats from the sanctioned North Korean company Green Pine Associated Corporation.[23] An anonymised member state reported to the UN Panel of Experts that approximately 80 North Koreans were based in the country to train the presidential guard and other units. It was alleged that, in 2017, this group had travelled from Angola to an unknown destination to conduct a military advisory mission, but this has been denied by the Angolan government. Nevertheless, the UN confirmed the presence of Green Pine representatives in Angola.[24] A North Korean diplomat accredited to Angola (who turned out to be working on behalf of Green Pine) was expelled from the country in 2017 following UN pressure.[25] After much insistence, the Angolan government considered the presence of North Korean nationals in Luanda 'to be in excessive numbers' and vowed to gradually reduce it.[26]

* * *

In recent years, Namibia has gained notoriety for hiring the North Korean art studio Mansudae Overseas Projects (MOP). Using North Korean forced labour, MOP has constructed several highly visible buildings in Windhoek, including the presidential palace and a history museum.[27] The UN revealed that the construction company was also active in military projects and was connected to KOMID, a sanctioned North Korean arms company. It turns out that MOP was also involved in the construction of the headquarters of the Namibian Ministry of Defence, a munitions factory in Windhoek (with the aim to produce small arms ammunitions of 7.62 mm calibre), the Military Academy and military bases.[28]

Furthermore, KOMID exported pressure tanks and machinery to the Namibian Defence Force in 2012, materiel that 'could be used for military explosives and production of propellants'.[29] Around this time, two North Korean diplomats from the North Korean embassy in Pretoria, South Africa, were operating as KOMID representatives in Namibia. Although they were officially accredited in Pretoria as Second and Third Secretary of the embassy, travel records showed that they spent most of their time in Windhoek.[30] Following international pressure, Namibia terminated the remaining construction contracts with MOP, sold their vehicles and equipment in an auction and repatriated 242 North Korean nationals in 2017.[31]

Patterns

Many nodes in the North Korean illicit networks that span the globe are relatively overlooked, claims Bechtol, and 'this is true nowhere more so than the continent of Africa'.[32] One important aspect of this network is the North Korean embassies in the African continent. The North Korean companies that violate UN sanctions are often supported by North Korean diplomats, who can travel on diplomatic passports and are less likely to be checked at customs.

In Southern Africa, the North Korean network of traditional embassies (which includes missions in South Africa and Tanzania) is supplemented by trade offices in Namibia, Zimbabwe and Zambia.[33] Such hubs are not bound to servicing only a single country but perform transnational or even regional roles. There are hundreds of North Korean trade companies active in the world and many, if not all, depend on diplomatic support.[34]

An exiled North Korean diplomat with extensive working experience in Africa told me that the illicit activities of North Korean diplomats can be explained through the concept of self-help. His former colleagues in the North Korean diplomatic service know that earning hard foreign currency sustains the diplomatic post that they occupy. Moreover, generating money may result in medals or other favours back home in Pyongyang. If diplomats outperform their peers in terms of finding revenue, they may even be allowed to stay longer abroad than the usual three years. For many North Koreans, this is a desirable objective as the living conditions within their home country are dire.[35]

This system of self-help was largely unnecessary during the Cold War, when the North Korean Ministry of Foreign Affairs had enough cash to fund embassies across the African continent. However, since the disastrous years of the famine and economic collapse of the 1990s, this system has become crucial for maintaining the status quo of North Korea's diplomatic structures—and, of course, for stuffing the revolutionary coffers of the Kim family. For example, when Kim Jong Un came to power and ordered the construction of flats for 10,000 households, the Ministry of Foreign Affairs in Pyongyang ordered all diplomatic posts to supply anything they could: cash, but also building materials. When Kim Jong Un wanted to expand the Pyongyang Zoo, the embassy in South Africa managed to obtain several lions. Those diplomats received a hero's welcome when they returned back home.[36]

North Korean diplomats 'continue to play key roles' in facilitating illegitimate activities in Africa.[37] Among the standard tasks of North Korean embassies in Africa are accommodating trade companies from Pyongyang and maintaining ties with the domestic military industry.[38] The analyst Andrea Berger notes that 'embassy representatives have on many occasions been caught facilitating arms deals'.[39] In addition to brokering services, the UN observes that North Korean diplomats 'often serve as shipping companies' agents or cash carriers'.[40] Moreover, North Korean officials have also been accused of dealing in counterfeited US dollars, methamphetamine and ivory (see Chapter 15).[41]

UN reports show that North Korea is incredibly skilled in circumventing sanctions by using 'increasingly sophisticated and diversified techniques'.[42] Recurring patterns include the extensive use of shell companies and front companies, which makes it difficult to trace individual companies as these often comprise numerous local subsidiaries and carry different names. Furthermore, North Korean trade can be facilitated through the use of local banks and the endorsement of local political elites.

The majority of recorded illicit North Korean transport involves containerised cargo. North Korean merchant ships use flags or maritime mobile service identity numbers from African countries while carrying out illegal operations.[43] The transport of prohibited goods is also facilitated through regular cargo services or chartered cargo flights.[44] In 2009, Ethiopian Airlines transported five tonnes of North Korean arms material through regular passenger flights, including tank engines and armoured vehicles.[45]

There is a difference between North Korean brokers who reside long-term in Africa and outsourced labourers. The brokers—diplomats or businessmen—are locally grounded. They usually stay in one place or region for several years, speak the *lingua franca* and they know how to navigate local politics, businesses and other stakeholders.[46] This is further illustrated in Chapter 15, through a discussion of North Korean businessmen in the Democratic Republic of Congo.

In contrast, the North Korean instructors, technicians or other kinds of labourers who are exported for specific projects usually have much less space to move around. A UN investigation from 2014 showed that, in the Republic of Congo, two refurbishment teams were lodged in secret compounds to ensure confidentiality. The teams were 'self-sufficient in terms of food and medical care with embedded cooks, doctors, and interpreters and virtually all food and supplies' came from the DPRK. Personnel rarely left the compound and were not rotated for years at a time in order to reduce expenses and increase secrecy.[47]

SURVIVAL

The UN noted that non-military sources of income—such as construction projects or medical cooperation—could be used to disguise the earnings from military activities.[48] While it is true that China is occasionally complicit in North Korean illegal ventures in Africa,[49] North Korea oversees its own foreign policy.[50] In that sense, the modus operandi remains the same as during the Cold War. North Korean activities in Africa no longer fit the description of 'two persons and a fax machine', observes the UN, but are part of a 'relatively mature, complex and international corporate ecosystem'.[51]

African motives for engagement

It is a safe assumption that the case studies covered at the start of this chapter—concerning Tanzanian F-7 fighter jets, Mozambican air defence systems, and Namibian munitions factories—only scratch the surface of North Korean military activities in Southern Africa. Future UN reports and media investigations will likely unearth new evidence of sanction-busting activities.

The UN Panel of Experts detected 'a general distaste for implementing sanctions regimes' in several countries.[52] In the past decade, the majority of Southern African states (including Angola, Botswana, Lesotho, Madagascar, Mozambique, Namibia, South Africa, Tanzania, Zambia and Zimbabwe) repeatedly failed to submit national implementation reports or did not respond to specific enquiries from the Panel.[53] The UN noted that the proportion on non-reporting states is 'higher in regions with a long history of cooperation' with the DPRK, which aptly describes Southern Africa.[54]

It is significant that North Korea seems to favour locations with historic business and political connections, as is the case in Southern Africa.[55] Shell companies often change and supply chains are thus complex,[56] but the 'trusted foreign parties' of North Korea remain the same for years.[57] Even though the UN estimates that its sanctions have cost North Korea 'hundreds of millions of dollars' in lost revenue, North Korea is largely immune to external pressure on its military programmes.[58]

169

COMRADES BEYOND THE COLD WAR

It is therefore more effective, according to Berger, to concentrate on the demand-side, by making 'North Korea and its products less appealing from the perspective of potential consumers'.[59] But why do African countries ignore UN sanctions against North Korea? This book offers three reasons why African countries continue to engage with North Korea: historical affinity (reciprocity), the practical issue of maintenance dependency (necessity) and the presence of weak enforcement regimes (opportunity).

* * *

The first reason is *reciprocity* and revolves around historical relationships. The North Korean assistance of the twentieth century is ingrained in the institutional memory of Southern African liberation movements. Chapter 3 described how African leaders travelled to Pyongyang in search of support. Sam Nujoma thanked Kim Il Sung in 1986 for his 'practical material assistance', after which Kim assured him that North Korea 'will firmly stand by you in the future too'.[60] This is exactly what happened after Namibia became independent, as North Korea offered training services, military hardware and construction expertise.

Nujoma's words were far from uncommon across Southern Africa and beyond. Several contemporary African leaders justify contemporary military relations with North Korea by referring to the historical relations of the past. In 2014, the Ugandan president and dictator Yoweri Museveni praised North Korea's assistance in the training of police officers. During a graduation ceremony of new recruits, Museveni said to the journalists in his audience: 'The DPRK always gives us technical support—I do not see any problem with them'.[61] Years earlier, in 1969, Museveni (then a guerrilla leader) received military training in Pyongyang, a milestone in his rise to the Ugandan presidency. 'It was the first time I had ever handled a weapon', Museveni recalled in his autobiography.[62]

The second reason is *necessity* and revolves around maintenance dependency. Contemporary African armies occasionally rely upon the repair services of North Korea, as they continue to use outdated military hardware from the Cold War era. The previous

170

SURVIVAL

chapter highlighted how African liberation governments benefited from North Korean weapons and training during the Cold War, which was often provided for free or cheaply. As time moves on, this material is prone to wearing out and breaking down and is therefore in need of repair or an upgrade. Who better to hire than North Korea?

Since the end of the Cold War, North Korea has maintained a profitable niche in the global arms market through the 'repair, servicing and provision of spare parts for ageing communist-bloc systems'.[63] It has an important advantage because a dwindling number of competitors offer similar services when it comes to vintage equipment.[64] In 2007, it was discovered that North Koreans were working in an Ethiopian arms factory that produced AK-47 rifles—the same factory had been set up by the North Koreans in the 1980s.[65] Moreover, North Korea has a reputation for selling its services at very competitive prices. Berger quotes an Ethiopian minister who explained that North Korea priced its goods 50% cheaper than China.[66] This attracts African countries that consider buying brand-new weapon systems as 'prohibitively costly'.[67]

The third reason is *opportunity* and revolves around weak enforcement regimes. North Korea is aided by African countries' lax attitude vis-à-vis the UN.[68] The UN argued that a 'lack of awareness and understanding' of the sanction regime allows North Korea to exploit its relationships 'with African countries for arms-related services and training'.[69]

This was demonstrated in 2014 when the South African authorities intercepted a ship destined for the Republic of Congo.[70] The cargo was labelled as 'spare parts of bulldozers' but in fact contained spare parts for T-54/T-55 military tanks.[71] These so-called 'knock-down kits' are a tried and tested method of North Korea to conceal arms exports.[72] At least this ship was caught, but the UN identified at least three other previous deliveries, which illustrates that it was not an isolated incident.[73]

In many cases, local regulatory authorities in African countries—such as port officials, customs offices at airports or bank regulators—are subject to underfunding or political pressure, and subsequently fail to consider North Korea as a high priority.

171

But even in the rare cases when whistle-blowers expose criminal behaviour, the results are distressing. Two Congolese auditors revealed that a Congolese bank hosted the bank accounts of two North Korean businessmen but were punished for their bravery (this incident is explored in Chapter 15). In 2020, the High Court of Kinshasa sentenced them to death—both men had already fled the country and found refuge in exile, in Europe.[74] This sets a chilling precedent throughout the African continent.

Conclusion

North Korea has mastered the art of survival, despite immense internal and external pressure. In that sense, it is an inspiration for African regimes that strive to do the same. This book seeks to lift the veil of the shadowy world of North Korean operations in Africa— not just by describing what happens, but *why* it happens. For this, the shared history of the liberation struggle is indispensable.

In 2002, the historian Stephen Ellis dared contemporary historians to think about the present character of Africa. He wrote that today is no longer the age of national liberation or national development, but concluded that 'the discussion is open as to what sort of an age it really is'.[75] I would argue that, in the case of Southern Africa, the start of the twenty-first century can be defined by the political survival of African liberation movements that have held on to power since independence.

Across the Southern African region, a party–military complex of liberation governments and the military defies popular challenge to enduring rule by emphasising their heroic role in the struggle, a fight that, in a way, continues up until this day.[76] In 1972, Agostinho Neto urged his followers to continue the armed struggle 'in the future, after political independence, in order to be completely free'. He not only desired political independence, but also economic and social independence. This ambition required a continuous revolution.[77]

African citizens sometimes loosely transliterate the famous rallying cry of the past, *A luta continua* (the struggle continues), as 'the looting continues'. It is a scathing critique on today's political elites, who seem mainly interested in enriching themselves rather than the idealistic values of the past.

African authoritarian leaders consider North Korea as a suitable partner in crime, a state that is also led by political elites who favour survival above all else. It is my impression that, today, North Korean businessmen and diplomats in Africa are chasing ad hoc and relatively small-scale profits instead of large, long-term contracts. In short, the modus operandi of many North Korean operatives appears to be opportunistic trade that exploits historic relationships, maintenance dependency and weak enforcement. Rather than a top-down approach directed from Pyongyang, it is more likely that we are witnessing a certain bottom-up approach to trade that is informed by local incentives.

The North Korean embassy system is a decentralised system of foreign missions that operate as companies and seek to earn money whenever the opportunity arises. The need for survival is also a motivating factor for traditional North Korean businesses, even for the North Korean doctors who reside across the African continent, from Mali to Mozambique.[78]

The impact of the Covid-19 pandemic on African–North Korean networks is uncertain. Given the fact that North Korea sealed off its borders in an attempt to keep the virus out, it is conceivable that the distance between Pyongyang and North Korean nationals residing in Africa widened considerably. This blockade prevented the repatriation of overseas workers, which may have been another incentive for North Korean operatives to find ways to earn cash, as the need for survival increased.[79] In 2023, North Korea's announcement that it would close several embassies, including in Angola, indicated economic trouble.[80] Income from abroad is of vital importance for the North Korean regime and UN sanctions make this endeavour more difficult. Nevertheless, a UN report from 2024 predicts that 'once the border reopens further, North Korea is expected to send a large number of additional workers overseas'.[81]

EPILOGUE

PARTY–MILITARY COMPLEX

Contemporary Southern Africa is ruled by a unique political constellation that may be described as a Party–Military Complex. Since independence, the majority of states have been governed by liberation governments that came to power on account of their military wings. When independence was secured, liberation movements were transformed into political parties and their armed wings were incorporated into the national army. Today, both entities remain closely intertwined, as was the case during the years leading up to independence.

If liberation is the fruit, then survival and control were its seeds. For the exiled liberation movements in Africa, forging unity before and after independence was crucial. During the second half of the twentieth century, the ebb and flow of violence that spilled across the region resulted in a military mindset among African political elites who determine much of today's political culture. Throughout this process, African nationalists were inspired by and received practical help from North Korea. In the best traditions of communism, Kim Il Sung presented an example of a successful party-state. However, African interest in North Korea was not fuelled by communist ideology, but by pragmatism.

Just as the Korean War is a foundational myth for North Korea, so is the armed struggle for many African governments. Robert

Mugabe said: 'The People's votes and the People's guns are always inseparable twins ... There is no better defender of political power won through the gun than the gun itself'.[1] This signifies the clearly militaristic discourse that pervades much of Southern Africa today. However, as his rival Joshua Nkomo rightfully pointed out, the Fifth Brigade was 'a ZANU (PF) army and not part of the Zimbabwe National Army'.[2] North Korea primarily supported parties instead of countries—liberation movements instead of states.

Kim Il Sung offered practical help for African revolutionaries who sought to achieve and consolidate political power, such as the gifting of military hardware and the export of military instructors. Moreover, North Korea presented a certain ideal of how a revolutionary army was embedded in the wider political struggle for self-reliance. It was an idea that resonated with African revolutionaries, who believed that 'the armed struggle is essentially a political struggle by other means'. Similar principles can be discerned in the military doctrines of MK and other liberation armies. 'It is not just a question of picking up a gun. What is paramount are ideas that guide the guns'.[3] Again, the mythology of the Korean War inspired the African guerrilla.

With today's knowledge, Kim Il Sung did not emerge out of this period as the anti-imperialist hero he claimed to be, but rather as a prince of darkness. Through his military help, North Korea fuelled the authoritarian tendencies of some of the central figures in the freedom struggles of Southern Africa. The *Gukurahundi* genocide in Zimbabwe is the most evident example, but this pattern can be witnessed in several other instances as well.[4]

Importantly, the military relationship between Africans and North Koreans continued into the twenty-first century. To understand this, liberation history is key—contemporary African governments legitimise their enduring rule on account of the glorious revolutions of the past. SWAPO predicted in 1988 that *after* the victory of independence its slogan 'The Struggle Continues' would assume 'a deeper revolutionary significance'.[5] Indeed, the idea that the revolution continues is prevalent among several liberation governments in Southern Africa (see Chapter 13).

EPILOGUE

As such, North Korea helps African liberation governments to maintain their power despite internal opposition and external pressure. Of course, North Korea is now primarily motivated by earning hard foreign currency. The UN stated that arms trade remains 'one of the most profitable revenue sources' for North Korea.[6] The UN, the United States and other actors are trying to curb North Korea's military earnings through an extensive sanctions regime. For a variety of reasons—historical affinity, maintenance dependency, weak enforcement regimes—African states have repeatedly ignored these sanctions in recent years.

The military alliance of North Korea and African states is evidence of diplomatic structures that voluntarily withdraw from the liberal world order. This can lead to ironic results, such as the discovery, in 2017, that Congolese units from the United Nations Multidimensional Integrated Stabilisation Mission in the Central African Republic (MINUSCA) were armed with North Korean pistols. The weapons were originally owned by the presidential guard of the Democratic Republic of Congo, who received them from North Korea between 2014 and 2015. The pistols, together with shipments of rifles and mines, were used by North Korean military instructors stationed at a military base outside Kinshasa.[7] This shows that patterns similar to those in Southern Africa can be discerned in other parts of the continent as well.

PART THREE

BRONZE

CULTURAL HERITAGE

When I return from the land of exile and silence
Do not bring me flowers.

Bring me rather all the dews,
Tears of dawns which witnessed dramas.
Bring me the immense hunger for love
and the plaint of tumid sexes in star-studded night.
Bring me the long night of sleeplessness
with mothers mourning, their arms bereft of sons.

When I return from the land of exile and silence,
no, do not bring me flowers …

Bring me only, this
the last wish of heroes fallen at day-break
with a wingless stone in hand
and a thread of anger snaking from their eyes.

—'Poem of Return', by Jofre Rocha, Angola

PROLOGUE

A MONUMENTAL RELATIONSHIP

In recent years, several striking monuments have been erected across the African continent that assert a confident vision of African identity. In 2010, Senegal unveiled the African Renaissance Monument which is, at 50 metres, the largest statue on the continent.[1] At the launch ceremony, the Senegalese president Abdoulaye Wade announced that 'Africa has arrived in the 21st century standing tall and more ready than ever to take its destiny in its hands'.[2] Decades earlier, Senegalese historian Cheikh Anta Diop coined the term African Renaissance to describe the continent's right to determine its own future (a concept later used by the South African president Thabo Mbeki and other leaders).[3] In 2022, Benin inaugurated a 30-metre-tall statue of an Amazon warrior—a legend recently featured in the Hollywood blockbuster *The Woman King*.[4] Despite the indigenous African message, these monuments have a surprising background: they are constructed by MOP, a North Korean art studio.[5]

'Bronze' symbolises the African heritage that is designed and built by North Korea. Construction work is the most important form of African–North Korean cooperation today. African governments use North Korean monuments to legitimise their enduring rule, while the North Korean regime is dependent on hard foreign currency from Africa to survive. Contrary to scholarship that situates the African–North Korean alliance within the Cold War time frame, this book consciously includes the trade relations of recent years in its analysis.[6] The Cold War time frame of existing scholarship is a largely Eurocentric device that distorts a proper understanding of African–North Korean relations—the events of the 1990s did not stop these interactions, they merely altered them.

In Southern Africa, North Korean monuments justify the ongoing rule of liberation governments by celebrating their victories in the liberation struggles. Richard Werbner highlighted the 'postwars of the dead' in Southern Africa, 'the intense peacetime struggles over the appropriation of the heroism, martyrdom or even last remains' of those that participated in the struggle.[7] The choice of African elites for a North Korean heritage model is significant: they have put their national history, acclaimed heroes, and origin myths in North Korean hands. As such, this final part of the book is framed around heritage. Incontrovertibly, heritage presents a narrow interpretation of history. The art historian Min-Kyung Yoon shows that North Korean monuments 'mould and cast the past along a fixed revolutionary trajectory ... By solidifying the past, there is no more doubt about the revolution'.[8] Therefore, this final part of the book reviews how North Korean monuments reveal or conceal the past in Africa.

Miloš Todorović argues that heritage is an important tool in cultivating soft power. Nevertheless, 'little attention has been paid to studying and understanding its role in diplomacy'.[9] The popularity of North Korea's monumental diplomacy is an overlooked aspect of North Korean soft power in the twenty-first century. The proliferation of North Korean aesthetics in Africa raises questions about the space that North Korea occupies in the Global South. Today, North Korean soft power is primarily manifested in tangible forms of architecture—the museums, statues, presidential palaces, cemeteries, parks and stadiums built by MOP.[10]

MOP is the international division of Mansudae Art Studio, a large art studio based in Pyongyang. Founded in 1959, Mansudae Art Studio has become a pillar of the state-sanctioned visual culture

PROLOGUE

that supports the North Korean regime. It is responsible for the design and production of major heritage sites in Pyongyang, as well as the production of paintings, sculpture, woodcuts, ceramics and various other art forms. Mansudae Art Studio is estimated to employ nearly 4,000 people and is well-known for its high quality and craftsmanship.[11] MOP, its international division, operates in countries around the world—including Europe, Asia and Africa. Due to the scale of constructions and the resulting large revenue streams, MOP's activities in Africa are increasingly receiving scholarly attention.[12]

The key to North Korea's success in the global heritage industry is its 'one size fits all' model. MOP's catalogue consists of designs that are inspired by—and sometimes direct copies of— monuments in North Korea. As this part will explore in further detail, North Korean visual aesthetics suit a variety of postcolonial governments in Africa.[13] As such, MOP operates transnationally. The Namibian office of MOP performed a regional role in Southern Africa and was also involved in operations in Angola, Botswana and Mozambique.[14] MOP employees operate as transnational artists and work on different projects in different countries, where they apply a similar artistic model.[15]

African governments have plenty of options for the construction of heritage, both local and international, but they deliberately choose the services of North Korea. This is a fascinating and overlooked aspect of South–South cooperation that wilfully bypasses the West. As South Korea is ramping up its investments in Africa, the historical competition between both sides of the peninsula is being continued by other means.[16] In recent years, North Korea constructed a national history museum in Namibia— at the same time, South Korea built a national history museum in the Democratic Republic of Congo.[17]

The previous two parts of this book focused on the twentieth century. Divided between blood and bullets, diplomacy and war, they reflected the two paths for African liberation movements towards independence as laid out by Julius Nyerere. In contrast, the current part ('Bronze') is situated in the twenty-first century and examines the outcome of the struggle through an analysis

183

of heritage.[18] 'When I return from the land of exile', wrote Jofre Rocha in a poem that captures the ambiguous memories from the struggle era.[19] In the 1960s, Rocha (a pseudonym of Roberto Francisco de Almeida) was imprisoned in Lisbon for his anticolonial activities and, in later years, became a successful MPLA politician.[20] His poem raises the question of how liberation movements look back at the recent past, upon their return from the land of exile.

The legacy of the liberation struggle pervades almost every aspect of political life in Southern Africa. The chapters in the final part of this book dissect how African liberation governments use North Korean heritage to legitimise their enduring rule. Chapter 11 sets the stage by explaining how the narratives that propelled liberation governments into power have become myths that are now remembered through North Korean art. Chapters 12–14 each review an overarching theme of African memorial culture (nations, violence and heroism) with reference to North Korean visual aesthetics.[21] Chapter 15 considers the advantage that North Korea derives from this business, namely, foreign currency. The conclusion examines how contemporary political issues in Southern Africa are viewed through the prism of the struggle, a 'liberation lens' that is strongly coloured by North Korean aesthetics.

11

MYTH

PATRIOTIC HISTORY FROM PYONGYANG

A short walk through downtown Windhoek, up the hill towards the Namibian parliament, brings you right into the political heart of the country. It is a highly evocative intersection of the past and the present. On the right, visitors encounter a 130-year-old German fort. On the left, just beyond the *Alte Feste*, visitors can spot the German *Christuskirche*, a quaint gingerbread church. Wedged between these two pillars of colonisation stands a North Korean history museum that is entirely devoted to the indigenous uprisings against foreign occupation.

The tension between the Independence Memorial Museum and its colonial surroundings is evident. It is a landmark building that stands out for its unusual North Korean design and meaningful location—the site of a former concentration camp during the Namibian genocide of 1904–08, when German *Schutztruppe* decimated large parts of the local population.[1] So, within a short walk through downtown Windhoek, visitors will experience a wide-ranging view of more than a century of the politics of memory. And it is a sight not to be forgotten.

Why would Namibia, a country that became independent in 1990 after 100 years of foreign rule, celebrate its victory of

185

independence with a North Korean museum? Museums are 'politically charged' institutions that present 'state-sponsored presentations of history'.[2] Renzo Baas describes them as 'sites of power where a governing system symbolically reproduces itself' and are thus a revealing window onto the myths that underpin African governments.[3] In the case of Southern Africa, these myths put liberation governments centre stage in the glorious revolutions that led to independence.

The Independence Memorial Museum symbolises the influence of North Korea in African mythmaking, in which the liberation movement becomes central. North Korea's role is significant because its help extends beyond providing the builders that lay bricks and shovel mortar—it can also design the narrative. North Korean artists not only created the exterior of the Independence Memorial Museum, but they also designed the exhibitions and were therefore responsible for the state-sanctioned narrative of Namibia's liberation history.[4] SWAPO's decision to put their national heroes into the hands of MOP speaks volumes about the trust between the ruling party and North Korea. It signifies that, in large parts of the world, North Korea is viewed differently than in the West. For SWAPO, Pyongyang's pariah status is largely irrelevant—the Independence Memorial Museum opened its doors in 2014, years after the first sanctions were implemented by the international community.[5]

With the Independence Memorial Museum as a case study, this chapter illustrates how North Korea's heritage expertise met the demand for African patriotic history. The first section describes how, during the struggle, African liberation movements forged narratives that advanced their cause. Over time, these narratives turned into myths—and are now eternalised through North Korean heritage. The second section highlights the mythical role ascribed to SWAPO in the Independence Memorial Museum. The third section discusses the role of patriotic history in Southern Africa.

MYTH

Narratives

Truth is the first casualty of war, and history—to paraphrase the Namibian historian Jeremy Silvester—is often its first conscript.[6] This is particularly true for wars of liberation, as history is a potent tool for the rejection or legitimisation of political regimes. In Southern Africa, the liberation wars were as much over information as they were wars on the battlefield. All actors in the Southern African liberation struggles tried to take control of the narrative. This resulted in, for example, the use of forgeries that discredited opponents by spreading false information—in particular, the South African government was known for its 'dirty tricks'.[7] More relevant for the focus of this book, however, are the labour-intensive efforts of liberation movements to produce propaganda in which they were portrayed as operating on the right side of history.

Even though many African liberation movements were forced to operate from exile, they nevertheless framed themselves as nationally rooted movements. Part One of this book discussed how the recognition of the UN and other actors was of paramount importance for the legitimacy of their organisations and, by extension, their wider cause. Similar to the North Korean campaign for statehood, it was essential to forge a narrative of a just revolution against oppression. For this reason, the departments of information within what were effectively militarily weak African liberation movements became institutions of central importance. These departments produced magazines, books, radio programmes, posters, poetry and songs, often from exile, which drove the dissemination of nationalist narratives.

It is no coincidence that many exiled African nationalists who took up scholarships in Europe and the United States decided to study history. Several key leaders in Southern Africa used their historical training to generate the narratives of liberation movements that prevail today. At the dawn of independence, many of them ended up in influential political positions.[8] Zimbabwe is but one example. 'There were so many historians in the cabinet and in charge of public institutions', joked Terence Ranger in 1980, then a University of Zimbabwe lecturer, 'that the new Zimbabwe was an experiment in rule by historiography'. Twenty years later, with the benefit of hindsight, he added that 'it is not so funny now'.[9]

With SWAPO's rise to power in 1990 came 'the duty of recording and preserving our nation's history', said Namibian president Hifikepunye Pohamba. The Independence Memorial Museum fulfilled the 'sacred task to tell, record and preserve our own history, as we perceive it, as we experience it, and as we see it with our own eyes'.[10]

Myths

The construction of national museums is a conventional method for governments to showcase their own interpretations of history. In Southern Africa, liberation governments produce historical myths about the struggle that legitimise their enduring rule. Naturally, their own organisations are central to these myths and obscure other actors and factors. This pattern can be observed in the Independence Memorial Museum in Windhoek, the first post-apartheid national history museum in Namibia and therefore the most prominent display of public history in the country.

The Independence Memorial Museum is funded by the SWAPO government and built by MOP. Construction work began in 2009 and the opening was originally planned for 2010 but ultimately delayed for four more years. The building has been described by academics as 'a futuristic design that celebrates and asserts the power of the modern post-colonial state' and by locals as 'the coffee pot' due to its peculiar shape.[11]

The collection of the museum is divided over three floors, each representing a chapter in Namibian history. The museum experience culminates in a large North Korean-style panorama that can be viewed from a special balcony. Access is free of charge, and the collection mainly consists of historical images, statues, firearms, pieces of clothing and other objects. Most strikingly, the museum is adorned by multiple life-sized painted murals that display coloured collages of starving and fighting Namibians. The museum makes 'no attempt to contextualise images with text

MYTH

beyond the use of brief labels', causing the historians Christian Williams and Tichaona Mazarire to conclude that 'history here works primarily at a symbolic level, supported by a simple underlying narrative of colonialism, resistance, and liberation'.[12]

The first floor is titled 'Colonial Repression' and displays a supposedly harmonious and peaceful Namibian society prior to the arrival of European oppressors. The exhibition visualises the resistance by Namibian leaders against the German occupation, with special reference to the 1904–08 genocide. The terror of this event is captured in a 'Chamber of Horrors': a dark space, closed off by thick curtains, furnished with terrifying sculptures of starving people in chains. The room aims to mimic the concentration camps used by the German *Schutztruppe*.

The second floor is titled 'Liberation' and narrates the struggle against the South African occupation. The floor pays attention to life under apartheid rule and national opposition against the National Party. Much attention is given to the Kassinga Massacre of 1978 (also known as the Battle of Cassinga) when South African airborne forces bombed and overran a SWAPO base in Angola killing hundreds of exiled Namibians. The prominent role of SWAPO becomes clear in this part of the museum, with a focus on the military dimension of the struggle. In addition to murals and photographs, visitors can observe weapon displays and a fake tank.

The third floor is titled 'Road to Independence' and details how SWAPO liberated Namibia. The importance of SWAPO's leader and first Namibian president Sam Nujoma is emphasised. Several national symbols are highlighted and explained via special displays, including the national constitution, the flag, the coat of arms and the president's flag. The walls display nationalist slogans, such as 'Long Live Namibian Independence!' This floor leads to the Panoramic Hall, the centrepiece of the museum. A viewing platform affords visitors an unrestricted view of an extensive North Korean-style painting that illustrates the struggle for Namibian freedom through emotional depictions of starving, fighting and, ultimately, cooperating Namibian citizens.

Soon after construction started, the museum became the subject of severe local criticism. From the outset, Namibians questioned the high costs (an estimated 60 million Namibian dollars; around 2010, this amounted to US$8.5 million but the exchange rate is volatile) and the peculiar decision to hire a North Korean art studio.[13] When the museum became accessible to the public, visitors complained about obvious historical mistakes and grammatical errors in the exhibition.[14] Williams and Mazarire noted that 'some portions of the exhibition even appear to fabricate historical events'.[15]

In former colonies in Africa, museums are an opportunity for independent governments to instil a new sense of nationalism among their populations.[16] 'Nation-building', writes Enid Schildkrout, 'involves a certain amount of amnesia and continual rewriting of history'.[17] The Independence Memorial Museum, for example, has been described by historians as presenting 'a narrow history of Namibia' with an 'exceptionally decontextualised and melodramatic presentation'.[18]

Critics' main concern was the overriding narrative focus of SWAPO as the main liberator of Namibia. Elke Zuern observes that memorial sites offer specific interpretations of the past, 'highlighting and glorifying certain actors and actions while purposely forgetting others'.[19] The focus on SWAPO naturally diminished the roles of other actors that fought and suffered during the decades-long liberation struggle. Examples of marginalised but important groups are women in general, traditional leaders, churches and trade unions, while the histories of the Herero, Nama and Damara peoples were allegedly diminished in favour of a narrative that privileged the Owambo people in the northern part of Namibia, which is the political base of SWAPO.[20] Christopher Steiner argues that in museums ethnic groups that are merged together into 'new' states are usually overrepresented or underrepresented, 'but always misrepresented'.[21]

Furthermore, the exhibition displays an evident 'cult of personality' of Sam Nujoma and a 'glorification of the military struggle' that is not recognised by large parts of the population.[22] The decision to narrate highly localised, indigenous African history in general North Korean terms causes friction. Heike Becker notes that it 'may come across as astounding' that the Genocide

MYTH

Memorial emphasises a form of 'martial, masculinist heroism' while it is meant to commemorate the victims of a brutal genocidal campaign.[23]

Patriotic history

Upon independence, SWAPO inherited a society that, like all African nations, could be characterised by its ethnic and linguistic diversity. The new government suppressed a secessionist uprising in the first years of its tenure.[24] SWAPO's main concern did not differ from neighbouring states, as it desired a sense of national unity and cohesion.[25] Today, half of the Namibian population is under the age of 25 and has no active recollection of the days of colonialism and foreign rule. This group increasingly relies on the consumption of public history in order to understand the recent past.[26] This history is often reframed as 'national heritage', and it takes on a deeply nationalist framing from public school textbooks to the physical monuments that dot the landscape.

The Independence Memorial Museum is a fitting example of the widespread propagation of patriotic history in Southern Africa. In the early 2000s, the historian Terrence Ranger—who was deported by the white Rhodesian government in 1963 for his African nationalist views—identified the emergence of patriotic history in Zimbabwe. While traditional nationalist historiography 'celebrated aspiration and modernisation', patriotic history is 'narrower'. It explicitly lifts the revolutionary spirits by referring to a glorious past, which, in turn, legitimises the ruling party and discards everything else.[27]

Ranger's analysis was confined to Zimbabwe but *mutatis mutandis* can be applied to other liberation governments in Southern Africa. Patriotic history simplifies the past and deliberately divides the nation between revolutionaries and sell-outs, between those on the right or on the wrong side of history. Political opponents of the liberation governments are mocked for not taking part in the liberation struggle and thus failing to understand history.[28] One's political power is partly determined by one's struggle credentials.[29]

Patriotic history is 'explicitly antagonistic to academic historiography' and 'confronts Western "bogus universalism"'. Ranger described how, in Zimbabwe, hundreds of thousands of UNESCO textbooks on *Education for Human Rights and Democracy in Zimbabwe* remained stuck in warehouses while the government distributed patriotic history books to schools instead.[30] Most prominent, however, is the propagation of patriotic history through the discourse of African political and intellectual elites, as shown by Blessing-Miles Tendi.[31] A similar refusal to accept a Western-liberal framework of history characterises the North Korean education system, argues Jiyoung Song.[32]

Ranger was criticised by the historian Ian Phimister, who believes that the historiographical roots of patriotic history 'merit closer scrutiny'. According to Phimister, much of the historiography of nationalism was determined by nationalism's 'praise singers', such as Ranger. The latter's 'fanciful extrapolations and factual misrepresentations' benefited the nationalist projects in the 1970s and 1980s. Ranger's ground-breaking studies of Zimbabwean history strengthened the idea of a united struggle against colonialism, which was 'perfectly attuned to the needs of new Jacobins'. In his account of Matabeleland, Ranger overlooked the atrocities of the Fifth Brigade and praised Robert Mugabe instead.[33]

Nevertheless, Phimister's critique of nationalist historiography does not disqualify the analytical strength of patriotic history as a concept. During times of crisis, the ZANU government in Zimbabwe has repeatedly emphasised heritage while ignoring economic problems. 'Whenever people sense danger they are reminded of some historical achievement', writes Erikana Haurovi. 'People are forced to remember the harshness of the historical colonial past whenever some crisis emerges'.[34] This is a powerful mechanism that occurs across the Southern African region when liberation governments are threatened by international or external pressures. Ranger's work has inspired a plethora of studies on patriotic history in Southern Africa, especially in Namibia, Mozambique and Angola.[35]

MYTH

For the transformation of history into heritage, and the transformation of patriotic narratives into nationalist monuments, African liberation governments continue to turn to North Korea. North Korea is perhaps the best example of a 'partisan state', argued the historian Wada Haruki. Its post-war development is characterised by the sublimation of Kim Il Sung's anticolonial guerrilla warfare 'into the single most important, most sacred, and all-encompassing saga of the nation's modern history'. Heonik Kwon and Byung-Ho Chung call North Korea a 'radical example of the use and abuse of postcolonial rhetoric', a discourse infused with 'the powerful drama of commemoration and longing'. This 'landscape of longing' is manifested through heritage, the 'material culture of commemoration'.[36]

Conclusion

Monuments signify the changing of the guards. African liberation governments want to announce to the world that they are now in charge—and want to remain in charge. The site of the Independence Memorial Museum in Namibia used to be the location of the *Reiterdenkmal*, a statue of a soldier on horseback that was erected in 1912 by the German authorities in commemoration of the Namibian genocide. According to the German governor, the statue symbolised 'that we are and shall remain masters here'.[37]

Roughly a century later, at the same spot, the Namibian president Pohamba announced that 'we became masters of this place, now and forever. Not the colonialists. Never again will our Motherland be colonised'. In a highly symbolic decision, the *Reiterdenkmal* was removed to make room for a large statue of Sam Nujoma, which was placed in front of the entrance to the Independence Memorial Museum.[38] According to Renzo Baas, the statue occupies 'a position within a historic space [that] emphasises its connection to both the past and the future'.[39]

The Independence Memorial Museum in Namibia demonstrates that African liberation governments hire North Korea to design and construct their own historical myths. The Independence Memorial Museum in Windhoek has a similar function as the

Victorious Fatherland Liberation War Museum in Pyongyang, which narrates North Korea's war experience through the heritage of anticolonial struggle.[40] The adoption of North Korea's heritage model occurs across Southern Africa. In these myths, the liberation governments become the sole actors in the revolutionary struggle and consequently marginalise all other actors. The party reigns supreme. What this means for the conceptualisation of the nation, violence and heroism, is explored in the next three chapters.

12

NATIONS

A FAMILY AFFAIR

The skyline of Luanda, the capital city of Angola, is dominated by an imposing obelisk. With a height of 120 metres, the Memorial António Agostinho Neto (MAAN) is the largest monument in Angola and one of the largest personal memorials in the world. Locals have nicknamed the building 'the rocket'.[1] The memorial is dedicated to Agostinho Neto—a poet, the leader of the MPLA and the first president of Angola.[2] Neto ruled the country from 1975 until his death in 1979 and is known as the father of the Angolan nation.[3]

The MAAN symbolises how African liberation governments imagine the nation as a family, using North Korean visual aesthetics. Unveiled in 2012, the futuristic shrine to Neto signifies the 'edification of the MPLA regime' and was designed by a North Korean company. The North Korean artists were inspired by Neto's poem 'The pathway to the stars' and the architecture of the heritage site represents how the statesman is elevated above the sky, watching over his people. Vasco Martins and Miguel Cardina noted that the MAAN is designed as a 'sacred ground for the birth of the Angolan nation'.[4]

The distinct form of nationalism that put most Southern African liberation movements into power is driven by the notion of family. Family became a powerful metaphor for the party organisation of liberation governments and, by extension, for the nation as a whole. 'Let us go forward as one Zambian family to find our destiny', urged Kenneth Kaunda at the declaration of Zambian independence in 1964.[5] If nations are families, leaders such as Neto and Kaunda are their fathers; the citizens are their children.[6] There is a distinct patriarchal quality to the idea of political fatherhood— the gendered dimension of liberation heritage is discussed further in Chapter 14.

With the MAAN as a case study, this chapter explores how the party and the nation can be understood through the prism of family. The first section dissects how notions of 'the party' and 'the nation' blended with the idea of 'family' from the perspective of African liberation movements. The second section shows that a similar process was ongoing in North Korea and highlights the anti-democratic tendencies of this approach. The metaphor of family is useful for understanding the desire of African revolutionaries to foster unity at all costs. The third section explores how North Korean heritage is instrumental in postcolonial nation building in Africa, reproducing the same ideas of family by elevating political leaders as the patriarchs that lead nations to prosperity.

To be born a nation

Years ago, my mentor Jan-Bart Gewald gifted me a copy of *To be Born a Nation: The Liberation Struggle for Namibia*, a book that now rests in obscurity but is nevertheless central to the Namibian liberation struggle. Published by SWAPO in 1981, it narrates the history of Namibia as perceived by the liberation movement. The title of the book is derived from the Mozambican saying, 'to die a tribe and be born a nation', a statement that eloquently captures the main mission of liberation movements during the twentieth century. According to historian and SWAPO official Peter Katjavivi, the book's title 'encapsulates the drive for unity and the bonds through common endeavour and sacrifice' that were essential during the

NATIONS

struggle. Coincidentally, *To be Born a Nation* also underlines the transnational dimension of African politics: a Namibian history, inspired by a Mozambican saying, published in exile in Angola.[7]

Colonial and settler regimes in Africa administered a divide and rule approach, utilising the presence of different ethnic groups to exercise control. Apartheid is an extreme example, but every colonial government in Africa utilised this approach to some extent. As such, anticolonial activists realised they needed to form *national* liberation movements and forge a sense of unity. 'Tribalism and regionalism were regarded as major nemeses of national liberation', hence the need for quarrelling tribes to die and unified nations to be born.[8] As such, parties became microcosms of the nation. Both were understood through the prism of the family.

'Participating in the struggle entailed a distinct notion of "family"', argues the historian and former ANC operative Raymond Suttner. During the struggle, 'family' was often a metaphor or code word for the party.[9] When the journalist Lisa Distelheim visited an ANC camp in Zambia, she described it as 'an overgrown family, funded by relatives abroad'.[10] Liberation movements were collectives that demanded personal sacrifices for the greater good. 'Single-mindedness' is one of the conditions of a successful revolution, stressed Suttner (and, coincidentally, one of the key terms of the North Korean revolution). This had far-reaching implications for the individuals that joined liberation movements, especially in exile. The collective was the most important; sacrifices and hardship were part of the deal. Personal love was supplanted by 'love for the people'. Suttner quotes a female ANC member who left her children behind in Tanzania to carry out work for the party, explaining to them that 'although I may be your mother, your real mother and father are the ANC. The ANC will look after you, feed you and clothe you'. Especially for young people in exile, who missed their family and longed for role models, the party fulfilled parental roles.[11]

The notion of family appeared in the discourse of all victorious liberation movements in Southern Africa. The ANC commemorated the death of its 'brave and gallant sons', who shed their 'precious blood ... in the cause of Africa's freedom'.[12] SWAPO called its soldiers 'the sons and daughters of Namibia'.[13] In a similar vein, FRELIMO celebrated how 'the sons of the Mozambican people began on their irreversible path towards independence'.[14] The MPLA believed that 'the blood shed by this country's finest sons and daughters is the price we paid to win our independence'.[15]

At the end of the civil war, the MPLA government introduced a scheme to reunite family members who had been separated during the course of the fighting. The scheme was aptly called 'the reunion of the big Angolan family' (*o reencontro da grande família angolana*) and required people to come to Independence Square in Luanda, in the hope of encountering their sorely missed relatives. The proceedings were televised for the public under the name 'Courage, Nation' (*Nação Coragem*). The historian Justin Pearce describes how the MPLA used this programme to foster national unity, with Neto as an icon.[16]

The family state

The idea that North Korean society is ruled as a family has long been recognised in the field of North Korean Studies. Lee Moon-Woong calls the political system of North Korea 'a family state', as the relationship between the people and the leader can be defined through kinship relations. The leader 'is akin to the role of a head of the household … the destiny of the state resembles the fate of a family'.[17] Bruce Cumings stipulates that 'family rearing principles can be extended to politics'.[18] Charles Armstrong argued that North Korea routinised family metaphors to such an extent that 'they no longer seemed metaphorical and took on a concrete literalness'.[19]

Crucially, the anticolonial struggle provided 'the origin myth for the patriarchal, familial-political order' in North Korea.[20] Just as Suttner described in the case of the ANC, Kim Il Sung's guerrilla unit, which led the struggle against Japanese colonisation, 'resembled a traditional family unit'. The guerrilla army largely consisted of poor peasants who viewed Kim as a father.[21] North Korean cultural propaganda views Kim's guerrilla unit as the ideal prototype of North Korean society. 'Family' is thus used 'as a

NATIONS

synonym for the nation'. Chapter 14 discusses how the succession of power in North Korea is not a family affair in the traditional sense of genealogical continuity, but 'a political event rooted in the modern history of political fatherhood'.[22]

The revolutionary family is guided by the two virtues of 'loyalty to the sovereign or country' (*ch'ung*) and 'filial piety' (*hyo*).[23] Suk-Young Kim argues that North Korean propaganda art reminds people 'of their national unity as one family', as patriotism is understood as the filial piety of children (the people) towards their parents (the leaders).[24] These displays of unity are designed against the backdrop of an ever-present struggle against external forces that aim to subdue the nation. As a result, writes the art historian Min-Kyung Yoon, the historical narrative of North Korean art is 'one of triumph against all odds, the intense struggles of heroic individuals, the unwavering loyalty and love for the homeland that is deeply seeped with revolutionary fervour'.[25] A similar message, but targeted for African audiences, is exemplified through North Korean heritage in Southern Africa.

However, the virtues of 'loyalty to the sovereign or country' (*ch'ung*) and 'filial piety' (*hyo*) harbour a dangerous tendency to stifle dissent. The almost sacred responsibility to the collective, Suttner noted in the case of South Africa, 'carries with it the possibility of abuse'.[26] Maintaining unity is always difficult in families, and political organisations are no different. The leadership of African liberation movements were gripped by 'spy fever', an obsession with 'the threat of spies and traitors' in their midst.[27] Betraying the party, and thus becoming a traitor to the nation, was the same as betraying your family—a sin for which there was no redemption. 'Loyalty to the liberation movement' was paramount.[28]

Some instances of spy fever during the liberation struggles have been documented—the paranoia concerning Andreas Shipanga of SWAPO and the Quatro camps of the ANC (discussed in Chapter 8) are some examples.[29] Crucially, liberation movements maintained this mentality of repression when they came into power. 'The unity of the party is the unity of the people', said the Zambian president and UNIP leader Kenneth Kaunda in 1971. When UNIP appeared to lose its majority in the elections a few years prior,

Kaunda warned that 'the nation caught a cold which has been difficult to cure for a long time'. Therefore, UNIP officials 'must act as doctors … to cure this cold, which has threatened the very fabric of our nationhood'.[30] Indeed, shortly after independence, a church rebellion threatened the authority of the ruling party—the opposition was violently crushed by UNIP and hundreds of people were massacred.[31]

When UNIP declared Zambia a one-party state in 1973, Kaunda argued that the 'one-party democracy', as he liked to call it, will 'enable us to deal with dissenters as members of the same family'. In a speech entitled 'The Nation Is You', Kaunda cautioned those that disagreed with the party line. 'It is one thing to criticise. But it is quite another to oppose'. The new era 'must mean an end to political prostitutes' who were 'living on cheap tissues of lies and propaganda'. Kaunda, who was continually referred to as the 'father' of the Zambian nation, promised tough measures against his opponents. 'I extend the warning to those who wish to operate underground that, if they should rear their heads above the ground, they will be crushed'.[32]

When a regime 'mobilises militant postcolonial rhetoric to bolster its legitimacy', observed Heonik Kwon and Byung-Ho Chung in the case of North Korea, 'the rhetoric can turn into a locally hegemonic force, thereby stamping out divergent voices and interpretations'.[33] Indeed, Kim Il Sung 'was quick to draw a clear boundary between those who were part of the family and those who were not'.[34] This is a key mechanism in the revolutionary state politics of former anticolonial movements. The 'One Zambia, One Nation' myth was cultivated by Zambian politicians, but also amplified by nationalist academics, including in the West, who 'glossed over the considerable violence and repression that had accompanied the birth of the nation'.[35]

Nation building

Nation building in postcolonial Africa is a challenging endeavour. In the first years of independent rule, victorious liberation governments navigated internal and external opposition to their

NATIONS

authority. The governments of Angola and Mozambique fought ruthless civil wars, the Zimbabwean government executed a genocide and the governments of Namibia and Zambia repressed secessionist uprisings.[36] However, with the ascension to power, liberation governments now had new tools at their disposal: state-funded heritage, designed and built by North Korea. The Neto memorial in Angola is illustrative of how North Korea provides inspiration for African nation building, as it uses North Korean aesthetics to display a narrow interpretation of the nation.

The main aim of the MAAN is to offer a narrative of the liberation struggle, the Angolan nation and the role of Neto himself. The 18-hectare memorial site is dominated by the 120-metre-high 'rocket' and includes a museum, an exhibition gallery, a library, a documentation centre, shops and the sarcophagus room containing Neto's body. A tribune area holds 2,000 seats that look out across an avenue for parades, of about 500 metres. The enormous 'rocket' in particular, which ostentatiously resembles the barrel of an AK-47, is an awe-inspiring feature. In North Korean visual culture, the importance of grandness (*ungjangsŏng*) is a 'vital aesthetic quality'. Yoon argues that North Korean monuments must 'evoke a wave of emotions that engulfs and overpowers ... further dwarfing the people under the great collective'.[37] This is, indeed, the response solicited by the MAAN and also by the other African monuments that are discussed in this book.

An intriguing part of the MAAN is the statue of a kneeling elephant. It represents 'the natural world paying homage' to the great leader, in the same way as in the film *The Lion King*, when the animal kingdom bows for Simba.[38] Ironically, the animal appears to be an Asian rather than an African elephant.

The contract for the MAAN was originally awarded to the Soviet Institute for Projects, and construction started in 1982, on the 60th birthday of the already deceased Neto. The work stopped in 1988, presumably as a result of the heavy fighting during the civil war. It resumed in 2005 when Mansudae Art Projects entirely redesigned the project. Finished in 2012, the design signals the 'political alliances of post-independent Angola'.[39]

Similar to other Southern African states, Angola's liberation struggle was marked by the competition between multiple liberation movements, 'each pushing their own vision of the nation'.[40] As part of its attempt to gain legitimacy, the MPLA claimed to represent the Angolan nation and designated Neto as its father. During the struggle, MPLA based its ideology on the idea that 'the MPLA is the people and the people is the MPLA'. In a eulogy printed by SWAPO, the MPLA described Neto as the 'uncontested leader of a heroic people', the 'father of all Angolan children, the son of all the mothers of Angola'.[41]

However, this particular vision of the Angolan nation as a family includes 'deafening silences'. The MPLA grappled with grave internal divisions throughout its history: there were splinter groups, defections and leadership contestations. In 1977, for instance, the MPLA purged and massacred thousands of people in response to a (failed) coup attempt.[42] The MAAN entirely avoids this complicated history, thus erasing a 'distinctive part of Neto's struggle' and excluding numerous well-known MPLA officials who do not fit into a harmonious narrative.[43] These taboos are in line with the government's policy to 'silence inconvenient versions of history'.[44]

Moreover, the MAAN omits the many different cultures, languages and other differences within the diverse nation(s) that make up modern Angola. Instead, the people are 'symbolically described as the ideological lever and motivator of the liberation struggle, the recipient of the gift of liberation and independence'. Vasco Martins and Miguel Cardina argued that the MAAN's marginalisation of certain parts of the population have hindered its 'ability to contribute to the new ways Angolans are imagining the nation'.[45] Pearce argues that the MPLA deflects the threat of opposition 'by claiming an exclusive role as the defender of the nation'. Conflicting voices are silenced.[46]

Conclusion

The introduction to this book describes how Kenneth Kaunda shouted the words 'One Zambia, One Nation!' in Pyongyang.

NATIONS

Similar slogans were adopted across Africa. SWAPO, for example, used the slogan 'One Namibia, One Nation'.[47] The reasoning behind this is evident: in order to gain authority and access to resources, it was vital for anticolonial leaders in Africa to display a sense of unity against the oppressor. As such, liberation governments in Africa portray themselves as the guardians of the nation. This state-sanctioned unity doctrine is encapsulated in North Korean monuments. The National Heroes' Acre in Zimbabwe (discussed in Chapter 13), for example, 'arouses national consciousness, forges national unity and identity', according to the ZANU government.[48]

For decades, liberation governments were imagined as families, before and after independence. Distinctions between the party, the nation and the notion of family became blurred. Like so many newly installed governments in Southern Africa, ZANU was quick to 'claim ownership of the birth of the nation' when it came to power in 1980.[49] North Korean monuments proved to be effective vehicles for disseminating the government's interpretation of what the nation entails. This follows a similar pattern, as discussed in the previous chapter, where the party obtains a central role in historical mythmaking of the struggle.

North Korean heritage in Southern Africa, such as the MAAN, offers an opportunity to analyse the dominant narrative about the nation: a harmonious family, with a founding father who leads his sons and daughters towards glory. However, the definition of what the family constitutes is determined by the party. The desire to put party leaders at the centre of memorial landscapes leaves 'large sections of society at the margins'.[50] Just as North Korea created 'a visible boundary between the legitimate members of the imagined family and the enemies of the family-nation', so did African governments.[51]

A more careful inquiry divulges that narratives such as the MAAN offer only a partisan interpretation of the nation. These narratives conceal the brutal repression of dissidents, those family members who were banned from the clan, in the name of unity.

13

VIOLENCE

ROMANTICISING THE REVOLUTION

Sequestered in the hills near Harare, Zimbabwe's capital city, lies a sacred burial ground. Not an ancient site where the traditional ancestors are remembered, but its modern equivalent: a cemetery for the freedom fighters of ZANU. The National Heroes' Acre of Zimbabwe is a copy of a revolutionary cemetery in Pyongyang and is created by a North Korean art studio. Built in the shape of two AK-47s lying back-to-back, each grave represents a bullet in the magazines of the two revolutionary guns.[1]

Weapons and armed struggle feature prominently in the African memorial landscapes that are designed by North Korea. Zimbabwe is not an exception; in fact, the National Heroes' Acre is 'a model' for memorial culture across Southern Africa.[2] The National Heroes' Acre of Namibia features the Statue of the Unknown Soldier in Namibia, who carries a Kalashnikov rifle in one hand and swings a grenade with the other (though he is unknown, the soldier bears a remarkable likeness to Sam Nujoma).[3] Similar examples can be found across the continent. In Egypt, the Battle of Ismailia Monument is shaped as a vertical AK-47 with a bayonet, pointing towards the sky.[4]

The National Heroes' Acre in Zimbabwe symbolises the importance of violence in the commemoration of the liberation struggles in Africa. Nations that were 'born from the barrel of the gun', to borrow Richard Werbner's phrase, place a high premium on romanticising the revolution.[5] North Korean visual aesthetics aptly value the military dimensions of the liberation struggle over the diplomatic dimensions. This reflects the experiences of African freedom fighters, many of whom believed that negotiations were insufficient to liberate their peoples. Freedom could only be achieved on the battlefield. Hence, North Korean heritage in Africa excels in glorifying violent resistance.

With the National Heroes' Acre in Zimbabwe as a case study, this chapter explores how North Korean heritage sites utilise the revolutionary past to suit incumbent liberation governments in Southern Africa. The first section discusses the continuity thesis, a process by which African nationalists connected their campaigns for self-governance to earlier historical uprisings. The second section considers how African governments use North Korean monuments to shrewdly appropriate early colonial resistance for their own benefit. The third section makes a comparison with North Korean political culture, which is infused with a militaristic ideology that resembles African statehood.

Continuity thesis

Modern liberation movements in Africa have legitimised their cause by referring to historical uprisings that far preceded the founding of their own organisations. African nationalists successfully conceptualised early resistance against colonial interference as 'a simple pre-history of mass nationalism'.[6] In other words, they developed a direct line between localised uprisings against foreign intervention in previous centuries to the campaigns for self-governance in modern times. In the mythology of liberation movements, the connection between 'primary resistance' of early colonialism and the 'secondary resistance' of recent times is key. This, in short, is the continuity thesis that forms the backbone of liberation heritage in Southern Africa.[7]

VIOLENCE

However, the continuity thesis is essentially a teleological view of the past. The 'primary resistance movements' indeed opposed foreign powers, but occasionally collaborated with them and were not motivated by nationalist ideas as we recognise them today.[8] Often, definitions of the nation state as 'Namibia' or 'Zimbabwe' did not yet exist. Applying them to the distant past is anachronistic, but academic complications matter little to African liberation movements. Appropriating historical events proved to be an effective way to rally support for their cause and inspire their followers.

As the oldest liberation movement on the continent, the ANC in South Africa provided the model of revisionist history that other nationalist groups in Africa followed. The ANC traces the roots of its armed resistance back to 1652 and the arrival of the Dutch. Its own official history of resistance conceptualises precolonial warfare between European settlers and indigenous groups as wars of resistance that had a direct connection to the twentieth century campaign for self-governance.[9] 'For centuries the African people shed their blood in armed combat in defence of their birth right', proclaimed the SACP in 1971.[10]

In 1980, ANC president Oliver Tambo used the Battle of Blood River of 1838 to justify the armed struggle against apartheid.[11] At the banks of the Ncome River, thousands of Voortrekkers defeated the army of the Zulu king Dingane. Even though the Zulu warriors 'heroically defended themselves with spears against the endless volley of cannon and guns', many were massacred, hence the name Blood River.[12] From a historical perspective, it is difficult to see this tragedy as a sign of nationalism, but the ANC mythologised the event as an act of national resistance, omitting details about the Zulu context: 'African people courageously defended their motherland', was the message.[13] Many years later, Tambo connected the battle of 1838 to 1961, when militants from ANC's armed wing, MK, started the armed struggle. MK 'once again started the process of washing out the blood from [the] Ncome River', said Tambo. 'Our people's heritage, which was stolen and held by the gun, would have to be repossessed by the gun'. Although both events are 123 years apart, they 'symbolise the drama and passion' of the South African struggle, according to Tambo.[14]

Another source of inspiration was the Battle of Isandlwana, a conflict between the Zulu Kingdom and the British Empire that occurred in 1879, long before the idea of a national South African identity existed. A hundred years later, the ANC nevertheless celebrated the battle as a victory in the pursuit of independence. It was 'one of the most glorious and spectacular achievements in the world struggle for racist foreign domination', said Tambo; 'they shed rivers of blood to remain a free people in the land which was theirs'.[15] ANC propaganda obscures the existence of the Zulu kingdom, but emphasised 'the thousands of spears' that 'wiped out' the British Army. The ANC proclaimed 1979 as Year of the Spear and cultivated Isandlwana as a courageous battle against foreign invasion, a fight for 'freedom, independence and peace'. For more than 200 years, the ANC reported, its people have fought against colonial aggression and national oppression 'with spears in hand'.[16] It is no coincidence that MK, the armed wing of the ANC, means 'Spear of the Nation' in Xhosa. Although MK was founded in 1961, under entirely different circumstances, it is deliberately connected to earlier uprisings.[17]

'We recall with pride the heroes of the centuries', announced Tambo in 1980. 'The ANC dips its banner in respectful memory of all those who have laid down their lives in the course of our struggle'.[18] ANC literature depicted local kings such as Shaka Zulu and Moshoeshoe I, who operated in the nineteenth century, as 'South African generals and freedom fighters', even though South Africa did not yet exist, and these leaders were not motivated by nationalist ideas. Nevertheless, the ANC believed that contemporary militants from the 1960s 'travelled this silent road carved by those great commanders', a struggle 'in the name of Africa for the national independence of future generations'.[19]

Similar patterns can be observed with other victorious liberation movements in Southern Africa. In Namibia, SWAPO traced the roots of its resistance back to 1670.[20] The party claimed to be 'the sons and daughters, the soldiers, the worthy heirs' of heroes such as Hendrik Witbooi, who opposed the Germans at the end of the nineteenth century.[21] Many SWAPO songs that were sung in

VIOLENCE

the 1970s were in fact derived from songs composed during the Herero and Nama resistance against German colonialism in the early 1900s, several decades before SWAPO was established.[22] The Youth League of TANU in Tanzania called its magazine *Maji*, after the armed rebellion against German colonial rule between 1905–07.[23] The deliberate connection between a primary and secondary resistance is perhaps most pronounced in Zimbabwe, where the ideology of *Chimurenga* serves the political goals of ZANU.[24]

Revolutionary heritage

The National Heroes' Acre of Zimbabwe was inaugurated in 1982, two years after Zimbabwean independence. For ZANU, it was one of the first and largest heritage projects it decided to undertake. The cemetery was designed by North Korea to honour the heroes of the Zimbabwean liberation struggle and is a surprisingly large site. The main attraction of the Heroes' Acre are the burial grounds: approximately 170 graves are arranged as bullets in two AK-47 rifles. Other features include a museum, the Tomb and Statue for the Unknown Soldier (featuring an AK-47), the 40-metre Freedom Tower (which recalls 'the military might of victory in the liberation war'), the Eternal Flame, national flags and the national coat of arms (again featuring the AK-47).[25] The site is regularly used for national commemorations and therefore includes a grandstand with 5,000 seats for visitors.[26]

The historical narrative presented by the National Heroes' Acre is centred around the ideology of *Chimurenga*. This is the 'rallying cry' of ZANU and underpins the belief that the party's legitimacy is not derived 'from elections but from active participation in the epic anti-colonial struggle'. The First *Chimurenga* dates back to the primary resistance from the 1890s, while the Second *Chimurenga* is the secondary resistance led by ZANU during the 1970s.[27] In this way, the history of Zimbabwe 'is reduced to a succession of *Chimurengas*', in which ZANU becomes 'the alpha and omega of Zimbabwe's past, present and future'.[28] It is no coincidence that ZAPU veterans subsequently boycotted Heroes' Acre commemorations and burials.[29]

Of particular interest in the National Heroes' Acre are two murals on the eastern and western flanks of the burial site, which depict the continuity between the primary and secondary resistance in Zimbabwe. The visual story starts with indigenous uprisings against British troops and seamlessly connects these events with the guerrilla fighting of the twentieth century against the Rhodesian regime. The final part of the murals depicts the independence celebrations of 1980, where a larger-than-life Mugabe leads his people to a liberated future.[30]

The continuity thesis can extend into the present, as a third resistance becomes necessary to ensure the relevance of liberation governments in this day and age. Because ZANU considered universities 'anti-Government mentality factories', the Zimbabwean government established youth militia camps in 2001. The primary aim of these camps was to teach patriotic history and to recruit the youth as 'warriors into the third *Chimurenga*'.[31] Also in Namibia, South Africa and other countries the ruling classes propagate the necessity of a continuing revolution.

Even though the National Heroes' Acre in Zimbabwe is presented as quintessential *Zimbabwean* history, it is, in fact, one of the best examples of the 'one size fits all' model of North Korean heritage. In 2002, 20 years after the inauguration of the Zimbabwean Heroes' Acre, the National Heroes' Acre of Namibia was consecrated in Windhoek. Both cemeteries were constructed by MOP and bear a striking resemblance to each other. Both are copies of the Revolutionary Martyrs' Cemetery of North Korea.[32]

Located on the outskirts of Pyongyang, the Revolutionary Martyrs' Cemetery commemorates the guerrillas that lost their lives for North Korea.[33] It has a similar physical layout as its African counterparts, including a Tomb of the Unknown Soldier (representing 'the soul of the nation') and graves that seem to be primarily reserved for the comrades of Kim Il Sung and the other 'founding heroes' of the North Korean state. According to Kwon and Chung, the cemetery is 'an important site in the political order' of North Korea as it 'embodies the principles of the partisan state'. Like its African counterparts, its narrative is grounded in the anticolonial struggle.[34]

VIOLENCE

The decision by Zimbabwean authorities to imitate North Korean heritage is an outcome of the fraternal diplomatic and military ties that were forged during the liberation struggles. Moreover, the cemeteries in Zimbabwe and Namibia are tangible evidence of the argument that North Korean visual aesthetics inspire African elites.

Military first

As with the African continuity thesis, North Korean art is organised around a teleological idea of 'a mythic historic destiny' that creates a direct link between anticolonial struggle and modern politics.[35] Kim Il Sung claimed that his grandfather led the resistance against American invaders in 1866, a courageous feat that was connected to the guerrilla fight against Japanese colonisation in the 1930s and the 'Victorious Fatherland Liberation War' against American imperialism in the 1950s.[36] These heroic exploits provide the script for new chapters of state-sanctioned revolutionary heritage, a narrative encapsulated in physical monuments. Kim Il Sung's grandfather is buried in the Revolutionary Martyrs' Cemetery in Pyongyang.

During Kim Jong Il's reign, North Korea introduced the 'military first' (*sŏn'gun*) policy that privileges the role of the army, and military power more generally, in times of crisis.[37] This policy is guided by an ideology called 'the philosophy of the barrel of a gun' (*ch'ongdae*), which seeks to create 'a moral and practical unity between the army and the society'. *Ch'ongdae* obviously refers to the glorious heritage of the anticolonial armed struggle, led by Kim Il Sung and sustained by the 'hereditary politics' of Kim Jong Il.[38] The practical outcome of unity between the army and the people is reminiscent of the party–military complex in Southern African states, as discussed in the second part of this book.

Kwon and Chung argue that military-first politics dominates political culture in North Korea. It is a deliberate instrument for the Kims' political succession process: the military-first ideology (*sŏn'gun*) distinguished Kim Jong Il's tenure from Kim Il Sung (described in Chapter 14), while the 'barrel of the gun' philosophy (*ch'ongdae*) emphasises continuity between the old and new regimes. North Korean literature stresses the 'moral imperative' to continue the revolution and maintain revolutionary heritage, 'privileging this imperative over questions of economic welfare'.[39] This approach is emulated by Southern African liberation governments, who urge their citizenry to believe in an ongoing revolution. There are compelling similarities between *sŏn'gun* in North Korea and *Chimurenga* in Zimbabwe.

In North Korea, the 'military first' idea is also an extension of the 'family state' as all key members of the Kim dynasty perform a role: Kim Il Sung as the leader of the armed struggle, his father Kim Hyung Jik as his teacher, his wife Kim Jong Suk as the Mother of *Sŏn'gun*, and his son Kim Jong Il (and now *his* son, Kim Jong Un), as his successors. In North Korea, this is called 'the barrel-of-a-gun family genealogy' (*ch'ongdae kamun*).[40]

North Korea's political culture celebrates the 'moral purity of revolutionary violence', an idea that is preserved in its militant architecture and is subsequently echoed in African heritage.[41] War is not necessarily a tragedy; victory is all that matters. While museums that commemorate genocide in Europe, such as Dachau, present a subdued account of warfare, the Independence Memorial Museum commemorates the terrors of the Namibian genocide in an almost exuberant manner.[42]

North Korea's 'determination to defend its revolutionary heritage', write Kwon and Chung, is 'nothing short of a political revolution'. Usually, charismatic authority is an unsustainable form of political power, for it is inherently temporary due to its impermanent nature. However, North Korea has succeeded in sustaining its hereditary ruling system through its memorial culture. No other socialist states of the Cold War were capable of achieving the same.[43]

Conclusion

In the relatively young political states in Africa, the nation is defined in terms of decolonisation. Especially in Southern Africa, 'political origin myths go back to a birth at the barrel of an anti-

VIOLENCE

colonial gun'. Richard Werbner describes how African national elites envision a 'monumentally centred, heroic nationhood' that is not only won by freedom fighters, but should also be defended by them.[44]

North Korean monuments remind African populations that they are part of a centuries-old tradition of resistance, one that extends into the present. 'We are saying, as a nation, that we emerged victorious', said Hifikepunye Pohamba at the opening of the North Korean museum in Namibia. 'We are fortified by the knowledge that the current and future generations will continue to carry the flame of the revolution forward'.[45] Carrying the flame forward is indeed the main message of African liberation movements. They are the flag bearers of resistance. Not for idealistic purposes, but simply because a continuing revolution ensures their continuing relevance. *A luta continua*.

African monuments reflect the military mindsets that were developed by political elites in exile (see Chapter 8). Military and political veterans have been dominant voices in debates about the past.[46] Importantly, this approach is congruent with historical commemorations within North Korea, where the violent uprisings against Japanese colonisation and American imperialism are the cornerstones of the prevailing regime. Whether in Africa or in Korea, referring to a glorious revolution is an effective strategy in the competition for power.

14

HEROISM

THE FOUNDING FATHERS

In the centre of Maputo, the capital city of Mozambique, stands an imposing statue of one of the most famous revolutionaries in Africa: Samora Machel. Over 9 metres tall, the monument shows Machel in his military attire, raising a finger in the air.[1] The statue was unveiled in 2011, on the exact spot where a statue of a colonial governor-general used to stand. This location carries symbolic weight, just as the Nujoma statue in Namibia does—former colonial spaces now occupied by the new heroes of the nation. Coincidentally, the statue of Machel is also a stone's throw away from the Avenida Kim Il Sung. Designed by MOP, the monument signifies the heroic leadership of Machel in the march towards freedom.

Machel's monument symbolises how African leaders are immortalised as the founding fathers of nations, following a North Korean model. Through North Korean visual aesthetics, the founding fathers display a distinct sense of heroism that must inspire the nation and legitimises the enduring rule of liberation governments in Southern Africa. They become larger than life— their legacies are now a key part of the mythology of the African liberation struggles that serve ruling elites.

COMRADES BEYOND THE COLD WAR

North Korea excels in producing personal statues of African leaders. The Tanzanian political giant Julius Nyerere, the Congolese leaders Patrice Lumumba, Joseph Kasavubu and Laurent-Désiré Kabila, and the Zimbabwean leader Joshua Nkomo were all cast in bronze by North Korean artists, in a similar way as Kim Il Sung and Kim Jong Il are presented in Pyongyang.[2] It has been rumoured that, in 2009, Robert Mugabe hired Mansudae Art Studios to design two giant personal statues for a total sum of \$5 million, although the monuments have not been revealed.[3]

Taking the Samora Machel statue as a case study, this chapter complicates the heroic role of individual leaders in liberation mythology in Southern Africa. The first section analyses the personal statues as a form of what Richard Werbner called 'elite memorialism'.[4] Rather than celebrating the people, North Korean heritage prioritises the individual. As such, we can observe the development of a certain cult of personality around the legacies of liberation leaders. The second section explores the 'heroic masculinity' that is a common feature of North Korean statues.[5] These monuments display a strong sense of masculinity, and this is not a coincidence. In Southern Africa, the nation is gendered and notions of heroism have a definitively male interpretation. The third section analyses how the memorialisation of past leaders can be a tool for incumbent leaders to strengthen their own position.

Cult of personality

The North Korean monument in honour of Machel, the former FRELIMO leader and first president of Mozambique, was erected in 2011. Marked by the government as the 'Year of Samora Machel', it was precisely 25 years since he died in a mysterious plane crash (widely thought to have been caused by South Africa). The year formally started on Heroes Day and included the construction of Machel statues in every provincial capital and the establishment of the Samora Machel Centre for Knowledge and Development. The Mozambican president Armando Guebuza announced that Machel 'is a hero in our history because of all the qualities and virtues that

HEROISM

we would like to see emulated by all Mozambicans, who are now engaged in the fight against poverty'.[6]

The Mozambican approach resonates with analyses of North Korean art. Kwon and Chung argue that North Korean art excels in communicating the 'charismatic authority' of its leaders.[7] Through North Korean monuments, the Southern African presidents of the past are glorified as fathers of the nation whose heroic leadership guides the people. Werbner's concept of 'elite memorialism' was coined for North Korean heritage in Zimbabwe but can also be applied to Mozambique, Namibia, Angola, Zambia and other states in Southern Africa.[8] Elite memorialism is essentially liberation hagiography.

The memorialisation of Sam Nujoma is another compelling illustration of an emerging personality cult in Africa. Nujoma's North Korean-made statue portrays him as the 'political father figure' of Namibian liberation, and, indeed, the Namibian parliament honoured Nujoma with the title 'Founding Father of the Republic of Namibia' following his retirement as president. The loyalty demanded by liberation movements 'leaves no space for retirement', notes Henning Melber. 'One can leave office, but still remain a leader with responsibilities'. SWAPO prefers to portray Nujoma in a military fashion rather than emphasising his (much more evident) diplomatic qualities—again a reflection of the violent overtones of liberation heritage, as discussed in Chapter 13.[9]

Agostinho Neto was immortalised as the father of the Angolan nation.[10] According to the MPLA, the Neto memorial in Luanda was constructed to perpetuate the image of him as the 'Immortal Guide of the Angolan Revolution' and the 'Founder of the Nation'. Intended as 'the central piece in the daily homage Angolan society was to pay Neto', the North Korean mausoleum (discussed in Chapter 12) portrays him as 'a solitary figure'. The adjacent museum covers four dimensions of his life—Neto as a poet, a healer, a liberator and a statesman. A key element is the sarcophagus room that holds his remains. Foreign dignitaries are required to pay homage to Neto by visiting the monument and depositing flowers at his tomb.[11] The same is applicable to North

Korea, where Kim Il Sung's body is embalmed and preserved in a mausoleum. The result is called 'legacy politics' (*yuhun chŏngch'i*), a central concept in North Korean politics.[12] The National Heroes' Acre in Namibia also accommodates tombs for the embalmed bodies of presidents.[13]

'UNIP has performed miracles', said Mainza Chona, the vice president of Zambia, in 1972. He declared Kenneth Kaunda 'Zambia's number one hero' and expressed the hope that 'the president will rule this country for many, many years to come— even forty more years, God willing'. Chona wanted Kaunda to become 'life-president of the republic ... A country without a strong political party is in chaos. We, his apostles should always solidly support him'. Indeed, Kaunda went on to serve almost 30 years before he relinquished power. 'The only legitimate criticism against UNIP and Kaunda', Chona went on, 'is the inability to teach the Zambian people to look back and see the terrible life before independence'.[14] This is precisely where North Korean heritage comes in.

The hero is a lone figure. Werbner called the National Heroes' Acre in Zimbabwe 'a cemetery for the elite ... glorying above all the individuality of great heroes of the nation'. The solitary statues of African leaders reiterate the special role assigned to elites in the memorialisation of the struggle. Through the portrayal of individual heroes instead of communal nations, North Korean heritage unintentionally visualises the growing division between the *chefs*, the leaders and the *povo*, the people.[15] Oftentimes, this division is reinforced through locations that are difficult to access for ordinary people. The Neto memorial is located in the Political Administrative Centre of Luanda, far away from the poor Angolans who constitute the majority of Angola.[16] The same is applicable to Pyongyang, where the majority of North Korean nationalist heritage is located: only the chosen North Korean elites are allowed to reside in this city, while the rest of the population is stowed away in other places and the countryside.[17]

218

HEROISM

Heroic masculinity

Through North Korean heritage, the founding fathers of postcolonial Africa are elevated to the status of heroes, which is a central notion in political remembrance cultures in Southern Africa. This is perhaps best observed through the celebration of national Heroes Days, which are held annually in Botswana (27 February), Zambia (3 July), Zimbabwe (11 August), Namibia (26 August), Mozambique (3 September) and Angola (17 September). These public holidays celebrate the recent victories in anticolonial struggles. The Heroes Day in Namibia, for example, marks the day of the beginning of the war for independence, on 26 August. In Angola, the Heroes Day is the birthday of Neto, 17 September.

In many of these countries, the choreography of nationalist commemoration is intrinsically linked to North Korean heritage. In Botswana, wreaths are laid at the Three Dikgosi Monument, designed by MOP.[18] In Namibia, similar events are organised around the National Heroes' Acre. In Zimbabwe, where the National Heroes' Acre acts as a 'shrine for the unity between personal and national identity', Mugabe has used Heroes Day to publicise his patriotic poetry about the 'gallant heroes' of Zimbabwe.[19] As Norma Kriger has shown, heroism is part of the fabric of Zimbabwean political discourse. The state adopted a ranking system for local, provincial and national heroes, and offers burials and payments for their dependants accordingly.[20]

Across Southern Africa, heroism is 'starkly gendered' as the hero is 'an essentially male figure'. There is a 'general tendency of liberation discourse to be masculinist' notes Raymond Suttner, the historian who used to be active in the ANC underground. For liberation movements, the recovery of freedom was similar to the restoration of manhood. Suttner traces the roots of this discourse to colonialism, which deliberately infantilised Africans by depicting them as 'a race of children'. African men, in particular, were called boys. As such, 'the assertion of manhood is in this context a claim for freedom'.[21]

The concept of the nation, writes Suttner, is therefore 'implicitly defined in terms of manhood'. The ANC originally only

219

accepted male members—joining the struggle was associated with attaining manhood. ANC members emulated the idea of the male warrior that can be traced back to the primary uprisings against colonialism. Nelson Mandela, for example, was explicitly inspired by 'continuing a tradition of martial heroism and resistance' that was essentially male.[22] In North Korea, the anticolonial resistance against Japan similarly provided Kim Il Sung's partisan fighters with 'a means to assert their manhood'. The art historian Suk-Young Kim argues that war gave these men 'a chance to bolster their lost masculinity'.[23]

However, the focus on masculinity distorts the representation of a factual history of the liberation struggle. As Melber has observed, females 'are conspicuously absent' in African nationalist discourse.[24] Oftentimes they are deliberately erased, or simply depicted as 'mothers in the struggle'.[25] A fitting example is Robert Mugabe's first wife, Sally Mugabe, buried in the National Heroes' Acre as the Mother of Zimbabwe.[26] North Korean society also presents itself as 'masculine or male-centred'.[27] A notable exception, one that mirrors the example of Sally Mugabe, is the wife of Kim Il Sun, Kim Jong Suk, buried in the Revolutionary Martyrs' Cemetery as the Mother of *Sŏn'gun*.[28] Virtually all other buried heroes, in both cemeteries, are male.

Suttner urges us to question the 'monolithic view of the heroic male' in the Southern African liberation struggles. There were important female contributions to the attainment of independence, many freedom fighters did not conform to traditional ideas of masculinity and, unfortunately, struggle memorialisation obscures the tragic occurrences of rape and other forms of gender-related abuse during war.[29]

Political afterlives

A striking feature of the Machel statue is not how the monument celebrates the memory of the deceased leader, but how it served the leader who commissioned the work, then-president Guebuza. The historian Albino Jopela shows how Guebuza turned FRELIMO's political ancestors into sacralised heroes, with the

HEROISM

aim to mobilise the Mozambican population for a 'new struggle', namely, Guebuza's political agenda. In addition, Guebuza 'claims for himself a prominent place in the pantheon of the liberators of the nation' through the memorialisation of Machel as the father of Mozambique. As ordinary Mozambicans were voicing widespread dissatisfaction with the 'generalised lethargy and corruption in the state apparatus', FRELIMO attributed new values to Machel's legacy 'that serve the cause of the current government'.[30]

Machel's memorialisation illustrates how the development of a personality cult around political veterans of the liberation struggle benefit contemporary elites.[31] African liberation governments appropriate the political afterlives of their founding fathers to smooth the transition of power from one generation to the next. This process is perhaps perfected in North Korea, where Kim Jong Il, the son and successor of Kim Il Sung, devised an elaborate personality cult around his father with the aim of strengthening his own position. As the formally declared 'eternal president' (*yŏnggu chusŏk*), Kim Il Sung's figure continues to loom large over North Korean mythology.[32]

Kim Jong Il could not claim political authority based on participation in the origin myth of anticolonial warfare. He was simply too young, as he was born in 1942. This meant that he had to find another way to gain legitimacy, which became the strategic deployment of revolutionary art (*hyŏngmyŏng yesul*). Kim Jong Il 'began his high political career as a pioneer of an artistic revolution' that used performative art to deify his father. As a result, Kim Jong Il manoeuvred himself into a central position of power, as he became the one person who could continue his father's legacy—a process that resembles the state hagiography of African liberation giants.[33]

It was no coincidence that Kim led two major renovations of the Revolutionary Martyrs' Cemetery in Pyongyang (discussed in Chapter 13), in celebration of his father's sixtieth and seventieth birthday. These decisions were a tribute to Kim Il Sung's glory and exemplified his son's respect for the memory of his leadership. As such, the monumental renovations were 'an important part of the process of political succession'.[34] African liberation governments

221

follow a similar pattern, where the afterlives of the founding fathers are used to enhance the legitimacy of those that follow in their footsteps.

Heonik Kwon and Byung-Ho Chung conclude that Kim Jong Il's 'artistic revolution in the 1970s was integral to the succession of power from the country's founding hero to his eldest son'.[35] It is important to note that North Korea's personality cult was not an original feature of the state system from its inception in 1948 but an outcome of succession politics years later. The construction of monuments, as Yoon points out, started in the 1960s, while the 'deification of Kim Il Sung' only started in the 1970s, under Kim Jong Il's guidance.[36]

Kim Il Sung's death in 1994 'was akin to the death of a father for many North Koreans'. Known as the Great National Bereavement, Kwon and Chung call this event 'a family affair'. A commemorative poem of the WPK described the North Korean people as wailing and crying children who have lost their father. Kwon and Chung point out that the poem mainly praises Kim Jong Il's 'heroic efforts to keep the family (of the nation) together after the founding father passed away'.[37]

The succession of Kim Il Sung further illustrates how the Western Cold War time frame 'comes up against serious conceptual problems in the context of East Asian history'. This political transition in North Korea must be situated in the 1970s, not the 1990s. Kwon and Chung therefore argue that 'Europe-centred temporality of the Cold War' does not do justice to the Korean context, a call that is equally applicable to Southern Africa.[38]

In the process of this political succession, North Korea increasingly relied on 'symbolic and theatrical means to demonstrate the power and authority of the partisan state'.[39] Wada Haruki and the North Korean exile Jang Jin Sung have developed the idea of North Korea as a 'theatre state', based on the work of Clifford Geertz.[40] Indeed, Keith Howard observes that 'North Korea behaves as if its whole territory is a theatre'.[41] The theatre is performed for both domestic and international audiences, a distinction that Brian Myers called the 'inside track' and 'outside track' of propaganda.[42] The ultimate mission of the North Korean

HEROISM

theatre state 'is to resist, via the man-made politics of art, the natural mortality of charismatic authority'.[43]

North Korean heritage imbues anticolonial heroism with new, contemporary meanings. In the 2000s, amid dire economic circumstances, North Korean literature on *ch'ongdae* began to articulate the idea that 'being a barrel of a gun', as the military-first doctrine requires of North Korean citizens, 'might involve overcoming the pain of hunger'. Rather than fighting an actual war, the current (ongoing) revolution demanded the North Korean masses to withstand stark economic pressure. Kwong and Chung explain that military-first politics 'provides a new formula for revolution', one that is cloaked in the discourse of the past but befits the priorities of the current regime.[44]

A similar pattern of performative politics can be recognised across Southern Africa, where liberation governments remodel revolutionary discourse to fit contemporary policy issues. The Namibian Heroes' Day is celebrated with a ceremony at the North Korean-built National Heroes' Acre—once described by Nujoma as 'sacred ground' for the Namibian nation. In 2015, President Hage Geingob used his first Heroes' Day speech to urge his followers to remain loyal to SWAPO despite difficult economic times. He reminded the Namibian people that 'only half the battle is won. The second phase of the struggle will determine the same sacrifice and selflessness that the first struggle demanded'.[45]

Geingob hereby invoked the continuity thesis (as discussed in Chapter 13) by linking past and present struggles. 'Independence was not handed to us on a silver platter', concluded Geingob, 'it was earned, and the currency was blood'. Now, he demanded that Namibians follow in the footsteps of anticolonial warriors by becoming 'economic heroes'.[46] This signifies the continuation of a tradition that is rooted in the struggle. African nationalism, argues Werbner, is 'not a spent force'. On the contrary, it is gaining strength against 'perceived continuities in oppression by its new elites and present global forces'.[47] It is the same old story, but now repackaged in North Korean aesthetics.

Geingob passed away in February 2024. It was the first time that a Namibian president had died, which is a fitting example of how

223

young the Namibian state is. The SWAPO government requested assistance from the Zambian Defence Force for Geingob's funeral, citing a 'lack of experience' as the main reason. Geingob was celebrated as a 'liberation struggle icon' by his successor, Nangolo Mbumba, and was conferred hero status. As befits his stature, Geingob was buried in a room dedicated to him in the National Heroes' Acre.[48]

Conclusion

All heroes need villains. In Southern Africa, the state presents its citizens with a simple dichotomy, between good and bad, which is rooted in the anticolonial experiences from the recent past. During the days of struggle, African liberation movements explained their cause by differentiating between the rightful liberators and evil oppressors, the comrades and the sell-outs, the revolutionaries and the reactionaries; in other words, the liberation movement and outside forces. It is part of the origin myths of African nations in which the incumbent regimes play a central role. Those that fall on the wrong side of the dichotomy are not part of the family that makes up the liberation movement and, by extension, the nation.

African freedom fighters-turned-politicians practise a style of government that the historian Timothy Snyder describes as the 'politics of eternity'. With their constant references to liberation, African elites champion a general anti-historical worldview that revolves around a distinct interpretation of the struggle. It is a mood, Snyder writes, which is defined by 'a longing for past moments that never really happened during epochs that were, in fact, disastrous'. For the eternity politicians in Africa, the past is 'a vast misty courtyard of illegible monuments to national victimhood', which are prone to manipulation.[49] This resembles the 'legacy politics' (*yuhun chŏngch'i*) that characterises North Korea.[50]

As such, politics becomes a discussion between good and evil, defined by external enemies that threaten the purity of the nation, with a sense of crisis that is not temporary but constant. It is justified by 'a masquerade of history', but has real-life consequences. The

HEROISM

contemporary 'seduction by a mythical past' restrains the ability to think about possible futures. Snyder describes eternity politics as a hypnosis: 'the spinning vortex of cyclical myth'.[51] The fact that African governments use North Korean art studios to construct the physical monuments to visualise those myths is a telling sign of the mutual trust between African and North Korean elites.

15

MONEY

NATIONALISM AS A BUSINESS MODEL

In 2022, a private university in Zambia's capital, Lusaka, opened a new campus in a bid to keep up with rising student numbers and academic success. The state-of-the-art facilities included student accommodation, sport fields, academic halls and a library. A year later, an attentive journalist made a surprising discovery while browsing through a recent issue of the propaganda magazine *Foreign Trade of DPR Korea*. It was an advert of a North Korean construction company bearing a photo of a recently completed job: the university library in Zambia.[1]

The university library symbolises the proliferation of smaller art studios and other North Korean companies that succeed in flying under the radar in Africa. The previous chapters of this final part of the book are centred around spectacular memorials that function on the national level. The UN now recognises MOP as an instrument in North Korea's economic toolbox. However, there also appears to be a multitude of smaller, generally unknown companies that operate on local or provincial levels in Africa.

This chapter explores the financial dimension of the relationships between African liberation movements and North Korea.[2] The first section describes how African demands for memorialisation

COMRADES BEYOND THE COLD WAR

have resulted in an attractive market for North Korean art studios. While the introduction of UN sanctions has seriously hampered this particular form of trade, African–North Korean ties remain intimate. The second section considers the African continent as a crucial node in the global illicit networks that fill the coffers of the Kim regime. Construction remains an important item in the North Korean portfolio, which is complemented by a host of illegal activities.

Heritage industry

The march of liberation movements towards the highest echelons of power heralded the start of a new memorial culture in Southern Africa. As the previous chapters have highlighted, the newly elected governments across the region constructed memorial landscapes that foregrounded their own crucial role in the liberation of their nations. In this context, Renzo Baas describes memorialisation as 'a state-sponsored domain, even an industry'.[3] Indeed, African heritage is booming business—and some of the profits flow towards Pyongyang.

The North Korean 'one size fits all model' for nationalist heritage is a lucrative business model. With the collapse of the North Korean economy in the 1990s, a desperate need for hard foreign currency arose. North Korean art studios tapped into profitable markets when they realised that governments in Africa were willing to pay good money for their services. In particular, MOP has had unrivalled access to Southern African liberation movements. In Angola alone, the UN confirmed that, until 2015, MOP had undertaken over 56 different construction projects.[4]

A recurring feature of North Korean construction projects is that they tend to cost much more than originally planned. The National Heroes' Acre in Namibia was initially budgeted for N$34 million but was realised for N$60 million. In 2006, the entrance fees amounted to N$64,188 while the upkeep costs were N$500,000 a year. These costs have been described as 'a drain on the National Monuments Council's already meagre finance'. Nevertheless, the Namibian government was prepared to spend considerable sums

228

MONEY

of money on nationalist heritage. The closed tender for the State House, where the Namibian president resides, was estimated at a whopping N$445 million—and again awarded to MOP.[5]

How much money does North Korea earn through its monumental diplomacy in Africa? Unfortunately, the financial dimension of African–North Korean relations is difficult to ascertain. African governments usually award Mansudae projects through closed tender procedures, which makes it impossible to determine a total number. The United Nations noted that the financial activities of North Korea are obscured by 'a general veil of secrecy'.[6]

The introduction of a sanctions regime against North Korea in 2006 did not criminalise construction work. Strictly speaking, the core business of MOP was perhaps controversial but not illegal. However, over the years, it appeared that MOP had not only built civilian monuments, but it had also ventured into military affairs. In Namibia, the art studio worked alongside KOMID, the North Korean arms company that supplied the Namibian Defence Force. The UN scolded MOP for 'assisting in the evasion of sanctions by providing services and assistance related to the manufacture and maintenance of arms and related material'.[7] In addition to nationalist heritage such as the Independence Memorial Museum, MOP was also responsible for the construction or augmentation of the headquarters of the Ministry of Defence, a military academy, a munitions factory to produce small arms ammunitions and several military bases.[8]

The UN Panel of Experts observes that the value of North Korean construction projects appears to be inflated and often takes place through joint ventures, which allows foreign partners to earmark funds for sanction-evading purposes. The Panel stresses that 'illicit earnings could be remitted in the guise of legitimate payments'.[9] In 2015, MOP had withdrawn US$280,000 in cash from a local Namibian bank and instructed its labourers to bring this back to Pyongyang, in increments of $20,000. The request was filed as 'travel expenses'.[10] In 2022, a North Korean diplomat smuggled hundreds of thousands of US dollars in cash from Niger to Nigeria, 'likely utilising diplomatic credentials to avoid scrutiny and baggage inspections'.[11] North Korea often makes use of bulk cash in order to circumvent the formal financial sector.[12]

An important but usually overlooked dimension of North Korean operations in Africa is the labourers. They are vital for the success of heritage construction and other business endeavours. In 2024, the UN reported that 100,000 North Korean nationals were working overseas, in approximately 40 countries.[13] Recent research on North Korean labourers in Europe shows that their working conditions amount to modern slavery. They work in dangerous circumstances, cannot move around on their own accord and have to yield the majority of their salaries to the regime.[14] There are signs that the circumstances in Africa are no different, which would not only violate international sanctions but also a wide range of (local) labour laws.[15] Forced labour is deployed in both civilian and military projects.[16] The UN estimated that the sanctioning of North Korean overseas workers may cost North Korea 'up to hundreds of millions of dollars', which underlines the importance of labour export as a revenue stream for Pyongyang.[17]

However, the financial net around North Korea is tightening. Between 2000–15, MOP won major tenders in Southern Africa, despite North Korea's increasing international isolation. While the original UN sanctions focused on curbing North Korea's arms trade, resolution 2321 (2016) explicitly prohibits member states from procuring North Korean statues.[18] In 2017, the Panel of Experts asserted that MOP had violated the UN resolutions against North Korea and recommended that MOP entities and staff members be designated. The UN Security Council resolution 2397 (2017) obligates member states to repatriate all North Korean overseas workers before 22 December 2019.[19]

The sanctions had an effect. Following international pressure, Namibia announced that it would terminate their contracts with MOP.[20] In 2017, Namibia repatriated 242 North Korean nationals.[21] All vehicles and equipment of MOP were sold off in a private auction, showing that the UN Security Council measures made it much more difficult for MOP to operate as usual.[22] In 2020, Angola repatriated 296 North Korean nationals following the UN deadline.[23] Across the Southern African region, North

MONEY

Korean projects were forced to a halt. But, as the next part of this chapter shows, there is compelling evidence that trade continues, nonetheless.

Soft power, hard currency

North Korea is a country that has moved beyond decline into despair. The increase of the sanctions regime in recent years has forced Pyongyang to rely increasingly on inventive sources of income. It is saved, in part, by the relations and experience it has amassed in Africa. The North Korean investments made during the African liberation struggles of the twentieth century are now paying off. As such, North Korea is successfully turning historical soft power into modern hard currency.

The library of the University of Lusaka provides a glimpse into the unexplored and myriad ways that North Korea earns money in the construction business in Africa. The library, Ifang Bremer reported for *NK News*, is designed by Moksong Overseas Construction & Economic Technology Cooperation Company. In *Foreign Trade of DPR Korea*, the company boasts to have 'agencies in several countries' to execute 'new architectural formation plans, construction methods and labour assistance' on a 'world level'.[24] The name of MOP is splashed across UN resolutions and global news reports. Until Bremer's discovery, few people outside of North Korea had heard of Moksong.

In 2020–21, the investigative collective The Sentry exposed the extensive reach of Korea Paekho Trading Corporation in the Democratic Republic of Congo and other African countries. Paekho is a North Korean art studio that has constructed several public works for local governments in Congo, such as roundabouts and fountains. The North Korean managers carried governmental passports and had adapted well to local circumstances: they were fluent in French and enjoyed access to local authorities. However, official Congolese documents recorded their nationalities ambiguously as 'Korean' while local news reports depicted them as South Korean.[25] This confusion worked to their advantage.

231

Following reporting from The Sentry, Paekho was designated by the UN. Nevertheless, the use of shell companies and different names makes it difficult to put a halt to companies such as Paekho.[26] North Korea exploits legitimate business structures to conceal illegal activities, using 'aliases, agents, offices and complicit companies based in multiple jurisdictions in ways that follow global trading patterns'.[27] North Korean companies exploit the time periods between Security Council designations and member state implementation 'by changing names, directors and addresses', which makes it difficult to track them.[28]

The construction projects that are executed by Moksong and Paekho are much smaller than the grand memorial sites of MOP. However, the combined sum of all these smaller projects is likely to be a significant number. This makes it an important lifeline of the North Korean regime.

I argue that contemporary North Korean criminal networks in Africa build upon decades of diplomatic experience.[29] During the twentieth century, embassies formed the basis of North Korea's diplomatic charm offensive (described in the first part of this book, 'Blood') and military cooperation (described in the second part of this book, 'Bullets') in Africa. The end of the Cold War and subsequent collapse of the North Korean economy transformed this diplomatic system from money-spending to money-earning entities. This network now constitutes the backbone of a sprawling web of corruption.

North Korea is not a truly socialist state, despite mainstream scholars and commentators depicting it as such. It is a kingdom first and a capitalist enterprise second.[30] Today, as mentioned in Chapter 10, North Korean embassies operate as a decentralised system that seeks to earn money whenever the opportunity arises.[31] They are money-spinners, as ambassadors are required to generate a certain amount of money each year.[32] This is not just an African phenomenon but occurs around the world: the North Korean embassy in Germany partly operated as a city hostel, the North Korean embassy in Bulgaria could be rented for weddings and the North Korean embassy in Pakistan turned out to be a bootlegging

MONEY

operation where thousands of bottles of Johnnie Walker Black Label were stashed.[33]

In Africa, the construction work of Moksong and Paekho is probably only the tip of the iceberg: evidence suggests that North Korean diplomatic staff are involved in a shadowy world of running illicit schemes. Cigarettes, counterfeiting dollars, producing top-notch crystal meth: North Koreans build upon years of experience in Africa.[34] As early as 1976, two North Korean diplomats were caught with 400 kilos of hashish in Egypt.[35] In 1989, the British foreign office reported a rhino horn smuggling ring in the North Korean embassy in Zambia, when 'a plastic horn was found flung out of one of the embassy windows' by an enraged North Korean diplomat who discovered that 'the embassy had been sold a fake'.[36] A report from 2000 estimated that, in the past decade, 'North Korean diplomats were the biggest buyer of African ivory' in the world.[37] In 2015, a North Korean diplomat and a taekwondo master were arrested in Mozambique while possessing $99,300 in cash and 4.5 kg of rhino horn.[38] In 2022, a North Korean diplomat in South Africa attempted to traffic rhino horn with a staggering worth of $65 million. The UN Panel of Experts reported that between 2022 and 2023 North Koreans were involved in the smuggling of rhino horns and elephant tusks 'from Botswana to Mozambique, via South Africa and Zimbabwe and involving Malawi citizens'. These operations reveal the existence of complex regional trading networks. All involved countries either replied to the UN that they did not possess relevant information about these activities, or failed to reply at all.[39]

Conclusion

Postcolonial African governments offer North Korea political support and sources of income beyond the reach of the UN sanctions regime. The role of North Korea on the world stage is poorly explained, as the survival of the 'hermit kingdom' being partly dependent on the support of African states is usually overlooked. Through historical relationships, maintenance dependency and weak enforcement (as discussed in Chapter 10), various forms of illicit trade continue to thrive between the African continent and North Korea. Pyongyang's status as a rogue pariah state is not widely recognised beyond the Western liberal world order.

However, UN sanctions do impact African–North Korean relations. The introduction of new punitive measures and tightening existing ones push North Korea into a different modus operandi. The grand, eye-catching heritage projects that were the focus of the previous chapters constitute but one area of African–North Korean ties. Naturally, on account of its visibility, such projects receive most attention in popular and academic analysis. This chapter, in contrast, argues that there is presumably a much larger undercurrent of smaller projects of North Korean operations in Africa that escape our attention.

With the UN sanctions system in place, illegal forms of cooperation are most likely the model for the immediate future of the African–North Korean alliance. To unearth this world of underground activities, more work and improved research methodologies are necessary. The UN is primarily targeting the supply side of this relationship, but, as Andrea Berger argues, North Korea 'is largely immune to external influence'.[40] I suggest that it is imperative to analyse the demand side by concentrating on African agency.[41] As such, this book has attempted to provide the historical contextualisation necessary to understand not only how, but *why*, this form of cooperation has survived the Cold War and extends into the present.

EPILOGUE

A LIBERATION LENS

Southern Africa is governed by the past. The nationalist heritage that is explored in the final part of this book is an outcome of the dominant political culture in Southern Africa, which is guided by the experience of struggle. After all, the majority of states in Southern Africa are ruled by former liberation movements. I argue that the past revolution is the prism through which they understand present-day politics—I coin this the 'liberation lens'. It is a lens that is strongly coloured by North Korean visual aesthetics.

As a result of the liberation lens, contemporary political discourse is pervaded by revolutionary rhetoric. In a debate about LGBT rights in June 2023, SWAPO official and member of parliament Jerry Ekandjo invoked his experience as a political prisoner on Robben Island in the 1970s: 'We cannot be a republic of homosexuals ... I went to Robben Island at the age of 26 not to promote homosexuality here. People died, and disappeared'. Ekandjo also referred to Sam Nujoma's viewpoints, even though the leader had left office in 2005: 'The founding father said no'.[1] The manner in which Ekandjo connects contemporary political issues to his struggle credentials is commonplace across Southern Africa.[2] Whether it is gender, economic woes, land redistribution or the Russian invasion of Ukraine—some of the most sensitive issues in Southern Africa today are debated through the liberation lens.

COMRADES BEYOND THE COLD WAR

This book has emphasised the transnational dimension of liberation politics, military and heritage. During the decades of decolonisation, the operations of liberation movements across the Southern African region were marked by a high degree of interaction. 'We consult with each other ... and teach what we have learned from our own particular struggles', said Shipanga about the relationship between SWAPO and the MPLA.[3] ZANU said that CCM 'fathered our struggle'.[4] FRELIMO paid tribute to TANU and UNIP, their 'comrades and friends ... [who] accepted any sacrifice to make our victory possible'.[5] The ANC and ZAPU issued a 'historical declaration of their alliance' against apartheid.[6] The ANC and FRELIMO signed a cooperation agreement to stimulate meetings and exchange of information.[7] 'FRELIMO equals ANC', declared the South African party, which also commemorated the 'indissoluble bonds of fraternity' with the MPLA, CCM and UNIP.[8] In the run-up to the total liberation of Southern Africa, the political bureaus of the leading nationalist movements attended each other's conferences and discussed areas of cooperation.[9] The result is a shared political culture that transcends national boundaries.

Nostalgia is a powerful drug. The history of liberation weighs heavily on the shoulders of today's African political elites. Richard Werbner describes how, in Southern Africa, 'the state has itself become the agent of nostalgia, for the sake of nation-building'. He adds that 'heritage is a state cultural policy, often in an anti-colonial appeal inventing tradition for an authentic past'.[10] Today, it is widely believed that the future lies ahead of us—we move towards the future, with our backs to the past. However, ancient Greek and Hebrew traditions envisaged temporality the other way around. They argued that history is right in front of us, as it is evidently the only thing we can see, while the future remains invisible, behind our backs.[11] Perhaps Southern African elites govern in a similar fashion, with a firm focus on the recent past.

It is important to note that the 'authentic past' encapsulated in North Korean heritage must serve the incumbent African elites, who wish to remain in power. In these origin myths, the party takes centre stage. It is a past that portrays the nation

EPILOGUE

as a harmonious family but conceals the brutal repression of dissidents, a past that glorifies violence but omits diplomacy, a past that memorialises elites and ignores the people. To this end, liberation governments adopt a heritage blueprint derived from North Korea—which means that Pyongyang is not only generating goodwill, but also cash.

North Korea does not have a monopoly on the construction of large-scale monuments. In fact, African states can theoretically choose from a large number of global competitors. Nevertheless, in Southern Africa, the critical infrastructure of nationalist heritage is not created by Africans, and not even by outsiders like China, Russia, Cuba or Western countries. The honour goes to North Korea, widely assumed to be an isolated pariah state. North Korean art studios produce the tangible outcome of Southern Africa's obsession with the past. Liberation heritage is a growth industry— the SADC's Southern African Liberation Struggles project, the African Liberation Project in Tanzania and the Museum of African Liberation in Zimbabwe are just a few government-sanctioned examples from recent years.[12]

There is a tension between the 'one size fits all' model of North Korean nationalism and the idiosyncrasies of African histories. Werbner describes how postcolonial monuments in Southern Africa combine precolonial symbolism and colonial stereotyping with North Korean aesthetics, 'a national imagery which is at once divisive and unifying'.[13] A recurring critique is that African governments overlook local architects in favour of North Korea.[14] As a result, the monuments look detached from their African contexts. The statue of Laurent-Désiré Kabila in Congo is said to have the head of Kabila but the body of Kim Jong Il.[15] The construction of the African Renaissance Monument in Senegal was delayed because the faces on the statue were deemed too Korean. President Abdoulaye Wade ordered a redesign to make them more African.[16]

The liberation movements that fought for democracy have been transformed into liberation governments that are guided by a desire for political survival and display anti-democratic behaviour. Henning Melber calls this 'the limits to liberation'.[17] While the nationalist monuments highlighted in this book are designed as symbols that celebrate independence, they inadvertently turn into places of mourning for the reduction of political space. The National Heroes' Acre in Zimbabwe is, after all, a cemetery—a resting place for party veterans, a graveyard for democracy. The conclusion of this book discusses the influence of North Korea on the authoritarian tendencies of Southern African political culture.

CONCLUSION

POWER TO THE PARTY

The rallying cry of national liberation movements across Southern Africa was 'Power to the people!' During the struggle for freedom, these words reverberated in liberation camps in exile, they were chanted during protest marches in global capitals and whispered by imprisoned freedom fighters on Robben Island, and they were included in every speech at independence celebrations.[1] Today, this slogan has been informally transformed into 'power to the party'. From Angola to Zimbabwe, liberation governments, rooted in the anticolonial organisations of the past, desperately cling to power.

A struggle for liberal ideals does not always result in a liberal outcome. African nationalists searched for freedom and eventually found power. In recent times, the once idealistic ANC has not been engaged in a contest over ideas but in a competition for the spoils that result from political influence. 'Ideology and programmatic issues have been supplanted by personal support and patronage', asserts the former ANC operative Raymond Suttner.[2] Similar criticism is applicable to the MPLA (Angola), FRELIMO (Mozambique), SWAPO (Namibia), ZANU (Zimbabwe) and could also have been applied to UNIP (Zambia) until the 1990s.

During the twentieth century, people dreamt of decolonisation as a road—it led somewhere. But what if there is no ultimate destination? What if the struggle necessarily carries on into perpetuity? African liberation governments have difficulty shaking the military mindsets from their days of exile and view contemporary politics through a liberation lens. They use the past to legitimise their claim to authority and have concocted the idea of a continuous struggle, which extends into the twenty-first century. In their quest for eternal rule, African liberation governments found an unexpected inspiration: North Korea.

Contrary to existing scholarship, which focuses on North Korean motives for engaging with the outside world, this book examines the question of how political elites in Southern Africa benefited from North Korean support. A focus on African agency reveals that liberation governments utilised diplomatic cooperation, military assistance and nationalist heritage offered by North Korea to further their own interests—not primarily the interests of the state, but the interests of their own parties. Importantly, the relationships that were forged in the early 1960s continue to thrive today. Therefore, this book argues that not the Cold War, but rather liberation itself was the leitmotif for African–North Korean relations.

In the remainder of this conclusion, I will review the three assumptions that were highlighted in the introduction: first, that Southern African political culture is rooted in the liberation struggle; second, that we must shift our analytical focus from states to regimes; and third, that the common periodisation of contemporary history is counter-productive.

Democratic backsliding

One of the most worrying developments in global politics is a gradual decline of democracy. Larry Bartels et al. show that, in recent years, 'more countries have moved away from democracy rather than toward it'.[3] Democratic backsliding manifests through a range of illiberal measures, including the manipulation of elections, the erosion of public institutions, the repression of political opponents and the marginalisation of minorities. Ursula Daxecker describes this development as 'a global threat'.[4]

CONCLUSION

With regard to the African continent, Leonardo Arriola et al. find that the period of democratisation that swept across the continent in the early 1990s appeared promising but soon came to a standstill. While a panoramic view of the continent reveals a remarkable stagnation in the level of African democracy, the authors note considerable cross-country variation vis-à-vis democratic progress or decline.[5] However, both a continental approach and methodological nationalism distort our understanding of regional patterns.[6] I would argue for precisely the latter: Southern Africa, as a region dominated by former liberation movements, is experiencing a general trend towards electoral autocracy.[7]

When liberation governments were first elected to power, following independence, they won comfortable majorities. However, after several decades of uninterrupted rule, they gradually approach the danger zone of electoral politics. 'The Western imperialist countries are working hard to reverse the gains of the revolution in Southern Africa', claimed Utoni Nujoma in 2022 (he is Sam Nujoma's son and now serves as a high-ranking government minister for SWAPO). He recognised that liberation governments were under threat, citing the examples of Namibia and neighbouring countries.[8] In 2019, SWAPO recorded its lowest vote share ever, losing its two-thirds majority in the National Assembly for the first time.[9] In 2021, the ANC—for the first time ever—received under 50% of the votes in local elections.[10] In 2022, the MPLA won the Angolan elections with just 51.2% of the votes, the lowest majority in its history.[11] The comfortable margins of the past are no more.

As summarised in the first assumption of this book, the anti-democratic reflexes of liberation governments are part of a political culture that is rooted in the experiences of the liberation struggle. Samora Machel warned the Mozambican people in 1974 that 'anyone who deforms our line can expect no tolerance from us. We shall be intransigent on this, as we were during the hard war years'.[12] The emphasis on the 'war years' is key. The exile dimension of liberation politics resulted in numerous interactions between different movements and a transnational culture in which the importance of unity is a common denominator. Whether it

241

was in diplomacy (discussed in the first part of this book) or in war (discussed in the second part of this book), nationalist parties envisioned themselves as the rightful flag bearers of freedom. This mentality carried on in postcolonial politics.

From the perspective of liberation governments, according to Ian Phimister, their removal from power would 'constitute a counter-revolutionary victory for reactionary forces'.[13] As such, liberation governments operate ruthlessly in the face of discord. The *Gukurahundi* genocide in Zimbabwe, the crushing of secessionist movements in Namibia and Zimbabwe, the civil wars in Angola and Mozambique: incumbent regimes in Southern Africa were not afraid to meet steel with steel. They had already done the same in exile when dissidents threatened to weaken the unity of their movements.

Like many of his contemporaries, Kenneth Kaunda feared the reintroduction of foreign rule in the years following Zambian independence.[14] 'Once you start on a revolutionary path, you have no alternative', Kaunda said in 1970. If you stray from this path, 'you are bound to lose control of the ship and it will sink'.[15] Consequently, two years later, Kaunda banned all other political parties in Zambia and proudly announced that 'parliament will be the midwife to the birth of a one-party participatory democracy'. He feared 'the reconquest of Zambia … the re-establishment of foreign rule' and thus changed the country into a formal one-party state.[16] Three decades later, in Zimbabwe, ZANU seemed to lose the parliamentary elections in 2000 to the rival Movement for Democratic Change. Robert Mugabe's government responded with such extensive electoral fraud and political violence that Zimbabwe de facto changed into a one-party state.[17]

Power reveals character. The president of SWAPO's youth league said in 2008 that 'we have a political religion called SWAPO … and the political hell is where all the other political parties are'.[18] In 2022, the SWAPO prime minister predicted that 'we will not allow SWAPO to be defeated until Jesus comes back'.[19] 'I agree with her', said a SWAPO governor Laura McLeod-Katjirua at a party event in 2023, 'because Jesus will not come'. She was dismayed at the opposition against the former liberation

CONCLUSION

movement: 'freedom and independence we brought, we brought along democracy, that same democracy that people are fighting us with'. If it were possible, the governor continued, she would abolish democracy altogether. McLeod-Katjirua said that 'power is sweet', and if another political party were to win the next general election, she 'will go back into exile'.[20]

These are the excesses of the 'limits of liberation' as described by Henning Melber, a political culture that transcends national boundaries in Southern Africa and conceptualises the party as the beginning and end of the nation state.[21] Blaauw and Zaire show that, across Southern Africa, the inability of erstwhile liberation movements to accept open contestation 'is embedded in the history and political culture of these parties-turned-government'.[22] In the historical development of this mindset, African nationalists were influenced by North Korea.

Party building

In their march towards power, African liberation movements claimed the nation and organised themselves as states-in-waiting. 'SWAPO is the people and the people are SWAPO' was the message in the case of Namibia.[23] Mugabe believed that 'the party and the people and the people and the party must have one and the same meaning'.[24] For him, this meaning was evident. 'Long live ZANU, long live Zimbabwe'.[25] It is a model widely applied in Southern Africa. 'Historically, to say FRELIMO was to say Mozambique. To say MPLA was to say Angola ... The names of our organisations signified the purest, most sacred interests of our peoples', said Machel.[26] The amalgamation of statehood and nationhood with the party draws attention to the importance of the development of the latter as an organisation.

As summarised in the second assumption of this book, we must shift our lens from countries to regimes. Rather than focusing on nation building or state building, we should analyse party-building to properly assess the impact of North Korea in Africa. Pyongyang excelled in assisting the transformation of African liberation movements into liberation governments. North Korea not only

243

exported the necessary tools to African freedom fighters—political pamphlets, cheap guns and nationalist heritage—but also the idea behind them, a vision of a singular regime that remains in power in perpetuity.

North Korea generally supported African regimes, not states. It is no coincidence that North Korea invested heavily in the training of African youth leagues of political movements.[27] Jide Owoeye argued that North Korea constructed 'party-to-party links' between the WPK and their African counterparts in anticipation of diplomatic ties.[28] However, there is evidence that this strategy continued even after formal diplomatic ties were established. In 1988, a Tanzanian delegation visited Kim Il Sung to learn about their 'experience in building the party'. Party building was the cornerstone of any successful revolution, according to Kim, who concluded that 'our two parties and peoples have a very close relationship'.[29] In the same year, an agreement was signed between the WPK and FRELIMO, rather than between the governments of North Korea and Mozambique.[30] This lasting fraternity is not inexplicable. North Korea is a true hereditary regime, where power is passed on within a single dynasty. Liberation governments are, in a sense, politically hereditary institutions, where it is simply expected that power stays within a single regime.

The idea that the people 'must be united into one organisation with one ideology under the guidance of the party and the leader' is equally applicable to Southern African and North Korean contexts.[31] In this case, the former quote is from Kim Jong Il, but similar sentiments were echoed in Africa. While still in exile, Agostinho Neto relayed a message through Radio Tanzania to his companions in the struggle. 'The experience of Africa has taught us many things', Neto confided to those listening in—including 'the lesson that the party must control the life of the country during every moment. The strength that gave us arms with which to defend ourselves from foreign occupation will also guarantee true independence in the future'. It was 1968 and it would take another few years before Angola would become sovereign. Yet, Neto was already predicting that 'it is necessary that the party constitute the backbone, the base and the principal element in the

CONCLUSION

life of the nation. Where there is no party', said the nationalist leader, 'anarchy enters ... instead of independence we will have neo-colonialism'.[32]

Again, the party-centred mindsets of African revolutionaries were carried into postcolonial politics. 'The party is supreme', said Kaunda in 1971, and 'the government is a product and a servant of UNIP. The strength of the government clearly depends upon the strength of UNIP'. In a speech titled 'a path for the future', Kaunda emphasised that the fight against colonialism was ongoing, albeit in a 'more subtle form'. The party that delivered independence was the only one that could be trusted to chart Zambia's course in the uncertain waters of postcolonial rule. 'We do not know what the future holds', said Kaunda, 'but we do know who holds the future. It is UNIP'.[33]

It goes too far to argue that African liberation governments mirror North Korean politics. Nevertheless, there are significant similarities in political strategies. Just like the North Korean political caste, Zimbabwean elites blame the economic ruin and human rights violations on 'the interference by imperialist agents and the persistent raft of Western sanctions'. Political opponents are branded as 'agents of the West' and brutally repressed.[34] Both states are increasingly isolated on the international stage. It is not unimaginable that North Korea's stubborn persistence in spite of enormous odds commands inspiration from African liberation movements that also feel threatened to give up rule.

Africa is not an exception—North Korea provides inspiration for states across the non-Western world. In 2009, a former Taiwanese national policy advisor argued that Taiwan 'should model its dealings with China on North Korea', as Pyongyang's diplomacy gained maximum benefits without sacrificing North Korean sovereignty.[35] In 2023, a former Indonesian president believed that Indonesia 'should emulate North Korea in building its nuclear capacity'.[36] 'Russia needs to live like North Korea for a certain number of years', said Russian warlord Yevgeny Prigozhin in one of his famous speeches about the invasion of Ukraine. 'Close all borders, stop playing nice, bring all our kids back from abroad and work our asses off. Then we'll see some results'.[37]

COMRADES BEYOND THE COLD WAR

Periodisation

As summarised in the third assumption of this book, the traditional periodisation of the past is counterproductive in the context of African–North Korean relations. A recurring motif throughout this book is the need to rethink the Cold War as a driver of events for South–South cooperation. Pragmatism, not ideology, was the determining factor behind African–North Korean relations.

North Korea deliberately followed its own path and moved away from China and the Soviet Union from the 1970s, but the Western world is late in catching up and persists in viewing the country as 'communist' or 'Stalinist'. Most existing scholarship adopts a Cold War era timeframe to study North Korea's relations with Africa, which suggests that the end of the Cold War in the 1990s signalled the end of the African–North Korean exchanges. As this book shows, this is not the case—just look at the growth of the North Korean heritage industry in Africa to see the evidence.

After the initial honeymoon period of newly installed African liberation governments, political difficulties and economic recessions eroded their mandate and legitimacy.[38] Richard Werbner argues that as the postcolonial state 'transforms from an early period of triumphalism to a current one of widespread disaffection' the controversies around remembered identity intensify.[39] It is therefore imperative for incumbent regimes to implement large-scale memorial policies that favour their own role in the recent past. As such, commemorating the past becomes a political strategy. Again, African liberation movements turned to Pyongyang for advice and help: hence, the proliferation of North Korean heritage in Africa.

North Korea is unique in maintaining its hereditary state system, 'longer than any other state entity born in the Cold War era'. While most charismatic state personalities of the communist world 'underwent a dramatic rise and fall', North Korea remained remarkably resilient, defying the norm found in other revolutionary societies.[40] From the perspective of African revolutionaries, North Korea differs from China and the Soviet Union: a former colonised nation, a state that is organised through Juche instead of

246

CONCLUSION

communism, and finally, a regime that has remained surprisingly stable. Pyongyang was able to maintain consistent relations with African liberation governments—which, as highlighted in this book, also remained remarkably consistent.

While North Korea's leadership formally changed with the death of Kim Il Sung in 1994, the real transformative decade for its state system occurred two decades before, in the 1970s. Kwon and Chung show that many of the 'striking features in today's North Korean political process took root during that process'.[41] Viewing these transformations through a Cold War periodisation therefore makes little sense. In short, the tumultuous events of the 1990s were not a turning point but a pivotal point—it altered but did not terminate African–North Korean exchanges. Continuity, not change, is what determines African–North Korean relations.

In the case of African politics, another unhelpful periodisation is the tendency to view African independence as the start of a new political era, while the conduct of liberation governments is, in fact, a continuation of political behaviour that is rooted in the decades before. Liberation governments, like political institutions, are shaped by African struggles for self-determination in the twentieth century. As their contemporary behaviour is determined by the experiences of exile politics, arguably the founding dates of liberation movements are the critical junctures, rather than the dates of independence.[42]

The institutional development of liberation governments cuts right through this artificial classification of colonial and postcolonial eras. Borrowing the idea of path dependency, which entails that 'institutions continue to evolve ... in ways that are constrained by past trajectories', liberation governments develop their own logic.[43] Over time, these organisations have showcased remarkably consistent political behaviour from their inception until the present. Anti-democratic measures in Namibia, Zimbabwe and other countries therefore do not fall from the sky but are rather rooted in the pre-independence era. This subscribes to Daxecker's observation that the current democratic recession 'takes the form of incremental decline from within rather than outright democratic collapse'.[44]

COMRADES BEYOND THE COLD WAR

Fritz Nganje argues that 'the choices and behaviour of political actors are mediated by institutions'.[45] This compels us to properly assess the character of said institutions, in this case liberation governments. Kathleen Thelen emphasises that institutions are to be understood as 'enduring legacies of political struggles'.[46] For liberation governments, the struggle is an essential and, in some ways, eternal experience. As Walter Kickert and Frans-Bauke van der Meer observe, historical traditions have a 'conserving influence on current developments ... long-term grown institutional patterns are not easily changed'.[47]

As discussed at length in this book, the Western world feared that African decolonisation masked a communist uprising. However, most Africans who joined left-leaning liberation movements were not primarily motivated by socialist worldviews but by a desire for political independence. Ideology was a vehicle towards power. If that is indeed the case, we must focus on who is behind the wheel. The political scientist Emmanuel Gyimah-Boadi calls attention to the 'waning commitment' of African political elites to democracy.[48] Southern African liberation movements illustrate that oftentimes the anti-democratic behaviour of leaders has longer historical roots.

* * *

The connections between African liberation governments and North Korea present an alternative history of decolonisation. This era was not wholly guided by the ideological conflict of the Cold War or the interests of powerful colonial empires. It was also driven by smaller actors who cultivated ties across geographical and cultural boundaries for their own benefit. It is important to recognise the complexity of this messy history by including more diverse actors and acknowledging their agency.

African leaders deliberately accepted diplomatic invitations to North Korea and largely ignored South Korean offers of aid. They preferred the potential of South–South Cooperation at the Pyongyang Conference of 1987 over the promises of the South Korean–American axis. African leaders deliberately accepted

248

CONCLUSION

North Korean military support and ignored foreign disapproval of their decisions. When Robert Mugabe contemplated the North Korean training of the Fifth Brigade, diplomats from various corners of the world tumbled over each other to offer him alternatives or threaten him into submission—to no avail. African leaders deliberately hired North Korean art studios to construct nationalist heritage and ignored local and international competitors. The Namibian history museum is not designed by Namibians, but by North Koreans. In each and every case, African leaders had *options*—and they chose North Korea.

Bound by blood, bullets and bronze, African liberation governments and North Korea form an overlooked alliance of hereditary political regimes. A brotherhood forged in the previous century during an age of optimism, when African freedom fighters and North Korean communists found each other in an earnest attempt at worldmaking.[49] They achieved and consolidated independence but ultimately failed to alter the global order. Now all that is left is a shadow system of semi-legal interactions, motivated by a mutual need for political survival. The prevailing age of cynicism is best captured in the blatant disregard for the UN sanctions regime, as evidenced through numerous sanctions violations and the general apathy of African governments towards submitting national implementation reports.[50]

The existence of African–North Korean relations is a largely unknown part of history. Yet, it has a profound effect on contemporary international relations: North Korea influences the postcolonial trajectories of Southern African states, while African states provide an indispensable source of income for North Korea.

NOTE ON ARCHIVES

While historians need enormous amounts of source material to write a book, most of the letters, telegrams and reports that flow through our hands in the archives never feature in the finished manuscript. Nevertheless, this material informs our thinking and is essential for the generation of new ideas. Extensive fieldwork is therefore indispensable, especially for the pursuit of global history. During the years that I spent researching this book, I had the good fortune of consulting dozens of repositories. As a result, this book is primarily based on insights gathered from declassified primary sources, some of which have now been used in scholarship for the first time.

One of my key takeaways is that truth is often stranger than fiction. If I were to write a thriller about the Korean crisis during the Cold War, and my cast of characters included an American General Bonesteel (sporting a scary eyepatch), an English diplomat who went by the name of Mr. England and a Russian counterpart called Mr. Smirnov, it would be completely unbelievable. Yet, I encountered each of these figures while I rummaged through dusty archival boxes in Seoul, London, Cape Town, Washington DC and other places. From these dry pages in near-abandoned reading rooms leapt a colourful cast of characters who have kindly accompanied me throughout my archival research. Their contributions were informative, often witty, and, above all, useful for understanding the diplomatic arrangements of the time.

251

However, I was mainly interested in the voices of African actors, such as Julius Nyerere, Kenneth Kaunda and Samora Machel, as I pondered the question of how they viewed and utilised Korean competition for influence. They feature prominently in my book, thanks to a year's worth of archival research.

Another takeaway is the realisation that there is a wealth of data on African–North Korean relations that awaits further scrutiny. This book deliberately omits West Africa, East Africa and North Africa, but the archival record is perhaps even richer for these regions than for Southern Africa. As diplomatic archives usually contain records of independent countries, the delayed independence of Southern Africa may have resulted in relatively fewer files compared with the rest of the continent. There are, therefore, tremendous opportunities for research on African–North Korean ties beyond Southern Africa.

The declassification of government materials merits special consideration. For this project, I have submitted an information request to the Stasi Records Archive in Germany, because I suspect that the Stasi archives might contain information about African–North Korean relations. The Ministry of State Security of the German Democratic Republic had a formal cooperation agreement with the Ministry of State Security of North Korea.[1] These records are closed to the public but can be accessed upon request. While my endeavour has, to date, not yielded significant surprises, it illustrates another way forward in the search for sources. It is a time-consuming process with uncertain results, as I found out when I submitted a FOIA request to the national archives of the United States (which was ultimately not granted). Nevertheless, future FOIA requests in the case of the United States, FOI requests at The National Archives of the United Kingdom and perhaps PAIA requests with the Department of Defence archives in South Africa, could generate new insights.[2]

Archives are vulnerable institutions that are increasingly threatened by political pressure, underfunding and climatological hazards. In Southern Africa, the space for researchers to move around and gain access to source material appears to be decreasing. Over the course of my research, the national archives of Namibia

NOTE ON ARCHIVES

and South Africa were temporarily closed because of dangerous working conditions.[3] In neighbouring countries, such as in Zimbabwe, historians have difficulty obtaining research permits and are therefore barred from entering archives in the first place.[4] Yet, I should stress that the deterioration of archives is not a purely African phenomenon: the national archives of the United States are equally imperilled by a shrinking budget, which has led to falling standards.[5] This research project has made me more aware of the trend in which our world is being darkened by an authoritarian turn—a process that, I fear, is connected to how nations treat their memory.

This book is based on the contents of 32 different archives, located across four continents, with sources in Afrikaans, Dutch, English, French, German, Korean (both Hangul and Hanja), Portuguese, Swahili and Swedish. I am extremely grateful to the African Studies Centre Leiden for supporting my archival research. The sections below discuss the most important African, Korean and Western repositories that I have used in the course of my work.

African sources

It is challenging to find African primary sources that shed light on the ties that bind liberation governments to North Korea. National archives in Africa proved to be largely irrelevant for my study. Colonial records deliberately marginalised the perspectives of African liberation movements, while postcolonial records are often not yet accessible to the public. The relatively recent independence dates of many Southern African countries, combined with long embargo periods for state records (often 30 years) means that historians have to practise patience. For example, the records of the first years of the SWAPO government in Namibia remained closed until the early 2020s, as Namibia became independent in 1990.[6]

In spite of these hurdles, I managed to locate two collections within African national archives that contain postcolonial records about North Korea. The Botswana Notes and Archives Records

Services holds a fascinating file on Seretse Khama's interactions with North Korea, mainly covering the 1970s.[7] The National Archives of Namibia have recently released two files on the SWAPO government's dealings with North Korea and South Korea in the 1990s.[8]

Given that the aim of this book is to shift the lens from states to regimes, it made sense to focus on the party archives of liberation governments rather than state archives. Unfortunately, the records of ruling parties in Southern Africa are generally inaccessible.[9] Notable exceptions are ANC collections of the Mayibuye Archives and the Fort Hare Archives in South Africa, and the UNIP archives in Zambia; but it must be acknowledged that these repositories have been cleaned by party officials and do not feature sensitive files related to intelligence and finances.[10]

Two viable alternatives for historians of African decolonisation are private collections in African university archives and exiled collections in Europe.[11] While the SWAPO party in Namibia hides its institutional archive from public view, the University of Namibia archives hold two private collections of high-ranking SWAPO officials, which contain useful material on the liberation movement (the Tjitendero Collection and the Katjavivi Collection). In addition, several European repositories preserve extensive records of liberation movements in Southern Africa. To stick with the Namibian example, Basler Afrika Bibliographien in Switzerland has a wonderful SWAPO collection.[12]

For anticolonial organisations more generally, the International Institute of Social History in the Netherlands and the Nordic Africa Institute in Sweden are stunning resources that feature African material. In particular, the latter's Pamphlet Collection was incredibly useful, with over 700 boxes of primary sources, spanning the period from the 1960s until the 1980s.[13] I spent a month in Uppsala working my way through the Southern African material, a moment that significantly altered the shape and contents of this book.

The transnational nature of African national liberation movements, in which exile and solidarity were key components, is reflected in the global scattering of their publications.[14] Inspired

254

NOTE ON ARCHIVES

by Brian Myers' typology of North Korean propaganda, we can make a distinction between the 'outside track' and the 'inside track' of the data produced by African liberation movements. To rally their bases and secure foreign support, liberation movements churned out publications on a regular basis. Crucially, this is the 'outside track' of the information produced by the bureaucracies of liberation movements.[15] Spread across numerous archives and even continents, this research project utilised speeches, bulletins, war communiques, messages of solidarity, conference documents, political programmes, press statements, brochures and informational booklets, photos and posters that were published by a wide variety of African anticolonial organisations. This laborious process yielded numerous references to interactions between Africans and North Korea. Most party bulletins, for example, include a brief 'international support' section—occasionally, North Korea would be featured through descriptions of meetings or photographs of visits.

However, the 'inside track' of liberation movements remains largely inaccessible as party archives are either closed or cleaned. As a result, the internal correspondence, policymaking and funding structures remain rather elusive.

Korean sources

What about Korean source material? The closest I could get to Pyongyang was Seoul. The Diplomatic Archives, located south of the Han River in the boisterous capital city of South Korea, proved to be an invaluable collection of primary sources. Throughout the Cold War, South Korean diplomats feverishly monitored the business of their northern rivals and reported any activity back home. The Diplomatic Archives constitute a unique perspective on the Global Cold War, as it provides a Korean perspective on the division of the Korean peninsula, which was one of the most decisive issues of the twentieth century.

As the African continent was an important theatre of inter-Korean competition, the Diplomatic Archives are a treasure trove of information about North Korea's charm offensive in Africa. The collection holds dozens of files related to African–Korean affairs. Because my translation progress is slow, I estimate that I have used only 20% of the files that I found in 2021. As there are many more relevant files available, and new ones are being released continuously, I expect that future diplomatic historians will find the contents extremely valuable.

The Diplomatic Archives come with their own set of challenges. South Korean diplomats sometimes spelled the names of African countries in various ways, which makes working through the catalogue a labour-intensive process. Botswana, for instance, is spelled as both 보츠나와 and 보츠와나 in different files.[16] A command of Korean is necessary in order to use the material, as they are mainly written in Hangul (older material is oftentimes written in Hanja). This likely explains why these sources have never been used by Africanists. I was lucky to have been allowed the chance to follow intensive Korean language lessons at the Korean Studies department at Leiden University.

In my particular case, negotiating access to the archives was difficult because I travelled to Seoul in 2021, at the height of the Covid-19 pandemic, and the South Korean government had imposed strict regulations on Seoul. In normal circumstances, the archives should be readily accessible. The records are digitised but only physically available in the reading room in Seoul, where they are stored on CD-ROMs and microfilm. While a copy of the entire archive is available in the library of Seoul National University, it is recommended to visit the Diplomatic Archives. Digitisation efforts are ongoing and historians are likely to find the most complete collections at the latter location.

Western sources

Finally, this book utilises material with a distinct Western perspective. The United Kingdom and the United States were not directly involved in African–North Korean relations but had a vested interest in the African continent. These 'third-party archives' are thus useful to determine factual details about developments that occurred within Africa, including North Korea's

NOTE ON ARCHIVES

campaign to win support. British embassies in Africa monitored the political situation in their former colonies and reported this back to Whitehall. Although it often appears that 80% of the correspondence within the National Archives of the United Kingdom consists of colonial officers politely thanking each other for the received correspondence, the remaining material includes fascinating details about African–North Korean relations. The Foreign Office records in London are among the best-organised archives in the world and include dozens of dossiers related to this study that are easily accessible.

While the National Archives and Records Administration of the United States holds an equally impressive amount of relevant source material on African–North Korean relations, these archives are much harder to navigate. The Cold War era records of the State Department are divided between three completely different systems. The 1963–73 diplomatic cables are organised in the Subject Numeric Files while the 1973–79 records are stored in the Access to Archival Databases. The records from 1980 onwards are not yet disclosed but researchers can submit FOIA requests, which, in my experience, is a useless exercise. During my time in Washington DC, I found the Subject Numeric Files in Record Group 59 the most valuable sub-collection, in contrast to the records of the Bureau of African Affairs, Bureau of East Asian and Pacific Affairs, and the Bureau of Intelligence and Research. It should be noted that policy files on North Korea are likely stored in presidential archives rather than in the National Archives.

NOTES

PREFACE

1. Van der Hoog 2024.
2. Van der Hoog 2022c.
3. Van der Hoog 2022d.
4. Van der Hoog 2022b.
5. Van der Hoog 2019a.
6. Myers 2015.
7. USA Today, 9 May 2018.
8. White 2021.
9. See for example [SNU] 비학렬 811.74 M929y 198, 영원히 당과 함께 : 시집.
10. Kim 2010.
11. Jang 2014.
12. [NAI] PC Mozambique NLM FRELIMO: Eduardo Mondlane, paper 27–28 February 1968.
13. Fanon 1961.
14. 'The Poet Must Die …', by Don Mattera. See Mattera 2011.
15. Moore and Beier 2007.

INTRODUCTION

1. The footage is available on YouTube: https://www.youtube.com/watch?v=Tda0e-M76a8.
2. Kim 1991, pp. 131–3.
3. Williams and Mazarire 2019.
4. Van der Hoog 2019b.
5. Van der Hoog 2023.
6. Van der Hoog 2019a.
7. Ellis 2000.

NOTES

pp. [3–19]

8. Roberts 2021.
9. [NAN] CCO 39/12/1/3/2.
10. Alexander et al. 2017.
11. Wada 2013.
12. Oberdorfer and Carlin 2013.
13. Walker 2019, p. 263.
14. Kwon and Chung 2012, p. 162.
15. Gewald 2014.
16. Melber 2002.
17. Southall 2013.
18. Ellis 2000; Ellis 2002.
19. Raymond Suttner argued that also in the case of ANC history, there is a need to rethink the standard periodisation by dates. 'History needs to be seen in a more fluid way without rigid separations between phases'. Suttner 2008, p. 17.
20. Lessing 1962; Brzezinski and Dallin 1963; De Villiers et al. 1975; Greig 1977; Henriksen 1981; Gann 1983.
21. Koh 1969; Kwak et al. 1983; Koh 1984; Scalapino and Lee 1986; Clough 1987.
22. Park 1978; Park 1987; Owoeye 1991.
23. Armstrong 2013.
24. Myers 2015.
25. Young 2021a.
26. Michishita 2010; Berger 2016b; Bechtol 2018.
27. Bermudez 1990.
28. DuPre et al. 2016; Rademeyer 2017; Mallory 2021; The Sentry 2020; The Sentry 2021; Ko 2022.
29. De Villiers et al. 1975.
30. Chipaike and Knowledge 2018, p. 1; Blaauw 2015; Brown 2012.
31. Dersso 2012, p. 14.
32. Fisher 2018.
33. Brown and Harman 2013, p. 1.
34. Van der Hoog 2020.
35. Van der Hoog 2018.
36. Higgins 2021.

PROLOGUE

1. Kornes 2010.
2. Tsoubaloko 2016.
3. [NAI] PC Namibia NLM SWAPO: SWAPO Statement.
4. [NAI] PC Angola NLM FNLA: G.R.A.E. Actualities N 3, Angola 10th Year.
5. [NAN] CCO, 39/12/1/3/1.

pp. [20–27]   NOTES

6.   [NAI] PC Zimbabwe NLM ZANU: press release, 30 November 1977.
7.   Chitando and Tarusarira, 2017, p. 11.
8.   [NAI] PC Angola NLM MPLA: speech by Neto, December 1972.
9.   [MA] ANC London Box 4, SACP: draft radio broadcast, undated.
10. [MA] ANC London Box 15: speech by Tambo, 16 December 1986.
11. [NAI] PC Namibia NLM SWAPO: statement by Hishongwa.
12. [NAI] PC Mozambique NLM FRELIMO: message from Machel, 20 September 1974.
13. [NAI] PC Southern Africa NLM: Shamuyarira and Leonard.
14. [NAI] PC Mozambique NLM FRELIMO: message from Machel, 20 September 1974.
15. [MA] ANC Lusaka Box 63: speech by Machel, September 1986.
16. [NAI] PC Angola NLM MPLA: speech by Dos Santos, 27 July 1983.
17. Kim 2010, p. 190; Kwon and Chung 2012, pp. 56–8.
18. David-West 2006, p. 77.
19. [NAI] PC Angola NLM MPLA: Angola in Arms, 15 April 1970; MPLA Informations, no. 2.
20. Myers 2011.

1.   SOLIDARITY

1.   Serpell 2019, p. 533.
2.   Passemiers 2019, p. 3.
3.   Correia and Verhoef 2009.
4.   Melber 2002.
5.   [NSS] SWAPO Information Bulletin: October 1986. Prior to Namibian independence, SWAPO officials were already trained as diplomats. See [SWAPOA] 02000009-9A/9C; [SWAPOA] 02000006. I want to thank Saima Ashipala for sharing these files with me.
6.   Meeting with Hugh Macmillan, 22 March 2022.
7.   Williams 2015.
8.   [MA] ANC Lusaka Box 46: Draft ANC code of discipline.
9.   [SEA] 2.5.4.3: Lisa Distelheim, 30 October 1986.
10. [NAI] PC Mozambique NLM FRELIMO: speech by Machel, 27 April 1984.
11. Suttner 2008.
12. Saunders 2010; Alexander et al. 2017; Alexander et al. 2020, p. 821.
13. For instance, the ANC-ZAPU alliance or the ZANU-FRELIMO alliance in the 1970s. See Macmillan 2017; Munguambe 2017.
14. Gewald 2014.
15. Melber 2002.
16. Burton 2019, p. 26.
17. [NAI] PC Angola NLM MPLA: speech by Neto, 8 September 1972.
18. Burton 2019, p. 29.

NOTES
pp. [27–33]

19. Roberts 2021.
20. Interview with an anonymous North Korean diplomat, Seoul, 19 July 2021.
21. *The Nationalist*, 13 January 1966. I wish to thank Brooks Marmon for sharing this file with me.
22. [NARA] RG 59, SNF Entry# 1613-D, Box# 2616, POL 19 TAIWAN—POL 6 TANZAN: Dar es Salaam to Department of State, 6 November 1973.
23. Alexander et al. 2017.
24. Khadiagala 1994, p. 24.
25. Khadiagala 1994, p. 24.
26. [NAI] PC Southern Africa NLM: Shamuyarira and Leonard.
27. Khadiagala 1994.
28. [NAI] PC Southern Africa NLM: Shamuyarira and Leonard.
29. Saunders 2018, p. 154.
30. [NAI] PC Southern Africa NLM: Shamuyarira and Leonard.
31. [NAI] PC Mozambique NLM FRELIMO: speech Machel, 8 January 1975.
32. [NAI] PC Southern Africa NLM: Shamuyarira and Leonard.
33. Alexander et al. 2017.
34. Saunders 2018, p. 154.
35. See Emmett 1999, pp. 315–37.
36. Armstrong 1989, pp. 84–85.
37. [BAB] PA.48: No 4.
38. [BAB] PA.48: No 5.
39. [NAI] PC History: Solana, January 1969.
40. Doran 2017a, p. 8.
41. [UNAM] PA1/20/13.
42. O'Malley 2018, p. 2.
43. Saunders 2007.
44. Walker 2019.
45. Park 1978, p. 73.
46. Saunders 2007.
47. O'Malley 2018, p. 2.
48. [UNAM] PA1/1/5; see also Armstrong 1989.
49. Walker 2019, p. 238; Saunders 2007.
50. 'Robben Island', by Mvula ya Nangolo. See Moore and Beier 2007.
51. Gurney 2000.
52. Thörn 2006.
53. [BL] MSS. AAM 2323.
54. Lee 2010, p. 3.
55. [NAI] PC Zambia Politics Kaunda: speech by Kaunda, 14–20 August 1967.
56. Dallywater et al. 2019, p. 7.
57. Fanon 1961, p. 315.
58. Prashad 2007.
59. Bianchini et al. 2023.

pp. [33–40]   NOTES

60. Khadiagala 1994, p. 1.
61. Melber 2004.
62. Melber 2002.
63. Khadiagala 1994, p. 18.
64. Mubako 1975, p. 9.
65. Kim 1984, pp. 338–9.

2.   COMPETITION

1. Stueck 2002, p. 1.
2. Stueck 2002.
3. Wada 2013.
4. Oberdorfer and Carlin 2013.
5. Jager 2013.
6. Clough 1987, p. 274.
7. United Nations 1950; Ministry of Foreign Affairs 1971; The Institute for East Asian Studies 1974.
8. Kerkhoff 2020, p. 50.
9. [NAUK] FCO 21/2319: Wenban-Smith to Elliot, 29 October 1982.
10. Pak 2000.
11. Lee 2010, p. 3.
12. Owoeye 1991, p. 632.
13. [NARA] RG 59, SNF Entry# A1 1613-A, Box# 3964, POL 17 Korea—POL Kuwait: New York to Seoul, 14 September 1963.
14. [NARA] RG 59, SNF Entry# 1613-C, Box# 2261, POL 32-4 KOR/UN—POL KOR N: Department of State Intelligence Note, 26 June 1969; [NARA] RG 59, SNF Entry# 1613-D, Box# 2420, POL 32-4 KOR—POL 16 KOR N: Ouagadougou to Washington DC, 2 March 1973.
15. [NAUK] FO 371/181117: North Korean advances in Africa, 2 March 1965.
16. [NARA] RG 59, SNF Entry# 1613-C, Box# 2398, POL 27-14 Korea, N-UN—POL 33-4 Korea, N-UN: Department of State to various diplomatic and consular posts, 8 September 1966.
17. [NAUK] FCO 31/3922: Whitehead, Research Department Note 16/83, September 1983.
18. Kim 1983, p. 72.
19. Owoeye 1991, p. 632.
20. Park 1987, p. 79.
21. Park 1978, p. 76–7.
22. Park 1978; Owoeye 1991.
23. Kerkhoff 2020, p. 56.
24. [SRA] MfS—HA II. Nr. 29133.
25. [DARK] 15765.

NOTES pp. [40–43]

26. [NARA] RG 59, SNF Entry# 1613-C, Box# 2406, POL 23-9 Korea, South— POL 32-4 Korea, S-UN: Blantyre to Department of State, 10 March 1965.

27. [NARA] RG 59, SNF Entry# 1613-D, Box# 2420, POL 32-4 KOR—POL 16 KOR N: Blantyre to Washington DC.

28. [NAUK] FCO 105/828: Danson to M.J. Long, 12 February 1982; P.J. Sullivan, Lilongwe, 30 June 1982.

29. [NARA] RG 59, SNF Entry# 1613-D, Box# 2420, POL 32-4 KOR—POL 16 KOR N: Blantyre to Washington DC.

30. [SRA] MfS—HA II. Nr. 29133.

31. [DARK[25089.

32. [NAUK] FCO 105/828: Danson to M.J. Long, 12 February 1982; P.J. Sullivan, Lilongwe, 30 June 1982.

33. [NAI] PC Angola Military: Anable, 2 January 1976.

34. [DARK] 15765.

35. [NAUK] FO 371/181130: Commonwealth Relations Office to Lusaka, 15 January 1965.

36. [NAUK] FCO 31/948: Hart to Hall, 7 June 1971.

37. [NAUK] FCO 105/1198: Varcoe to Clemens, 6 July 1983; FCO to Victoria, 18 May 1983; Smedley to Elliot, 28 July 1983; Thorpe to Leahy, 10 August 1983; Smedley to Dewberry, 1 September 1983; Smedley to Dewberry, 19 September 1983.

38. Owoeye 1991, p. 631; Shen and Xia 2018, p. 12.

39. [SRA] MfS—HA XXII. Nr. 1610/72.

40. [NAUK] FCO 31/948: Hart to Hall, 7 June 1971.

41. [NAUK] FCO 31/948.

42. [NAUK] FCO 21/3231: Giles, North Korean military assistance, 20 November 1984; [NARA] RG 59, SNF Entry# 1613-C, Box# 2263, POL KOR N-AFR—POL 31-1 KOR N-US: Department of State to Monrovia, 23 August 1967.

43. [NAUK] FCO 21/2866: Goodworth to Currie, 27 September 1984.

44. Park 1978, p. 76; Owoeye 1991, p. 633.

45. [NAUK] FO 371/181117: North Korean advances in Africa, 2 March 1965.

46. [NARA] RG 59, SNF Entry# 1613-D, Box# 2423, POL KOR N-US—POL 7 KOR S: Yaounde to Washington DC, 20 July 1971.

47. Owoeye 1991, p. 634.

48. [NARA] RG 59, SNF Entry# 1613-C, Box# 2398, POL 27-14 Korea, N-UN—POL 33-4 Korea, N-UN: Dar es Salaam to Department of State, 16 June 1966.

49. [NARA] RG 59, SNF Entry# 1613-C, Box# 2260, POL 32-4 KOR—POL 32-4 KOR/UN: Department of State, Memorandum of Conversation: 4 April 1967.

50. [NARA] RG 59, SNF Entry# 1613-C, Box# 2262, POL 7 KOR N—POL 7 KOR N: Department of State, 'North Korean Efforts', 18 June 1968.

264

pp. [43–47] NOTES

51. Interview with James E. Hoare, London, 28 August 2019.
52. [NARA] RG 59, SNF Entry# 1613-C, Box# 2405, POL 15-2 Korea, South—POL 23-8 Korea, South: Seoul to Department of State, 20 July 1964.
53. [NARA] RG 59, SNF Entry# 1613-C, Box# 2397, POL 14 Korea, N—POL 27-14 Korea, N-UN: Department of State, Memorandum of Conversation, 3 February 1966.
54. [NARA] RG 59, SNF Entry# 1613-C, Box# 2261, POL 32-4 KOR/UN—POL KOR N: Department of State to Seoul, 17 May 1968.
55. [NARA] RG 59, SNF Entry# 1613-C, Box# 2398, POL 27-14 Korea, N-UN—POL 33-4 Korea, N-UN: Dar es Salaam to Department of State, 16 June 1966.
56. Kim 2022, p. 41.
57. Interview with an anonymous North Korean diplomat, Seoul, 19 July 2021.
58. [NAI] PC Mozambique NLM FRELIMO: Black Liberation Press, 1977.
59. [NAI] PC Mozambique NLM FRELIMO: Frelimo Party, June 1983.
60. [NAI] PC Zambia Politics Kaunda: speech Kaunda, August 1976.
61. [NAI] PC Angola NLM MPLA: MPLA, 14 January 1985.
62. Geldenhuys 2005, pp. 150–3.
63. [UWC] ANC Lusaka Box 65: memorandum, 22 September 1986; letter, 25 May 1990; Sechaba, April 1972.
64. [NAI] PC South Africa NLM ANC: statement, 26 June 1969.
65. Personal correspondence with Ronnie Kasrils, 31 March 2022.
66. Interview with an anonymous North Korean diplomat, Seoul, 19 July 2021.
67. Lodge 2022.
68. Interview with an anonymous North Korean diplomat, Seoul, 19 July 2021.
69. [NAUK] FCO 45/1680.
70. Temu and Tembe 2014, pp. 354–5 [vol. 8].
71. Bermudez 1990; [NAUK] FCO 21/3595.
72. Interview with an anonymous North Korean diplomat, Seoul, 19 July 2021.
73. [SADOD] CSI GP 3 Box 1091. I want to thank Brooks Marmon for generously sharing this file with me.
74. [NAI] PC Zimbabwe NLM ZAPU: circular 3/1970, August/September; [NAI] PC Angola Military: Anable, 2 January 1976.
75. [NAUK] FO 371/154940: Cairo to London, 5 June 1961; [NAUK] FCO 31/1866: Priestley to Southworth, 10 April 1975.
76. Armstrong 1989, p. 102.
77. Lewis and Stolte 2019.
78. Kwon and Chung 2012, pp. 139–40.
79. *Korea Times*, 27 November 2007.
80. [NAI] PC Southern Africa NLM: Shamuyarira and Leonard.
81. Abou-El-Fadl 2019, pp. 157–8.
82. Koh 1969, p. 175.
83. Temu and Tembe 2014, pp. 354–67 [vol. 8].

NOTES

pp. [47–51]

84. [NARA] RG 59, SNF Entry# A1 1613-A, Box# 4040, POL 26 South Korea—POL S Korea-US: Dar es Salaam to Secretary of State, 8 May 1963.

85. [NAUK] FCO 141/14087: Communist Activities in Africa, February 1964; Communist Activities in Africa, March 1964.

86. [DARK] 25146.

87. [NAI] PC Regional Cooperation AAPSO; [JSTOR] Zimbabwe News, 1987.

88. [NAI] PC Regional Cooperation AAPSO.

89. [UNIP] EAP121/2/5/4/31.

90. [NAI] PC Regional Cooperation AAPSO.

91. [MA] ANC Lusaka Box 63: AAPSO 14th session.

92. [NAI] PC Regional Cooperation AAPSO: Respected and beloved leader, 7 September 1978.

93. [DARK] 1448.

94. [NAI] PC Regional Cooperation AAPSO.

95. Kerkhoff 2020, pp. 41–3.

96. Kerkhoff 2020, pp. 50–1.

97. [NAI] PC Tanzania Politics Nyerere: speech Nyerere, 13–17 April 1970.

98. Kerkhoff 2020, pp. 53–8.

99. [NAI] PC Zambia Politics Kaunda: speech Kaunda, August 1976.

100. [MA] ANC Lusaka Box 63: speech Machel, September 1986.

101. [NAI] PC Regional Cooperation: conference New Delhi, 9–13 February 1981.

102. [NAUK] FCO 31/3263: Codrington to Cox, 9 November 1981.

103. [NAUK] FCO 31/3674: Codrington to Huckle, 2 November 1982.

104. Kerkhoff 2020, p. 65.

105. Kerkhoff 2020, p. 41.

106. [NAUK] FCO 21/2876: Elliot to Wilson, 20 November 1984.

107. See for extensive documentation of the conference the Diplomatic Archives of the Ministry of Foreign Affairs of South Korea, which closely monitored North Korean activities during the Cold War: [DARK] 25166 (and the next 16 volumes).

108. Kim 1987, p. 1.

109. Getachew 2019, p. 2.

110. [NUL] L968.91005 Z711 v.20: Zimbabwe News, 1989.

111. Soulé-Kohndou 2013.

112. [NAUK] FCO 21/3602.

113. [DARK] 23558.

114. [NAUK] FCO 21/3602: Goodworth to Bowie, 25 September 1986.

115. [SRA] MfS—HA II. Nr. 29133.

116. During the establishment of the AAPSO, Egypt was ruled by the anti-imperialist icon Gamal Abdel Nasser. However, during the time of the Harare Summit Egypt was ruled by Hosni Mubarak, a staunch United States ally.

117. [NAUK] FCO 21/3602: Goodworth to Bowie, 25 September 1986.

pp. [51–58] NOTES

118. Kerkhoff 2020, p. 65.
119. [NAUK] FCO 21/3602: Goodworth to Bowie, 25 September 1986.
120. Interview with an anonymous North Korean diplomat, Seoul, 19 July 2021.
121. [UNAM] PA4/1/2/73/22.
122. [UNDL] A/42/411; [UNDL] TD/339.
123. [UNAM] PA4/1/2/73/22; [UNDL] A/AC.131/260: 5 October 1987.
124. Kim 2022, p. 39.
125. [NAI] PC Namibia NLM SWAPO: Tanga consultative congress, 26 December 1969—2 January 1970.
126. [NAI] PC Mozambique NLM FRELIMO: Frelimo Party, June 1983; [NAI] PC Angola NLM MPLA: president, 14 January 1985.
127. [NAI] PC Zambia Politics Kaunda: speech Kaunda, 7 January 1970.
128. [NAI] PC Angola NLM UNITA: Kwacha, January–February 1968.
129. [NAI] PC Angola NLM MPLA: Angola in Arms, 15 April 1970.
130. [NAI] PC Zimbabwe NLM ZAPU: The Zimbabwe People's Voice, 31 March 1979.
131. [NAI] PC Zimbabwe NLM ZANU: Zimbabwe News, 'Ideological and Revolutionary Education'.
132. [NARA] RG 59, SNF Entry# A1 1613-A, Box# 3999, POL 24 Nigeria—POL North Korea-US: Department of State to Kampala, 18 March 1963.
133. [NARA] RG 59, INR, Entry# P 15, Box# 10, AFRICA MISCELLANEOUS: Bureau of Intelligence and Research, Report No. 489, 16 June 1976.
134. Koh 1984, 148-149.

3. DIPLOMACY

1. Kwon and Chung 2012, pp. 131–5.
2. Kim and Rim 2022.
3. Kwon and Chung 2012, pp. 131–4.
4. Kim and Rim 2022.
5. Kwon and Chung 2012, p. 134.
6. [IISH] ZH 67293: 9 October 1985. I want to thank Brooks Marmon for sharing this file with me.
7. Park 1978.
8. Shillington 2014, p. 224.
9. Koh 1969, pp. 178–84.
10. Kim 1986, p. 327.
11. [NARA] RG 59, SNF Entry# 1613-D, Box# 2420, POL 32-4 KOR—POL 16 KOR N: Kinshasa to Washington DC, 5 March 1973.
12. Kirkwood 2013, p. 551.
13. Kim 2021, pp. 272–4.
14. Van der Hoog 2024.
15. [NAUK] FCO 21/3602.

NOTES   pp. [58–63]

16. [UNAM] PA3/6/89.
17. [UNAM] PA1/14/1/1.
18. Kim 1997, pp. 54–7.
19. [NAUK] FCO 21/4436.
20. [UDSM] *Daily News*, 23 July 1989. I wish to thank Yasmina Martin for sharing this file with me.
21. Temu and Tembe 2014, p. 366 [vol. 8]; [MA] ANC Lusaka Box 4 Correspondence: ANC (SOMAFCO, Mazimbu) in Tanzania 1979–1981; 190-1981 [files 4.3 and 4.4].
22. North Korea partly used its membership of the Non-Aligned Movement to invite as many foreign delegations to Kim's birthday parties as possible. [WCDA] MOL, XIX-J-1-j Korea, 1982, 80.
23. Kwon and Chung 2012, pp. 46–8.
24. Suh 1988, pp. 262–3.
25. [SRA] MfS—HA II. Nr. 29133. Algeria established diplomatic relations with North Korea in 1958, and Mauritania in 1964.
26. Interview with an anonymous North Korean diplomat, Seoul, 19 July 2021.
27. Parts of this video can be watched on YouTube, both in English and Korean: see https://youtu.be/MgX8Je-BRrE or https://youtu.be/Tda0e-M76a8.
28. Kim 1987, p. 297.
29. Interview with an anonymous North Korean diplomat, Seoul, 19 July 2021.
30. See https://youtu.be/MgX8Je-BRrE or https://youtu.be/Tda0e-M76a8.
31. [NAUK] FCO 21/2319.
32. See https://youtu.be/MgX8Je-BRrE or https://youtu.be/Tda0e-M76a8.
33. [WCDA] BStU, MfS, HA II/10.
34. Suh 1988, p. 262.
35. Kwon and Chung 2012, p. 131.
36. Yoon 2014, p. 202.
37. Kwon and Chung 2012, p. 131.
38. See https://youtu.be/Tda0e-M76a8.
39. Scott 2018, p. 215.
40. [NAUK] FCO 106/850.
41. [NAUK] FCO 45/536; [NAUK] FCO 106/850; [NAUK] FCO 21/2527.
42. [NAUK] FCO 106/850.
43. Rotberg 2012, p. 66.
44. Kirby 2020, pp. 12–16.
45. Including Daniel Kwelagobe (Minister for Public Broadcasting and Information) and Simon Hirschfield. Manatsha 2018, p. 143.
46. Manatsha 2018.
47. Manatsha 2018.
48. [BNARS] OP.1375: Khama to Kim, 26 August 1976. I wish to thank Given Matopote for his assistance in retrieving this file.
49. Parsons et al. 1995, p. 334.

pp. [63–68]   NOTES

50. Kirby 2020, p. 15.
51. Manatsha 2018.
52. Parsons 2006, pp. 679–80.
53. Christie 1989, p. 74.
54. [NAI] PC Mozambique NLM FRELIMO: message from Machel, 25 September 1973.
55. [NAI] PC Mozambique NLM FRELIMO: message from Machel, 25 September 1973.
56. Temu and Tembe 2014, p. 357 [vol. 8].
57. Temu and Tembe 2014, p. 249 [vol. 2].
58. Machel 1985, p. 57.
59. Kim 1987, p. 145.
60. [UWC] Você da Revolução, July 1978.
61. [WCDA] TELEGRAM 066.712.
62. Tempo Magazine, available at: http://www.mozambiquehistory.net/moz-dprk.php.
63. Temu and Tembe 2014, p. 358 [vol. 8].
64. [NAUK] FCO 21/2527.
65. UN PoE S/2014/147; S/2018/171; S/2019/171.
66. Choi and Jeong 2017, p. 345. Zimbabwe's first president, Canaan Banana, visited Pyongyang in 1982 and 1983. Banana fulfilled a largely ceremonial position, while the true executive power was consolidated within Mugabe's premiership. In 1987 Mugabe took over the formal presidency. See also [IISH] ZH 67293: 25 January 1984. I wish to thank Brooks Marmon for sharing this file with me.
67. [BAB] Speech Mugabe, 9 October 1980.
68. [NAUK] FCO 36/2764.
69. Choi and Jeong 2017.
70. [BAB] Speech Mugabe, 9 October 1980.
71. Van der Hoog 2018, p. 76.
72. Van der Hoog 2019a.
73. Pyongyang Sunan International Airport, available at: https://www.pyongyang-airport.com/en/visa_on_arrival_korea.php.
74. Temu and Tembe 2014, p. 363 [vol. 8].
75. Godwin 2016; Temu and Tembe 2014, p. 47 [vol. 3]; Temu and Tembe 2014, p. 93 [vol. 9].
76. Van der Hoog 2019a, pp. 47–9.
77. [NSS] SWAPO Information Bulletin, June 1986.
78. [NAN] MFA PE/083.
79. Van der Hoog 2019a.
80. [NAUK] FCO 21/2527.
81. Wallace 2011.
82. Suh 1988, pp. 30–1; Buzo 1991, p 1.

NOTES

pp. [68–76]

83. [DARK] 18677.
84. Myers 2015.
85. [BAB] AA1.
86. Scott 2018, p. 216.
87. Some examples can be found in [UNAM] PA4/5/421.
88. Free Korea 2009. See for a full interview: https://freekorea.us/2009/05/memories-of-an-african-student-forced-to-study-in-north-korea-during-the-1980s/.
89. Macías 2013; Macías 2023.
90. Che 2015; Choi and Jeong 2017; Young 2019.

4. DOCTRINE

1. Korea Times, 27 November 2007.
2. Kwon and Chung 2012, p. 80.
3. Myers 2015, p. 5.
4. Chan 2021, p. 44; Manatsha 2018, p. 145.
5. Myers 2015, p. 5.
6. Kwon and Chung 2012.
7. [UNAM] PA3/6/117; PA4/5/421.
8. Parts of this chapter are based on Van der Hoog 2022c.
9. [UNAM] PA4/5/421: No. 45, April 1989.
10. [SRA] MfS—HA II. Nr. 29133.
11. [UNAM] PA4/5/421: No. 45, April 1989.
12. These countries include Angola, Benin, Burkina Faso, Cameroon, Chad, Congo Brazzaville, Egypt, Equatorial Guinea, Ethiopia, Gambia, Ghana, Guinea, Guinea-Bissau, Lesotho, Madagascar, Mali, Mauritius, Mozambique, Namibia, Nigeria, Senegal, Sierra Leone, Sudan, Tanzania, Togo, Tunisia, Uganda, Zaire, Zambia and Zimbabwe. [WCDA] MOL, XIX-J-1-j 1977, 24; [UNAM] PA4/5/421.
13. Interview with an anonymous North Korean diplomat, Seoul, 19 July 2021.
14. Dobrzeniecki 2019.
15. [UNAM] PA4/5/421: Vol. 2, No. 1, April 1979.
16. [UNAM] PA4/5/421: No. 48, January 1990; Vol. 2, No. 1, April 1979.
17. [NAUK] FCO 95/860: Hart to Bryan, 28 September 1970; see also Dobrzeniecki 2019.
18. [UNAM] PA4/5/421: No. 24, January 1984.
19. Quoted in Park 1978, pp. 73–88; Owoeye 1991, pp. 630–45.
20. [NLN] F001—LCA/06128; F001—LCA/01319.
21. [NAN] F002-AA/0251; [NAN] F002-PA/0805; [NARA] RG 59, SNF Entry# 1613-D, Box# 2421, POL 16 KOR N—POL KOR N-KOR S: Bujumbura to Department of State, 28 July 1971.

pp. [76–81] NOTES

22. [NARA] RG 59, SNF Entry# 1613-D, Box# 2616, POL 19 TAIWAN—POL 6 TANZAN: Dar es Salaam to Department of State, 6 November 1973.
23. Mitchell 2021, p. 225.
24. [NAUK] FCO 95/860.
25. [IISH] ZH 67293: 28 August 1985. I want to thank Brooks Marmon for sharing this file with me.
26. Roberts 2023, p. 9, 11.
27. [UNAM] PA4/5/138.
28. Young 2018, p. 106.
29. [UNAM] PA4/5/421: No. 45, April 1989.
30. [NAUK] FCO 45/1283: Anderson to Cook, 8 March 1973.
31. [NAUK] FCO 21/2319: Wenban-Smith to Elliot, 29 October 1982.
32. [UNAM] PA3/6/67; [UNAM] PA3/5/3/273.
33. Another feature of North Korean art was the deployment of performing troupes, which regularly travelled to African countries. For example, in 1975 North Korean artists visited ten African states in just six months. See Suh 1988, p. 266.
34. [NAUK] FCO 31/948; [NAUK] FCO 105/1889; [NAUK] FCO 106/850; [NAUK, FCO 36/2764.
35. [UNAM] PA4/5/421: No. 33, April 1986.
36. [NAUK] FCO 45/1283; [NARA] RG 59, SNF Entry# 1613-D, Box# 2420, POL 32-4 KOR—POL 16 KOR N: Gaborone to Department of State, 5 March 1973.
37. [NARA] RG 59, SNF Entry# 1613-C, Box# 2263, POL KOR N-AFR—POL 31-1 KOR N-US: Bamako to Department of State, 1 May 1968.
38. For example, in Young 2018, pp. 107–08.
39. Kim 1989.
40. Yoon 2014; Kim 2010, p. 13.
41. Young 2018, pp. 110–11.
42. [UNAM] PA3/6/89: Vol 5 No 2, September-December 1987.
43. [NAUK] FCO 31/692, Hart to Bryan, 17 April 1970.
44. [NARA] RG 59, SNF Entry# 1613-D, Box# 2616, POL 19 TAIWAN—POL 6 TANZAN: Dar es Salaam to Department of State, 31 March 1970.
45. [NAUK] FCO 31/692, Hart to Bryan, 17 April 1970.
46. Dobrzeniecki 2019.
47. [UNAM] PA4/5/421: No. 33, April 1986.
48. [UNAM] PA4/5/421.
49. [UNAM] PA4/5/421: No. 46, April 1989.
50. Mupawaenda 1987, pp. 44–5.
51. [UNAM] PA4/5/421: No. 40, January 1988.
52. Kwon and Chung 2012.
53. [UNAM] PA4/5/421: No. 40, January 1988.
54. Larmer 2008.

NOTES

pp. [81–89]

55. [UNAM] PA4/5/421: No. 40, January 1988.
56. [UNAM] PA4/5/421: No. 33, April 1986.
57. [UNAM] PA4/5/421: No. 33, April 1986.
58. [UNAM] PA4/5/421: Vol. 4, No. 3, October 1981.
59. [UNAM] PA4/5/421: No. 40, January 1988.
60. *The Herald*, 24 November 2017.
61. Clapham 2008, p. 364.
62. Data from 2018, see Dobrzeniecki 2019; and also www.juchea.com.
63. Hirai 2023.
64. Pambi 2023, especially pp. 177–235.

5. DEVELOPMENT

1. Parts of this chapter are based on Van der Hoog 2022d.
2. Rodney 1972, p. 285. I want to thank Moe Taylor for bringing this to my attention.
3. [UNAM] PA3/6/121.
4. Cumings 1997, p. 423.
5. Robinson 1965, p. 542.
6. [NAUK] FCO 31/948.
7. For literature on Sino-Soviet rivalry in Africa and other places during the Cold War, see Friedman 2015; Brazinsky 2017.
8. Lankov 2013, p. 19.
9. [NAUK] FCO 21/3213.
10. Mytelka 1989, p. 78.
11. Yu 2007, p. 90.
12. Szalontai 2005, pp. 63–65.
13. CIA 1978. However, it must be noted that higher production levels did not automatically result in higher living standards. I want to thank Bill Brown for his helpful suggestions on this matter.
14. Yu 2007 , p. 90.
15. Kim 1990, pp. 218–30.
16. Agarwala 2014.
17. [NAUK] FCO 21/2876.
18. [UNAM] PA4/5/421.
19. [UNAM] PA4/5/421.
20. [DARK] 25182.
21. Kim 1987, p. 10.
22. Lankov 2013, p. 75.
23. [NAUK] FCO 31/3922.
24. [NAUK] FCO 105/1889; FCO 105/2183.
25. [NAUK] FCO 31/2433.
26. [WCDA] MOL, XIX-J-1-j 1977, 24; [NAUK] FCO 21/3884.

pp. [89–93]   NOTES

27. [UWC] Você da Revolução, July 1978.
28. [UNISA] Spotlight on Zimbabwe, 1981. I want to thank Brooks Marmon for sharing this file with me.
29. [NARA] RG 59, SNF Entry# 1613-D, Box# 2420, POL 32-4 KOR—POL 16 KOR N: Lusaka to Department of State, 24 March 1972.
30. This probably concerned a rice-production scheme near Mumbwa. [NAUK] FCO 21/4124; FCO 106/850.
31. Grilli 2018.
32. [NAI] PC Regional Cooperation AAPSO. The AAPSO 'fully supported' the plans of Kim Il Sung for the reunification of the Korean peninsula and condemned the 'fascist rule' of the US government and the 'puppet clique' of the South Korean government.
33. [DARK] 1448.
34. [DARK] 25146.
35. [NAUK] FCO 31/3263; FCO 31/3674; [DARK] 8253.
36. [NARA] RG 59, SNF Entry# 1613-D, Box# 2420, POL 32-4 KOR—POL 16 KOR N: Dar es Salaam to Department of State, 22 March 1973.
37. [TNA] ACC 622 S/10/16: Ntiro, 30 May 1970 (I wish to thank Yasmina Martin for sharing this file with me); [NAUK] FCO 31/692.
38. [NARA] RG 59, SNF Entry# 1613-D, Box# 2616, POL 19 TAIWAN—POL 6 TANZAN: Dar es Salaam to Department of State, 7 April 1970.
39. [SNU] 17450.
40. [DARK] 26593.
41. [NAI] PC Tanzania NLM TANU: Arusha Declaration, 1967.
42. [DAF] 193PO/1-26. I want to thank Eric Burton for sharing this file with me.
43. [DARK] 23558; [NAUK] FCO 31/3674.
44. [NARA] RG 59, SNF Entry# 1613-D, Box# 2616, POL 19 TAIWAN—POL 6 TANZAN: Dar es Salaam to Department of State, 6 November 1973; RG 59, SNF Entry# 1613-C, Box# 2001, POL COM BLOC N—POL 2-3 COM BLOC-ZAMBIA: Dar es Salaam to Department of State, 25 January 1968.
45. [NARA] RG 59, SNF Entry# 1613-C, Box# 2263, POL KOR N-AFR—POL 31-1 KOR N-US: Dar es Salaam to Department of State, 5 August 1967.
46. [DARK] 23558.
47. British diplomatic staff observed that 'the North Koreans will no doubt continue to gain cheap credit here by providing experts to superintend projects financed from other sources'. [NAUK] FCO 21/1879.
48. [DARK] 23558.
49. [NAUK] FCO 31/3674.
50. [NAUK] FCO 21/1879; [NAUK] FCO 31/3674; [DARK] 23558.
51. [DARK] 23558.
52. [NAUK] FCO 31/3674.
53. [NARA] RG 59, SNF Entry# 1613-D, Box# 2616, POL 19 TAIWAN—POL 6 TANZAN: Dar es Salaam to Department of State, 7 April 1970.

NOTES

pp. [93–103]

54. [DARK] 6029; [UDSM] Sunday News, 1 March 1973. I wish to thank Yasmina Martin for sharing this file with me.
55. [UDSM] *Daily News*, 5 December 1988. I wish to thank Yasmina Martin for sharing this file with me.
56. [DAF] 193PO/1-26.
57. [DARK] 23558.
58. [SNU] 17450.
59. Bobiash 1992.
60. [SNU] 17450.
61. Bobiash 1992.
62. Bobiash 1992.
63. The project was further discussed during high-level meetings between the North Korean Foreign Economic Business Department and the Ghanaian State Committee for Economic Cooperation. [SNU] 17450.
64. [SNU] 17450.
65. Bobiash 1992, pp. 87–88.
66. Bobiash 1992.
67. [DARK] 23558.
68. [DARK] 28215.
69. [SNU] 17450.
70. [NAUK] FCO 31/3674.
71. Buzo 1991, pp. 204–23.
72. NK News, 19 April 2022 (b).

EPILOGUE

1. [NAN] CCO, 39/12/1/3/1; [NAI] PC Zambia Foreign Relations: transcript of interview with Mwaanga, 10 April 1975.
2. Mwaanga originally used this metaphor to defend Zambia's contacts with South Africa during the period of détente. [NAI] PC Southern Africa NLM: Shamuyarira and Leonard.
3. Myers 2015.
4. Khadiagala 1994, p. 30.
5. [NAN] CCO, 39/12/1/3/1.
6. [NAN] CCO, 39/12/1/3/1.

PROLOGUE

1. [NAI] PC South Africa NLM ANC: The African Nationalist, November 1976; [NAI] PC Namibia NLM SWAPO: statement by Hishongwa; [NAI] PC Zimbabwe NLM ZANU: Conference on the Development of Zimbabwe, 23–24 February 1979; [NAI] PC Mozambique Foreign Relations: meeting

pp. [103–112] NOTES

between Samora and Military and Security Delegation of Zimbabwe; [MA] Sechaba, April 1972.

2. Lekgoathi and Mukonde 2024, p. 32.
3. Holtland 2021.
4. 'Poem for a Militant', by Jorge Rebelo. See Moore and Beier 2007.
5. White 2009, p. 238.
6. Kwon and Chung 2012, pp. 83–4; 87–8; 101–02.
7. Kwon and Chung 2012, p. 84.
8. Jang 2014, p. 19.
9. Bermudez 1990.
10. Temu and Tembe 2014, Vol. 2, Vol. 3, Vol. 5, Vol. 6, Vol. 8.
11. On the relationship between Kim and Mao, see Shen and Xia 2018.
12. Park 1983, p. 92.

6. WAR

1. [NAI] PC South Africa Foreign Relations: Suzman, November 1978.
2. [NAI] PC South Africa Foreign Relations: Suzman, November 1978.
3. [NAI] PC History: Solana, January 1969.
4. Chan 2021, p. 40.
5. [NAI] PC Southern Africa NLM: Shamuyarira and Leonard.
6. [NAI] PC Southern Africa NLM: Shamuyarira and Leonard; speech Nyerere.
7. Walker 2019.
8. Burns, quoted in Pearson 2017, p. 526.
9. International Court of Justice, South West Africa (Liberia v. South Africa).
10. Venzke 2019, p. 13.
11. [NAI] PC Southern Africa NLM: Shamuyarira and Leonard.
12. [NAI] PC Southern Africa NLM: Shamuyarira and Leonard; speech Nyerere.
13. For a nuanced history about the ANC's deliberations about the armed struggle, see Ellis 2011.
14. [MA] Sechaba, April 1972.
15. [MA] ANC London Box 15: The building of a nation, undated.
16. [NAI] PC Southern Africa NLM: Shamuyarira and Leonard.
17. Telepneva 2022, p. 2.
18. Khadiagala 1994, p. 21.
19. [NAI] PC Southern Africa NLM: Shamuyarira and Leonard; speech Nyerere.
20. [NAI] PC Mozambique NLM FRELIMO: speech by Machel, 15 September 1978.
21. [NAI] PC Southern Africa NLM: Shamuyarira and Leonard; speech Nyerere.
22. [NAI] PC Southern Africa NLM: Shamuyarira and Leonard; speech Nyerere.
23. [NAI] PC Southern Africa NLM: Shamuyarira and Leonard; speech Nyerere.
24. [MA] ANC London Box 15: statement by Nzo, 11–13 March 1982.
25. Alexander et al. 2017, p. 3.

NOTES pp. [112–120]

26. [MA] ANC London Box 15: statement by Nzo, 11–13 March 1982.
27. Marmon 2023.
28. White 2015.
29. Wessels 2017.
30. Baines and Vale 2008.
31. Wallace 2011, p. 305.
32. Jentzsch 2022, pp. 9–10.
33. Robinson 2006, p. 329.
34. Telepneva 2022, p. 2.
35. Guimaraes 2016.
36. Miller 2013.
37. Freeman 1989.
38. Visser 2004, p. 119.
39. Douek 2020, p. 63.
40. Armstrong 1989, p. 51.
41. [NAI] PC Southern Africa NLM: Shamuyarira and Leonard; speech Nyerere.
42. Armstrong 1989, p. 51.
43. [NAI] PC Zimbabwe NLM ZANU: Zimbabwe News, November 1972.
44. [NAI] PC Tanzania Politics Nyerere: speech by Nyerere, 15 October 1970.
45. [NAI] PC History: Solana, January 1969.
46. [NAI] PC History: Solana, January 1969.
47. [NAI] PC Angola NLMA MPLA: speech by Neto, 8 September 1972.
48. [NAI] PC Zimbabwe NLM ZAPU: speech by Nkomo, March 1979.
49. [NAI] PC Tanzania Politics Nyerere: speech by Nyerere, 15 October 1970.
50. [NAI] PC Namibia NLM SWAPO: statement by Hishongwa.
51. [NAI] PC Angola NLMA MPLA: speech by Neto, December 1972.
52. Temu and Tembe 2014, p. 28 [Vol. 5].
53. Dabengwa 2017, pp. 218–19.
54. Dabengwa 2017, p. 216.
55. *The Nationalist*, 8 January 1966. I wish to thank Brooks Marmon for sharing this file with me.
56. Kim 1985, p. 346.
57. Venzke 2019, p. 13.

7. WEAPONS

1. [NAI] PC Socialism: Department of State, Current Policy No. 99, 18 October 1979.
2. Stueck 2002, p. 5.
3. Alexander et al. 2017.
4. Stueck 2002, p. 4.
5. Stueck 1995, p. 74.
6. Abebe 2019.

pp. [121–127] NOTES

7. Park 2009.
8. [NARA] RG 59, SNF Entry# 1613-C, Box# 2259, POL KENYA-SOMALI—POL 27-14 KOR: Addis Ababa to Washington DC, December 1968; Department of State to Addis Ababa, 22 January 1969.
9. [UFS] M.B.4/750. I wish to thank Brooks Marmon for sharing this file with me.
10. [NARA] RG 59, SNF Entry# A1 1613-A, Box# 3964, POL 17 Korea—POL Kuwait: Pretoria to Secretary of State, 26 June 1963; New York to Seoul, 14 September 1963.
11. Ri 2012, p. 4.
12. Van der Hoog 2022d.
13. Ri 2012, p. 7. Interestingly, South Korea did the same. The difference between both Koreas, however, is the fact that North Korea actively reached out to African states while South Korea did not. See Kwon 2020.
14. Berger 2016b, p. 36.
15. Berger 2016b.
16. [NAUK] FCO 21/3231: North Korea, arms supplies.
17. Berger 2016b.
18. [NAUK] FCO 21/3231: North Korea, arms supplies.
19. Kerkhoff 2020, p. 56.
20. [NAUK] FCO 21/3231: North Korea, arms supplies.
21. Kwon and Chung 2012, pp. 88–9; 101.
22. Armstrong 1989, p. 82.
23. Stueck 2002, p. 1.
24. Hobsbawm and Ranger 1983.
25. Kwon and Chung 2012, pp. 88–9.
26. Dabengwa 2017, p. 219.
27. [MA] ANC London Box 4: Communist call to Africa.
28. [NAI] PC Angola NLM MPLA: declaration, 4 February 1971.
29. [NAI] PC Tanzania Politics Nyerere: speech Nyerere, 15 October 1970.
30. [NAI] PC Tanzania Politics Nyerere: speech Nyerere, 21 October 1969.
31. [NAI] PC Regional Cooperation AAPSO: statement by Nwako, April 1970.
32. Sapire 2009, p. 272.
33. [MA] ANC Lusaka Box 62: message from Nzo, 1987.
34. [MA] ANC London Box 7: Shakti, July-August 1978.
35. [NAI] PC Zimbabwe NLM ZAPU: Nkomo, March 1979.
36. [NAI] PC Zambia Politics Kaunda: speech Kaunda, 14–20 August 1967.
37. [UNAM] PA1/1/5.
38. Urquhart 1991, p. 321.
39. [UNAM] PA1/1/5.
40. [MA] ANC Lusaka Box 58: Thabetha, report, 15 March 1988.
41. [NAI] PC Socialism: Department of State, Current Policy No. 99, 18 October 1979.

NOTES

pp. [127–133]

42. [MA] ANC London Box 197: *Journal of African Marxists*.
43. [NAI] PC Tanzania Politics Nyerere: speech Nyerere, 21 October 1969.
44. [NAI] PC Mozambique NLM FRELIMO: Mozambique Revolution, July-September 1974.
45. [NAI] PC Tanzania Politics Nyerere: speech Nyerere, 21 October 1969.
46. [MA] ANC London Box 7: Unity in Action.

8.   TRAINING

1. It should be noted that Nujoma's autobiography, for a large part ghost-written by Randolph Vigne, is selective. See for a thoughtful review Saunders 2003.
2. Nujoma 2001, pp. 129–31.
3. Moorcraft 2011.
4. See also White and Larmer 2014.
5. Personal correspondence with John Grobler, 23 November 2023.
6. [NARA] RG 59, SNF Entry# A1 1613-A, Box# 3999, POL 24 Nigeria—POL North Korea-US: Department of State to various posts, 30 April 1963.
7. [NARA] RG 59, SNF Entry# 1613-C, Box# 2398, POL 27-14 Korea, N-UN—POL 33-4 Korea, N-UN: Algiers to Department of State, 6 May 1965; Algiers to Department of State, 10 August 1965.
8. [NARA] RG 59, SNF Entry# 1613-C, Box# 2400, POL 2 Korea, South—POL 2-1 Korea, South: Seoul to Department of State, 28 May 1965.
9. [NARA] RG 59, SNF Entry# A1 1613-A, Box# 3964, POL 17 Korea—POL Kuwait: Paris to Secretary of State, 16 September 1963; Algiers to Secretary of State, 19 September 1963.
10. RG 59, INR, Entry# P 15, Box# 10, AFRICA MISCELLANEOUS: Bureau of Intelligence and Research, Report No. 489, 16 June 1976.
11. Mandela 1995.
12. Youcef 2014, p. 67.
13. Drew 2015, p. 28.
14. Youcef 2014.
15. Drew 2015.
16. Youcef 2014.
17. [NAI] PC Zimbabwe NLM ZAPU: History of the armed struggle in Zimbabwe.
18. Grilli 2020.
19. Drew 2015.
20. Fanon 1961.
21. Armstrong 1989, pp. 68–72.
22. Armstrong 1989, p. 85.
23. [MA] ANC Lusaka Box 58: Ronnie Kasrils, Politics and the armed struggle.
24. SWAPO 1981, p. 262.
25. [NAI] PC Zimbabwe NLM ZANU: ZANU Political Programme, 1973.
26. Melber 2009.

pp. [134–138] NOTES

27. [NAI] PC Angola NLMA MPLA: speech by Neto, December 1972.
28. [NAI] PC Zimbabwe NLM ZANU: conference 23–24 February 1979; Zimbabwe News.
29. [NAI] PC Angola NLM MPLA: report to the UN Committee on Decolonisation.
30. [NAI] PC Angola NLM FNLA: The Angola Revolution and Education.
31. SWAPO 1981, p. 262.
32. [MA] ANC London Box 9: speech, June 16th detachment of MK.
33. [MA] Dawn: Vol. 2, No. 5, November 1978.
34. Landau 2022, p. 119, 229.
35. [NAI] PC Angola NLM MPLA: Victoria ou Morte, 14 April 1973.
36. SWAPO 1981, p. 262.
37. [NAI] PC Zimbabwe Military/Special Forces: Zimbabwe People's Army, September 1976.
38. [NAI] PC Zimbabwe NLM ZANU: conference 23–24 February 1979; Zimbabwe News.
39. Bermudez 1990.
40. *The Nationalist*, 8 January 1966. I wish to thank Brooks Marmon for sharing this file with me.
41. Bermudez 1990.
42. [NAUK] FCO 31/948.
43. Interview with an anonymous North Korean diplomat, Seoul, 19 July 2021; [NAUK] FO 371/181130; [NAUK] FO 371/170810; [NAUK] FO 371/181117.
44. [NAUK] FCO 21/3231.
45. Bermudez 1990.
46. Bermudez 1990.
47. Temu and Tembe 2014, p. 181, 377 [Vol. 6].
48. This was not exceptional. In 1986, North Korean trainers were also involved in the Basutoland National Party Youth League, the ruling party of Lesotho. After the coup on 15 January 1986, which deposed of the government of Leabua Jonathan, the trainers were reported to hide in the North Korean embassy and subsequently left the country. [NAUK] FCO 31/976; [NAUK] FCO 31/3263; [NAUK] FCO 105/2183; [NAUK] FCO 105/1889; [NAUK] FCO 31/3674; [DAF] 193PO/1-26.
49. Temu and Tembe 2014, p. 356 [vol. 8].
50. [NAUK] FCO 21/5260; Bermudez 1990; Bechtol 2018.
51. Owoeye 1991, p. 641.
52. [UNAM] PA44/1/4/115.
53. [NSS] SWAPO Information Bulletin: June 1986.
54. [NAUK] FCO 21/3231.
55. Greig 1977, p. 173.
56. [UML] MUM.00767. I wish to thank Brooks Marmon for sharing this file with me.

NOTES

pp. [138–146]

57. [NAUK] FCO 31/948; [SADIRCO] 1.1191.1 (I wish to thank Stuart Doran for sharing this file with me).

58. Another guess, reported in the press and based on anonymous 'Asian diplomatic sources', estimated that 3,800 African soldiers were trained in Pyongyang between 1971 and 1981. Bermudez 1990; [SADIRCO] 1.1191.1; [DARK] 18677.

59. [DARK] 23571; footage of Zulu's visit to Pyongyang can be found on YouTube: https://www.youtube.com/watch?v=bsz8NWLQxJU.

60. [NAUK] FCO 21/3231.

61. [NAUK] FCO 21/3231; [NAUK] FCO 31/3922.

62. Armstrong 1989, p. 82; Leys and Saul 1994.

63. Trewhela 2009.

9. VICTORY

1. Kim 1984, p. 345.

2. [UNAM] PA3/6/117.

3. Bermudez 1990.

4. [NAUK] FCO 21/2319.

5. [NAUK] FCO 21/2876.

6. [NAUK] FCO 21/3231.

7. Doran 2017a, pp. viii–ix; Catholic Commission for Justice and Peace in Zimbabwe 1997.

8. Karekwaivanane 2017, p. 191.

9. [NAUK] FCO 36/2764.

10. [SADIRCO] 1.191.1.

11. [DARK] 15765.

12. [NAUK] FCO 106/464.

13. Formally the name of the army division is '5 Brigade', yet in practice the name 'Fifth Brigade' has become common. This book therefore uses the latter.

14. Doran 2017a, p. 285.

15. [NAUK] FCO 21/1988.

16. [NAUK] FCO 106/758.

17. [NAUK] FCO 106/464; [DARK] 15765.

18. [NAUK] FCO 106/464; [DARK] 15765.

19. [DARK] 15765.

20. [SADIRCO] 1.191.1; Doran 2017a, p. 283.

21. [DARK] 15765.

22. Tendi 2020, p. 201.

23. Doran 2017a, p. 285.

24. [NAUK] FCO 106/464.

25. [NAUK] FCO 21/3231.

26. [DARK] 20368.

NOTES

27. Todd 2007, p. 36.
28. Nyathi 2018, p. 50.
29. Tendi 2020, p. 203.
30. [NAUK] FCO 106/464; [DARK] 15765.
31. Catholic Commission for Justice and Peace in Zimbabwe 1997; *Daily Maverick*, 25 October 2017.
32. Doran 2017a, pp. 283–4.
33. [NAI] PC Zimbabwe NLM ZANU: speech Mugabe, 1979.
34. Werbner 1998b, p. 94.
35. Tendi 2020, p. 203.
36. Werbner 1998b, p. 94.
37. Alexander 2021, p. 763.
38. Doran 2017a, p. 429.
39. Doran 2017a, p. 283.
40. Doran 2017a, p. 434.
41. Cheeseman and Tendi 2010, p. 215.
42. Macmillan 2017.
43. Mazarire 2010, p. 97.
44. Alexander 2021, p. 763.
45. 'Outrage spreads over Gukurahundi remarks'. Available at: https://www.zimbabwesituation.com/old/oct27_2006.html.
46. *Daily Maverick*, 25 October 2017.
47. Todd 2007, p. 374; A BBC transcript including Shiri's quote is available at: http://news.bbc.co.uk/hi/english/static/audio_video/programmes/panorama/transcripts/transcript_10_03_02.txt.
48. Kwon and Chung 2012, p. 140.
49. Werbner 1998b, p. 73; see also the reporting from Zenzele Ndebele and the Genocide Against the Ndebele Memorial Centre, https://twitter.com/zenzele/status/1397470081362374656 and https://twitter.com/Gukurahundizim.
50. Doran 2017a, pp. 460–1; see also the following message from Hopewell Chin'ono: https://twitter.com/daddyhope/status/1397569773177823241.
51. [NAI] PC Mozambique NLM FRELIMO: message from Machel, 8 January 1975.
52. Southern Africa Report 1986, available at: https://www.mozambiquehistory.net/history/mbuzini/8_victims/19861200_isaacman_on_fernando_honwana.pdf.
53. [NAUK] FCO 21/2527.
54. [DARK] 9351.
55. [DARK] 20368.
56. Bermudez 1990.
57. Tendi 2020, pp. 208–09.

NOTES
pp. [151–155]

58. [NAI] PC Mozambique Military/Conflicts: The Campaign Against Zimbabwean Aggression in Mozambique.
59. Bermudez 1990.
60. [NAUK] FCO 21/3231.
61. Bermudez 1990.
62. [DARK] 11727. For more background on Soviet activities in Africa, see Shubin 2008.
63. [NAUK] FCO 21/3231; [NAUK] FCO 31/3922.
64. [NAUK] FCO 31/2433.
65. Ellis 1996, pp. 172–4.
66. Bermudez 1990.
67. [NAUK] FCO 21/3217; [NAUK] FCO 21/3231; [NAUK] FCO 31/3922.
68. [DARK] 18677.
69. [SADIRCO] 1.191.1.
70. Jonathan had declared a state of emergency following signs that his party, the Basotho National Party, was losing control over Lesotho. At the same time, South Africa pressured Jonathan because Lesotho harboured ANC-operatives. A scenario similar to the military coup in the Seychelles was a threatening prospect for Jonathan.
71. [DARK] 20368.
72. [NAUK] FCO 105/1198.
73. [NAUK] FCO 105/1198.
74. [DARK] 20368.
75. [NAUK] FCO 21/2866.
76. [NAUK] FCO 105/1198.
77. Leistner 1983, p. 209.
78. [DARK] 18677.
79. [NAUK] FCO 105/1198: Varcoe to Clemens, 6 July 1983.
80. [NAI] PC Namibia NLM SWAPO: Legum, 13 December 1989.
81. [NAUK] FCO 21/4953.
82. Doran 2017a, p. 461.
83. Doran 2017a, pp. 302–03.
84. Doran 2017a, p. 285.
85. In the early days of an independent Botswana, North Korea had stationed several unarmed combat instructors in Botswana to train local police forces, but the cooperation between both groups was unsuccessful and the Koreans returned to Pyongyang fairly soon. [BNARS] OP-1375; NAUK FCO 45/1283. See for more details about Botswana's balancing of Eastern and Western allies: Kirby 2020; Franklin 1996; [DARK] 9351.
86. Doran 2017b.
87. [NARA] RG 59, SNF Entry# 1613-C, Box# 2399, POL 27-7 Korea, N-US— POL 2 Korea, South: Dar es Salaam to Department of State, 26 January 1965.

pp. [156–165]   NOTES

88.   [NARA] RG 59, SNF Entry# 1613-C, Box# 2396, POL 17-5 Kenya-US—POL 12-6 Korea, North: Dar es Salaam to Department of State, 28 June 1966.
89.   [NARA] RG 59, SNF Entry# 1613-C, Box# 2398, POL 27-14 Korea, N-UN—POL 33-4 Korea, N-UN: Dar es Salaam to Department of State, 2 July 1966.
90.   [NAUK] FCO 21/3231.
91.   [NAUK] FCO 105/1198.
92.   [NAUK] FCO 106/464: Henshaw to MacKellar, 11 September 1981.
93.   [NAUK] FCO 106/850.
94.   Owoeye 1991, p. 642.
95.   [NAUK] FCO 106/850.
96.   [DARK] 20368.
97.   [NAUK] FCO 106/850.
98.   Scott 2018, p. 211.
99.   Davidson 1992, p. 190.
100. Harrison 2023.

10.   SURVIVAL

1.   Melber 2002.
2.   Melber 2010, p. 42.
3.   Ranger 2004; Ndhlovu 2021.
4.   Kriger 2005.
5.   Blaauw and Zaire 2023.
6.   Blaauw and Zaire 2023, p. 3.
7.   UN PoE S/2014/147.
8.   Parts of this chapter are based on Van der Hoog 2022b.
9.   UN PoE S/2010/571.
10.   Berger 2016b; Ballbach 2022.
11.   Kim Yong Nam was President of the Presidium of the Supreme People's Assembly and previously served as the Minister of Foreign Affairs. [SNU] Vantage Point: Vol. 31, No. 4, April 2008.
12.   Bechtol 2018, p. 55.
13.   Berger 2016b, p. 62.
14.   Berger 2016b.
15.   UN PoE S/2016/157.
16.   UN PoE S/2014/147.
17.   While Tanzania reported that it had terminated their business relationship with Haegeumgang in 2014, it was alleged by the UN that the military cooperation was resumed in 2016. UN PoE S/2018/171.
18.   UN PoE S/2019/171.
19.   UN PoE S/2017/150; UN PoE S/2018/171; UN PoE S/2019/171.

NOTES

pp. [165–169]

20. UN PoE S/2018/171.
21. UN PoE S/2017/150.
22. UN PoE S/2019/171.
23. UN PoE S/2016/157.
24. It seems that Green Pine was using Angola as a base for international operations, as several North Korean diplomats in Angola travelled multiple times to Sri Lanka in order to discuss the building and sale of naval patrol vessels. UN PoE S/2017/150.
25. UN PoE S/2019/171.
26. UN PoE S/2018/171.
27. Van der Hoog 2019a.
28. UN PoE S/2016/157.
29. UN PoE S/2017/150.
30. UN PoE S/2016/157.
31. UN PoE S/2018/171; UN PoE S/2019/171.
32. Bechtol 2018, p. 118.
33. UN PoE S/2013/337.
34. Interview with an anonymous North Korean diplomat, Seoul, 19 July 2021.
35. Interview with an anonymous North Korean diplomat, Seoul, 19 July 2021.
36. Interview with an anonymous North Korean diplomat, Seoul, 19 July 2021.
37. UN PoE S/2015/131.
38. Interview with an anonymous North Korean diplomat, Seoul, 19 July 2021.
39. Berger 2016b, p. 8.
40. UN PoE S/2015/131.
41. [SNU] Vantage Point: Vol. 23, No. 5, May 2000; Chestnut 2007.
42. UN PoE S/2016/157.
43. Bechtol 2019; UN PoE S/2021/211.
44. UN PoE S/2013/337.
45. UN PoE S/2013/337.
46. The Sentry 2020.
47. UN PoE S/2015/131. These findings concur with our recent investigations on North Korean forced labour around the world, see Breuker and Van Gardingen 2018.
48. [SNU] Vantage Point: Vol. 36, No. 4, April 2013; UN PoE S/2020/151.
49. Young 2021b.
50. Ko 2022.
51. UN PoE S/2014/147.
52. UN PoE S/2012/422.
53. Berger 2016b; Bechtol 2018; UN PoE S/2023/171.
54. UN PoE S/2014/147.
55. UN PoE S/2014/147.
56. See for a comprehensive summary: UN PoE S/2010/571.
57. UN PoE S/2015/131.

pp. [169–181]   NOTES

58. UN PoE S/2020/151.
59. Berger 2016b, p. 8.
60. Van der Hoog 2019a, pp. 47-49.
61. Berger 2016a, p. 101.
62. Museveni 1997, p. 32.
63. Berger 2016a, p. 105.
64. UN PoE S/2014/147.
65. Berger 2016b, p. 46.
66. Berger 2016a, p. 116.
67. Berger 2016a, p. 120.
68. Mallory 2021.
69. UN PoE S/2015/131.
70. UN PoE S/2015/131.
71. UN PoE S/2010/571.
72. UN PoE S/2010/571.
73. UN PoE S/2012/422.
74. PPLAAF, available at: https://www.pplaaf.org/whistleblowers/koko-malela.html#.
75. Ellis 2002, p. 26.
76. Southall 2013.
77. [NAI] PC Angola NLM MPLA: speech Neto, December 1972.
78. NK News, 31 March 2022 (a).
79. UN PoE S/2022/132.
80. NK News, 1 November 2023.
81. UN PoE S/2024/215.

EPILOGUE

1. [NAI] PC Zimbabwe NLM ZANU: speech Mugabe, 1979.
2. Doran 2017a, p. 284.
3. [MA] ANC London Box 4, SACP, Inkululeko—Freedom, April 1975.
4. Catholic Commission for Justice and Peace in Zimbabwe 1997.
5. [NAI] PC Namibia NLM SWAPO: SWAPO Educational Political Calendar, 1988.
6. UN PoE S/2014/147.
7. UN PoE S/2017/150.

PROLOGUE

1. Van der Hoog 2018.
2. *The Guardian*, 4 April 2010.
3. Chan 2021, pp. 160–1; Diop 2000; Bongmba 2004.

285

NOTES

pp. [181–190]

4. VOA, 12 January 2023; see also Un PoE S2020/840 for information about a statue of Akhosu Behanzin.
5. The subtitle of this prologue, 'A Monumental Relationship', is borrowed from Van der Hoog 2023.
6. Bechtol 2018; Young 2021a.
7. Werbner 1998a, p. 7.
8. Yoon 2014, p. 140.
9. Todorović 2022.
10. PoE S/2017/150; Che 2022.
11. Kirkwood 2013.
12. Kirkwood 2013; Van der Hoog 2018; Kornes 2019; Che 2022.
13. In recent years, several texts have emerged that illuminate the relationship between North Korean art and political indoctrination. See Portal 2005; Kim 2010; Myers 2010; Kwon and Chung 2012; Frank 2012; Meuser 2012; Ryang 2012; Yoon 2014.
14. UN PoE S/2017/150; S/2018/171; S/2019/171.
15. One of the artists who worked on the mausoleum of Agonstinho Neto in Angola also worked at the Angkor Panorama Museum in Cambodia. El Periódico, 22 December 2015.
16. Kim 2014; Cho 2018; Chang 2020.
17. Cho 2018.
18. This final part of the book builds on Van der Hoog 2019a.
19. 'Poem of Return', by Jofre Rocha. See Moore and Beier 2007.
20. Costa 2013, p. 141.
21. This comparison derives much inspiration from Kwon and Chung 2012.

11. MYTH

1. Pohamba 2014; Wallace 2011.
2. Ang 2017, pp. 1–2; Williams and Mazarire 2019, p. 1809.
3. Baas 2022, p. 51.
4. Van der Hoog 2019b.
5. Indeed, one could argue that it is precisely the pariah status that makes North Korea so attractive to SWAPO.
6. Silvester 2015.
7. [UNAM] PA1/16/8/15; [NAN] A.0570, 4/1, A04.4C.003: Windhoek Advertiser, 12 July 1974; Potgieter 2007.
8. Van der Hoog 2019a, pp. 22–4. In Namibia, Peter Katjavivi is a fitting example.
9. Ranger 2004, p. 224.
10. Pohamba 2014.
11. Elago 2015, p. 289.
12. Williams and Mazarire 2019, p. 1810.
13. *Allgemeine Zeitung*, 8 December 2011.

pp. [190–197]   NOTES

14. *Allgemeine Zeitung*, 10 October 2013; *Die Republikein*, 31 March 2014.
15. Williams and Mazarire 2019, p. 1811.
16. Adedze 1995, p. 58.
17. Schildkrout 1995, p. 67.
18. Williams and Mazarire 2019, pp. 1809–10.
19. Zuern 2012, p. 494.
20. *Allgemeine Zeitung*, 23 October 2009; *Die Republikein*, 18 October 2013; *Die Republikein* 23 April 2014.
21. Steiner 1995, pp. 3–6.
22. *The Namibian*, 4 April 2014; *The Namibian*, 1 October 2014.
23. Becker 2020, p. 368.
24. Kangumu 2011.
25. Schildkrout 1995, p. 65.
26. Silvester 2015.
27. Ranger 2004, p. 218.
28. Ranger 2004.
29. Kriger 2006.
30. Ranger 2004, p. 218.
31. Tendi 2010.
32. Song 2011, p. 176.
33. Phimister 2012.
34. Ranger 2004, p. 232.
35. Schubert 2015, pp. 839–40.
36. Kwon and Chung, 2012, pp. 15–18, 30.
37. Zeller 2008, p. 231.
38. Pohamba 2014.
39. Baas 2022, p. 57.
40. Kwong and Chung 2012, p. 112.

12. NATIONS

1. Martins and Cardina 2019.
2. Ball 2019, p. 830.
3. Pearce 2015, p. 111.
4. Martins and Cardina 2019, p. 47.
5. Macpherson 1974, p. 453.
6. Melber 2009, pp. 456–8.
7. SWAPO 1981.
8. Becker 2015, pp. 29–30.
9. Suttner 2008, pp. 138–43.
10. [SEA] 2.5.4.3: Lisa Distelheim, 30 October 1986.
11. Suttner 2008, pp. 138–43.
12. [NAI] PC South Africa NLM ANC: press statement, Josiah Jele.

287

NOTES   pp. [198–203]

13. [NAI] PC Namibia NLM SWAPO: SWAPO statement, 26 August 1986.
14. [NAI] PC Mozambique NLM FRELIMO: report by Armando Gueboza.
15. [NAI] PC Angola NLM MPLA: speech by Alexandre Rodrigues 'Kito', 4 February 1987.
16. Pearce 2015, p. 112.
17. Lee Moon-Woong, quoted in Kwon and Chung 2012, p. 18.
18. Cumings 1997, p. 11.
19. Armstrong 2004, p. 222.
20. Kwon and Chung 2012, p. 26.
21. Kim 2010, p. 173.
22. Kwon and Chung 2012, p. 26.
23. Kwon and Chung 2012, pp. 60–1.
24. Kim 2010, p. 6, 166, 176.
25. Yoon 2014, p. 33.
26. Suttner 2008, p. 135.
27. Douek 2020, pp. 303–07.
28. Phimister 2012, p. 1.
29. Leys and Saul 1994; Trewhela 2009.
30. [NAI] PC Zambia Politics Kaunda: speech, 8 May 1971.
31. Gordon 2008, pp. 45–76.
32. [NAI] PC Zambia Politics Kaunda: speech, 4–6 March 1972.
33. Kwon and Chung 2012, p. 15.
34. Kim 2010, p. 194.
35. Gewald et al. 2008, p. 9.
36. Zeller and Melber 2019.
37. Yoon 2014, p. 141.
38. Martins and Cardina 2019.
39. Martins and Cardina 2019.
40. Martins and Cardina 2019, p. 47.
41. [UNAM] PA3/3/1/1: SWAPO Information and Publicity Department, approx. 1979.
42. Birmingham 1978.
43. Martins and Cardina 2019; Ball 2019, p. 831.
44. Pearce 2015, p. 112.
45. Martins and Cardina 2019, p. 59.
46. Pearce 2015, p. 103.
47. [UNAM] PA1/14/1/1: Namibia Today.
48. Ministry of Information, quoted in Werbner 1988, p. 77.
49. Ndlovu-Gatsheni 2012, p. 1.
50. Martins and Cardina 2019, p. 63.
51. Kim 2010, p. 18.

pp. [205–211]   NOTES

13. VIOLENCE

1. Van der Hoog 2019a, p. 33.
2. Martins and Cardina 2019, p. 48.
3. Van der Hoog 2019a, pp. 28–9; Becker 2011, pp. 523–7; Park 2021.
4. The Battle of Ismailia Monument is a gift from North Korea to Egypt. During the Yom Kippur War of 1973, North Korean pilots aided Egyptian armed forces. *New York Times*, 3 March 2018.
5. Werbner 1988, p. 77.
6. Ndlovu-Gatsheni 2007, p. 173.
7. Van der Hoog 2019a, pp. 67–8.
8. Ranger 1968.
9. [MA] ANC London Box 7: Unity in Action.
10. [MA] ANC London Box 4: SACP, Inkululeko—Freedom, No. 1, July 1971.
11. Just as the ANC mythologises Blood River, so did the Nasionale Party through the Voortrekker Monument in Pretoria.
12. [MA] ANC London Box 15, speech Oliver Tambo, 16 December 1980.
13. [NAI] PC South Africa NLM ANC: press statement, Josiah Jele.
14. [MA] ANC London Box 15, speech Oliver Tambo, 16 December 1980.
15. [MA] ANC Lusaka Box 8, speech Oliver Tambo, January 1979.
16. [MA] ANC Lusaka Box 8, NEC directive.
17. Ellis 2011.
18. [MA] ANC London Box 15, speech Oliver Tambo, 16 December 1980.
19. [NAI] PC South Africa NLM ANC: ANC statement, 26 June 1969.
20. SWAPO 1981, pp. 151–76.
21. [NAI] PC Namibia NLM SWAPO: SWAPO Educational Political Calendar, 1988.
22. SWAPO 1981, p. 231.
23. [NAI] Tanzania NLM TANU.
24. Ndlovu-Gatsheni 2012.
25. Van der Hoog 2019a, pp. 32–5; Werbner 1998b, pp. 84–5.
26. Van der Hoog 2019a, p. 32.
27. Ndlovu-Gatsheni 2012, pp. 2–3.
28. Phimister 2012, p. 2; Tendi 2010, p. 4.
29. Werbner 1998b, p. 91.
30. Van der Hoog 2019a, p. 33.
31. Ranger 2004, p. 219.
32. Van der Hoog 2019a, pp. 28–37; see also [NAN] AACRLS.023.
33. Kim 2010, p. 183.
34. Kwon and Chung 2012, pp. 103–21.
35. Yoon 2014.
36. Song 2011, p. 159; Wada 2013.
37. Denney et al. 2016.

NOTES

38. Kwon and Chung 2012, pp. 88–90.
39. Kwon and Chung 2012, pp. 75–87.
40. Kwon and Chung 2012, p. 85.
41. Kwon and Chung 2012, p. 91.
42. Becker 2020, p. 368.
43. Kwon and Chung 2012, p. 189.
44. Werbner 1998b, p. 75.
45. Pohamba 2014.
46. For a Zimbabwean case study, see Kriger 2006, p. 1154.

14. HEROISM

1. Jopela 2017.
2. UN PoE S/2017/150.
3. AsiaNews, 25 March 2014; Bloomberg, 27 March 2014.
4. Werbner 1998a, p. 8.
5. Suttner 2008, p. 121.
6. Jopela 2017, pp. 344–9.
7. Kwon and Chung 2012, p. 143.
8. Werbner 1998a, p. 8.
9. Melber 2009, pp. 456–8.
10. [UNAM] PA3/3/1/1: SWAPO Information and Publicity Department, approx. 1979.
11. Martins and Cardina 2019; Kwon and Chung 2012, p. 72.
12. Kwon and Chung 2012, pp. 72–3.
13. [NAN] AACRLS.023: The Patriot, 2 August 2018.
14. [NAI] PC Zambia Politics Kaunda: Speech, 1–3 December 1972.
15. Werbner 1998b, pp. 72–3.
16. Martins and Cardina 2019, p. 61.
17. Radio Free Asia, 28 March 2022.
18. Xinhua, 28 February 2020.
19. Werbner 1998b, pp. 86–9.
20. Kriger 1995.
21. Suttner 2008, pp. 105–08, 116, 349.
22. Suttner 2008, p. 112.
23. Kim 2010, p. 173.
24. Melber 2009, p. 457.
25. Suttner 2008, pp. 107–18.
26. Werbner 1998b, p. 84.
27. Kim 2010, p. 6, 166, 176.
28. Kwon and Chung 2012, pp. 114–15.
29. Suttner 2008, pp. 121–9.
30. Jopela 2017, p. 299.

pp. [221–230]

NOTES

31. Ironically, Machel disliked a North Korean-style cult of personality during his lifetime. Albino Jopela notes how 'Samora is celebrated in the same way that he strongly opposed during his life'. See Jopela 2017, p. 351.
32. Kwon and Chung 2012, pp. 71–2.
33. Kwon and Chung 2012, p. 26, 183.
34. Kwon and Chung 2012, p. 114.
35. Kwon and Chung 2012, p. 4.
36. Yoon 2014, p. 146.
37. Kwon and Chung 2012, pp. 22–4.
38. Kwon and Chung 2012, p. 49.
39. Kwon and Chung 2012, p. 44.
40. Kwon and Chung 2012, pp. 4–5; Breuker 2018.
41. Howard 2020, p. 3.
42. Myers 2015.
43. Kwon and Chung 2012, pp. 4–5.
44. Kwon and Chung 2012, p. 83, 95.
45. Geingob 2015, speech is available on Facebook at: https://www.facebook.com/DrHageGeingob/posts/my-first-heroes-day-speech-as-president-of-the-republic-of-namibia-heroes-acre-n/522485504574611/.
46. Geingob 2015, speech is available on Facebook at: https://www.facebook.com/DrHageGeingob/posts/my-first-heroes-day-speech-as-president-of-the-republic-of-namibia-heroes-acre-n/522485504574611/.
47. Werbner 1998b, p. 90.
48. *The Namibian*, 16 February 2024; *The Namibian*, 22 February 2024.
49. Snyder 2017, pp. 121–4,
50. Kwon and Chung 2012, pp. 72–3.
51. Snyder 2017, pp. 121–4.

15. MONEY

1. NK News, 24 May 2023.
2. Parts of this chapter are based on Van der Hoog 2022b.
3. Baas 2022, p. 64.
4. UN PoE S/2017/150.
5. [NAN] AACRLS.023: *The Namibian*, 5 July 2002; *The Namibian*, 6 May 2005; *The Namibian*, 19 October 2006.
6. UN PoE S/2017/150.
7. UN PoE S/2017/150.
8. UN PoE S/2016/156; UN PoE S/2017/150; UN PoE S/2022/132.
9. UN PoE S/2014/147.
10. UN PoE S/2017/150.
11. UN PoE S/2024/215.
12. UN PoE S/2017/150.

NOTES

pp. [230–236]

13. UN PoE S/2024/215.
14. Breuker and Van Gardingen 2016.
15. Van der Hoog 2018.
16. UN PoE S/2017/150.
17. UN PoE S/2020/151.
18. UN resolution 2321 (2016), in particular article 29.
19. NK News, 22 December 2019.
20. UN PoE S/2017/150.
21. UN PoE S/2018/171.
22. UN PoE S2019/171.
23. NK News, 5 August 2020.
24. NK News, 24 May 2023.
25. The Sentry 2020; The Sentry 2021.
26. UN PoE S/2021/211.
27. UN PoE S/2015/131.
28. UN PoE S/2017/150.
29. Rademeyer 2017.
30. Breuker 2018.
31. Salisbury 2021, pp. 313–30.
32. Interview with an anonymous North Korean diplomat, Seoul, 19 July 2021.
33. *New York Times*, 7 October 2017; Reuters, 8 November 2017; Reuters, 28 January 2020; see also UN PoE S/2018/171, especially pp. 75–7.
34. Chestnut 2007; Rademeyer 2017.
35. [SADIRCO] 1.191.1.
36. [NAUK] FCO 21/412: Smith to Broomfield, 11 December 1989.
37. [SNU] Vantage Point, Vol. 23, No. 5, May 2000; Chestnut 2007, pp. 80–111.
38. Rademeyer 2016, pp. 23–7.
39. UN PoE S/2024/215.
40. Berger 2016b, p. 8.
41. See also Van der Hoog 2022b, pp. 7–8.

EPILOGUE

1. *The Namibian*, 8 June 2023.
2. Ekandjo's proposal subverts the Namibian constitution and a recent ruling of the Namibian Supreme Court. The Namibian, 10 July 2023.
3. [NAI] PC Namibia NLM SWAPO: LSM Information Center, 1973.
4. [NAI] PC Zimbabwe NLM ZANU: speech Robert Mugabe, 1979.
5. [NAI] PC Mozambique NLM FRELIMO: speech Samora Machel, 8 January 1975.
6. [NAI] PC South Africa NLM ANC: Guerrilla Warfare, August 1970; [MA] Sechaba: Vol. 4, No. 4, April 1970.
7. [MA] ANC Lusaka Box 66: Ngcobo to Nzo, February 1990.

pp. [236–241]   NOTES

8. [MA] Sechaba: Vol. 4, No. 4, April 1970; ANC Lusaka Box 62: Tambo to Dos Santos, undated; Tambo to Mwinyi, undated; Tambo to Kaunda, undated.

9. [MA] ANC London Box 44: MPLA Partido do Trabalho, undated; [MA] ANC Lusaka Box 71: meeting between ANC and SWAPO, 27 January 1989; ANC Lusaka Box 62: Mabizela to Kawawa, 9 October 1987.

10. Werbner 1998a, p. 1.

11. Knox 1994; Borman 1960, p. 51; Steiner 1975, p. 157.

12. Temu and Tembe 2014; Saunders 2017; Limb 2018; see also Jopela 2017, pp. 195–258; [UNESDOC] 0000154025; African Liberation Museum, available at: https://www.africanliberation.museum/. The Hashim Mbita Project contains a section on North Korea, written by Alicia Altorfer-Ong (see Temu and Tembu 2014, vol. 8, pp. 342–67.

13. Werbner 1998a, p. 8.

14. [NAN] AACRLS.023; Werbner 1998b.

15. Atlas Obscura, 25 August 2014.

16. *BBC News*, 16 February 2016.

17. Melber 2004.

CONCLUSION

1. [NAI] PC Mozambique NLM FRELIMO: speech Machel, 20 September 1974; PC Zimbabwe NLM ZANU: ZANU 1976; speech Mugabe 1 January 1978; PC Angola NLM MPLA: speech Dos Santos, 27 July 1983.

2. Suttner 2008, p. 137.

3. Bartels et al. 2023, p. 1.

4. Bartels et al. 2023, p. 5.

5. Arriola et al. 2022.

6. Wimmer and Schiller 2003.

7. Melber 2004; Southall 2013; Blaauw and Zaire 2023.

8. Speech available via the X (Twitter) account of *The Namibian*: https://twitter.com/TheNamibian/status/1574364951438925824.

9. Melber 2020; Melber 2021, p. 142.

10. *Al Jazeera*, 4 November 2021.

11. *BBC News*, 29 August 2022.

12. [NAI] PC Mozambique NLM FRELIMO: speech Machel, 20 september 1974.

13. Phimister 2012, p. 27.

14. [NAI] PC Zambia Politics Kaunda: speech Kaunda, 1 December 1972.

15. [NAI] PC Zambia Politics Kaunda: speech Kaunda, 7–10 November 1970.

16. [NAI] PC Zambia Politics Kaunda: speech Kaunda, 1 December 1972; Mushingeh 1993.

17. Kriger 2005.

18. Elijah Ngurare, quoted in Melber 2009, p. 454.

19. *The Namibian*, 25 April 2022.

NOTES

20. *Namibian Sun*, 31 July 2023.
21. Melber 2009.
22. Blaauw and Zaire 2023, p. 12.
23. [NAI] PC Namibia NLM SWAPO: SWAPO Educational Political Calendar, 1988.
24. [NAI] PC Zimbabwe NLM ZANU: speech Mugabe 1 January 1978.
25. [NAI] PC Zimbabwe NLM ZANU: 'Call to all Africans of Zimbabwe', 19 June 1964.
26. [NAI] PC Mozambique NLM FRELIMO: speech Machel, 26 April 1984.
27. [SNU] 17450.
28. Owoeye 1991, p. 635.
29. Kim 1996, p. 90.
30. [NAUK] FCO 21/4124.
31. [UNAM] PA4/5/421: No. 40, January 1988.
32. [NAI] PC Angola NLM MPLA: Speech Neto, December 1972.
33. [NAI] PC Zambia Politics Kaunda: speech Kaunda, 8 May 1971.
34. See the 'Cry Freedom: Trends of Repression and Resistance in Five African Countries' investigative project of ZAM, in particular Malaba 2023.
35. *Taipei Times*, 18 August 2009.
36. *The Jakarta Post*, 13 June 2023.
37. *Ukrainska Pravda*, 24 May 2023.
38. Blaauw and Zaire 2023,
39. Werbner 1998a, p. 8.
40. Kwon and Chung 2012, pp. 2–3.
41. Kwon and Chung 2012, p. 127.
42. This section is inspired by the field of historical institutionalism. See Sanders 2009, p. 39 and Erdmann et al. 2011.
43. Thelen 1999, p. 387.
44. Bartels et al. 2023, pp. 4–5.
45. Nganje 2016, p. 154, referring to Steinmo.
46. Thelen 1999, p. 388.
47. Kickert and Van der Meer 2011, pp. 476–7.
48. Gyimah-Boadi 2015, p. 101.
49. Getachew 2019.
50. UN PoE S/2017/150; S/2016/157; S/2010/571.

NOTE ON ARCHIVES

1. [SRA] MfS—Sekr. Mittig. Nr. 98
2. Marmon 2022.
3. Van der Hoog 2022a; Breckenridge 2014.
4. Pritchard 2019.

pp. [253–256]   NOTES

5. *The Washington Post*, 7 May 2019.
6. Van der Hoog 2022a. See for example [NAN] MFA, PE/082; MFA, PE/083.
7. [BNARS] OP.1375.
8. [NAN] MFA PE/082; [NAN] MFA PE/083.
9. Alexander et al. 2017, p. 3.
10. The UNIP Archives are now digitised through the Endangered Archives Programme with the British Library, but I also visited the physical archives in Lusaka (Zambia), in 2014.
11. Alexander et al. 2020, p. 823.
12. [BAB] AA.3.
13. Van der Hoog 2022e.
14. Van der Hoog and Moore 2022.
15. Myers 2015.
16. [DARK] 8186; [DARK] 7013.

PRIMARY SOURCES

Basler Afrika Bibliographien [BAB], Switzerland
AA.1   Bilaterale Beziehungen.
AA.3   SWAPO Collection.
PA.48   Tony Emmett, Kozonguizi Documents, No 4: Kozonguizi, J.: The
              Namibian political situation. Undated (circa 1975).
PA.48   Tony Emmett, Kozonguizi Documents, No 5: Kozonguizi, J.:
              Brief outline of the history and international action by Namibians.
              January 1976.
Policy Statement No. 1, Prime Minister Addresses State Banquet in North Korea,
    9 October 1980.

Bodleian Libraries [BL], University of Oxford, United Kingdom
MSS. AAM 2323   Jamaica, Japan, Kenya, Democratic Peoples' Republic
                       of Korea, Laos, Lesotho, Liberia, Luxembourg, Malawi,
                       Malaysia, Malta, Morocco, Mozambique, Namibia, the
                       Netherlands, New Zealand, Nigeria, Pakistan, Peru,
                       Poland, Portugal, Rumania, Senegal, Spain, Sudan,
                       Sweden, Swaziland, Switzerland, Tanzania, United Arab
                       Republic, Union of Soviet Socialist Republics, Venezuela,
                       Vietnam, Zaire, Zambia and Zimbabwe, 1961–1995.

Botswana National Archives and Records Services [BNARS]
OP.1375   North Korea.

Diplomatic Archives of France [DAF]
193PO/1-26   Ministère des Affaires Étrangères, Dar es Salam, Ambassade, 1961–
                 1977.

297

PRIMARY SOURCES

Diplomatic Archives of the Republic of Korea [DARK]

11727	북한·아프리카 관계, 1978. 전2권 (V.2 남동아프리카).
15765	북한의 대짐바브웨 군사고문단 파견, 1981.
18677	북한·동부아프리카 관계, 1983.
20368	북한·아프리카지역 관계, 1983–84.
23558	북한·탄자니아 관계, 1985–86.
23571	북한·동부아프리카 관계, 1986.
25146	북한 일반(대내외 동향), 1987.
26593	북한·가나 관계, 1987–88.
28215	북한.가나 관계, 1989.
6029	북한 · 탄자니아 관계.
8253	북한·탄자니아 관계.
9351	북한의 대 아프리카지역 국가 군사 및 경제 원조 현황.
8186	북한 · 보츠나와 관계.
7013	북한 · 보츠와나 관계.
1448	AAPSO (아·아인민단결기구)회의, 제4차. Accra(가나) 1965.5.9-16.
25089	북한.말라위 관계, 1982–87.
25166	남남협력에 관한 비동맹 특별 각료회의. 평양, 1987.6.9-6.13. 전17권 (V.1 기본대책).
25182	남남협력에 관한 비동맹 특별 각료회의. 평양, 1987.6.9-6.13. 전17권 (V.17).

International Institute of Social History [ISSH],The Netherlands
ZH 67293   The People's Weekly.

JSTOR Primary Sources [JSTOR], Struggles for Freedom: Southern Africa
Zimbabwe News, Vol. 18, No. 11, 1987.

Mayibuye Archives [MA], South Africa

ANC London Box 4	SACP: Underground Publications Etc. (1960s–1980s)
ANC London Box 7	ANC: Internal Propaganda (1960s–1980s)
ANC London Box 9	ANC: Internal Propaganda (1972–1979)
ANC London Box 15	ANC: General (1971–1988)
ANC London Box 44	Armed Struggle Etc. (Bibliographies) (1970s–1980s)
ANC London Box 197	Documents (1977–1984).
ANC Lusaka Box 4	Correspondence.
ANC Lusaka Box 8	Documents (ANC General; 1977–1982)
ANC Lusaka Box 46	Organisations Information Conference (Various).
ANC Lusaka Box 58	Departments of Political Education and Health (1986–1990)

PRIMARY SOURCES

ANC Lusaka Box 62   Department of International Affairs + Relations With African Countries (1986–1991).

ANC Lusaka Box 63   International Relations: International Organisations (1986–1990)

ANC Lusaka Box 65   International Relations: America and Asia (1986–199).

ANC Lusaka Box 66   Political Military Council/Department of National Intelligence And Security (1985–1987).

ANC Lusaka Box 71   SACP, SWAPO and PAC (1986–1991).

Dawn (periodicals)

Sechaba (periodicals)

Namibia Scientific Society [NSS]

SWAPO Information Bulletin (periodicals).

National Archives and Records Administration [NARA], United States

NARA RG 59, INR, Entry# P 15, Box# 10, AFRICA MISCELLANEOUS.

RG 59, SNF Entry# 1613-C, Box# 2001, POL COM BLOC N—POL 2-3 COM BLOC-ZAMBIA.

RG 59, SNF Entry# 1613-C, Box# 2259, POL KENYA-SOMALI—POL 27-14 KOR.

RG 59, SNF Entry# 1613-C, Box# 2260, POL 32-4 KOR—POL 32-4 KOR/UN.

RG 59, SNF Entry# 1613-C, Box# 2261, POL 32-4 KOR/UN—POL KOR N.

RG 59, SNF Entry# 1613-C, Box# 2261, POL 32-4 KOR/UN—POL KOR N.

RG 59, SNF Entry# 1613-C, Box# 2262, POL 7 KOR N—POL 7 KOR N.

RG 59, SNF Entry# 1613-C, Box# 2263, POL KOR N-AFR—POL 31-1 KOR N-US.

RG 59, SNF Entry# 1613-C, Box# 2396, POL 17-5 Kenya-US—POL 12-6 Korea, North.

RG 59, SNF Entry# 1613-C, Box# 2397, POL 14 Korea, N—POL 27-14 Korea, N-UN.

RG 59, SNF Entry# 1613-C, Box# 2398, POL 27-14 Korea, N-UN—POL 33-4 Korea, N-UN.

RG 59, SNF Entry# 1613-C, Box# 2399, POL 27-7 Korea, N-US—POL 2 Korea, South.

RG 59, SNF Entry# 1613-C, Box# 2400, POL 2 Korea, South—POL 2-1 Korea, South.

RG 59, SNF Entry# 1613-C, Box# 2405, POL 15-2 Korea, South—POL 23-8 Korea, South.

RG 59, SNF Entry# 1613-C, Box# 2406, POL 23-9 Korea, South—POL 32-4 Korea, S-UN.

RG 59, SNF Entry# 1613-D, Box# 2420, POL 32-4 KOR—POL 16 KOR N.

RG 59, SNF Entry# 1613-D, Box# 2421, POL 16 KOR N—POL KOR N-KOR S.

PRIMARY SOURCES

RG 59, SNF Entry# 1613-D, Box# 2423, POL KOR N-US—POL 7 KOR S.
RG 59, SNF Entry# 1613-D, Box# 2616, POL 19 TAIWAN—POL 6 TANZAN.
RG 59, SNF Entry# A1 1613-A, Box# 3964, POL 17 Korea—POL Kuwait.
RG 59, SNF Entry# A1 1613-A, Box# 3999, POL 24 Nigeria—POL North Korea-US.
RG 59, SNF Entry# A1 1613-A, Box# 4040, POL 26 South Korea—POL S Korea-US.

National Archives of Namibia [NAN]

A.0570 4/1A04.4C.003	News cuttings: Namibia Liberation Struggle—Foreign Relations.
AACRLS.023	Heroes Acre.
CCO 39/12/1/3/1	Vredesoffensief in Afrika/Zambia, 1975.
CCO 39/12/1/3/2	Vredesoffensief in Afrika/Tanzania/Koerant uitknipsels, 1975–1976.
F002-AA/0251	Basiese beginsels van die opbou van die revolusionere party: verhandeling geskryf ter geleentheid van die 47ste herdenking van die stigting van die Werkersparty van Korea/Kim Jong Il;
F002-PA/0805	Die historiese les van die opbou van sosialisme en ons party se algeme lyn : toespraak voor die senior amptenare van die Sentrale Komitee van die Werkersparty van Korea, 3 Januarie 1992 / Kim Jong Il;
MFA PE/082	Bilateral relations with Korea democratic people republic, 1990–1992.
MFA PE/083	Bilateral relations with South Korea / Bilateral relations with Korea republic, 1990–1991.

National Archives of the United Kingdom [NAUK]

FCO 105/1198	Relations between Lesotho and communist countries and South Korea.
FCO 105/1889	Bilateral relations between Lesotho and communist countries.
FCO 105/2183	Relations between Lesotho and communist countries.
FCO 105/828	Relations between Malawi and North Korea.
FCO 106/464	Military assistance to Zimbabwe from North Korea.
FCO 106/758	Political relations between Zimbabwe and communist countries.
FCO 106/850	Political relations between Zambia and communist countries.

PRIMARY SOURCES

FCO 141/14087 — Northern Rhodesia: survey of communist activities in Africa.

FCO 21/1879 — Foreign policy of North Korea.

FCO 21/1988 — Foreign policy of North Korea.

FCO 21/2319 — Relations between North Korea and countries other than the UK.

FCO 21/2527 — Relations between North Korea and other countries.

FCO 21/2866 — Relations between North and South Korea and sub-Saharan African countries.

FCO 21/2876 — North Korea and the Non-Aligned Movement.

FCO 21/3213 — Relations between Uganda and North Korea.

FCO 21/3217 — Relations between North and South Korea and the Seychelles.

FCO 21/3231 — North Korean military assistance and arms sales to developing countries.

FCO 21/3595 — Relations between North and South Korea and African countries.

FCO 21/3602 — North and South Korea and the Non-Aligned Movement Summit, Harare, August-September 1986.

FCO 21/3884 — External relations of North Korea.

FCO 21/4124 — External relations of North Korea.

FCO 21/4436 — World Youth Festival, Pyongyang, North Korea, July 1989.

FCO 21/4953 — Relations between North Korea and other countries.

FCO 21/5260 — Arms sales to and from North Korea.

FCO 31/1866 — Liberation movements in Zaire.

FCO 31/2433 — Relations between the Seychelles and the Communist states.

FCO 31/3263 — Visits between Tanzania and communist countries.

FCO 31/3674 — Relations between Tanzania and North and South Korea.

FCO 31/3922 — Political relations between Ethiopia and North Korea.

FCO 31/692 — Relations between North Korea and Tanzania.

FCO 31/948 — Political relations between Somali Democratic Republic and North Korea.

FCO 31/976 — Tanzania's relations with Communist countries.

FCO 36/2764 — Involvement of Korea in Rhodesian problem.

FCO 45/1283 — Diplomatic relations between Botswana and other countries.

FCO 45/1680 — Relations between Angola and communist countries.

FCO 45/536 — Communist activities in Zambia.

FCO 95/860 — Tanzania: relations with North Korea.

FO 371/154940 — Political relations between Belgian Congo and other countries: North Korea.

FO 371/170810 — North Korean foreign policy.

301

PRIMARY SOURCES

FO 371/181117	Foreign policy: North Korea.
FO 371/181130	North Korean goodwill mission to east and central Africa.

National Library of Namibia [NLN]

F001—LCA/06128	On carrying forward the Juche idea / Kim Jong Il.
F001—LCA/01319	On the Juche idea of our party / Kim Jong Il.

Nordic Africa Institute [NAI], Sweden

Pamphlet Collection	Angola: Military.
Pamphlet Collection	Angola: National Liberation Movements: FNLA.
Pamphlet Collection	Angola: National Liberation Movements: MPLA.
Pamphlet Collection	Angola: National Liberation Movements: UNITA.
Pamphlet Collection	History.
Pamphlet Collection	Mozambique: Foreign Relations.
Pamphlet Collection	Mozambique: Military/Conflicts.
Pamphlet Collection	Mozambique: National Liberation Movements: FRELIMO.
Pamphlet Collection	Namibia: National Liberation Movements: SWAPO.
Pamphlet Collection	Regional Cooperation.
Pamphlet Collection	Regional Cooperation: AAPSO.
Pamphlet Collection	Socialism.
Pamphlet Collection	South Africa: Foreign Relations.
Pamphlet Collection	South Africa: National Liberation Movements: ANC.
Pamphlet Collection	Southern Africa: National Liberation Movements.
Pamphlet Collection	Tanzania: National Liberation Movements: TANU.
Pamphlet Collection	Tanzania: Politics: Nyerere.
Pamphlet Collection	Zambia: Foreign Relations.
Pamphlet Collection	Zambia: Politics: Kaunda.
Pamphlet Collection	Zimbabwe: Military/Special Forces.
Pamphlet Collection	Zimbabwe: National Liberation Movements: ZANU.
Pamphlet Collection	Zimbabwe: National Liberation Movements: ZAPU.

Northwestern University Libraries [NUL], United States

L968.91005 Z711 v.20 Zimbabwe News, Vol. 20, No. 11.

Seoul National University [SNU] Library, South Korea

17450	북한.가나관계.1982.
비학렬 811.74 M929y 198	영원히 당과 함께 : 시집.

Vantage Point (periodicals).

PRIMARY SOURCES

South African Department of Defence Archives [SADOD]
CSI GP 3 Box 1091   Front for the Liberation of Zimbabwe [FROLIZI].

South African Department of International Relations and Cooperation [SADIRCO]
1.1191.1.   North Korea Political Situation & Developments.

South West Africa People's Organisation Archives [SWAPOA], Namibia
02000009-9A/9C   Seminar on Training in Diplomacy for SWAPO Representative and Officials 1988.
02000006   Seminar: Training in Diplomacy.

Stasi Records Archive [SRA], Germany
MfS—HA II. Nr. 29133   Ländermappe. Koreanische Demokratische Volksrepublik.
MfS—HA XXII. Nr. 1610/72   Länderinformation.
MfS—Sekr. Mittig. Nr. 98   Vereinbarung.

Stephen Ellis Archive [SEA], African Studies Centre Leiden, The Netherlands
2.5.4.2.3   Lisa Distelheim, 'A state within a state waiting to go home', 30 October 1986.

Tanzania National Archives [TNA]
ACC 622 S/10/16   Chama cha urafiki Korea/Tanzania.

University of Mississippi Libraries [UML]
MUM.00767   H. Townsey Collection.

United Independence National (UNIP) Archives, Zambia
EAP121/2/5/4/31   'Afro-Asian Peoples Solidarity, Papers [1977-1979]' (1977–1979).

United Nations Digital Library [UNDL]
TD/339   Pyongyang Declaration and Plan of Action on South-South Co-operation: note by the UNCTAD Secretariat.
A/AC.131/260   Report of the Delegation of the United Nations Council for Namibia to the Extraordinary Ministerial Conference of the Movement of Non-Aligned Countries on South-South Co-operation, held at Pyongyang, from 9 to 13 June 1987.

PRIMARY SOURCES

A/42/411 Letter dated 87/07/06 from the Permanent Representative of Zimbabwe to the United Nations addressed to the Secretary-General.

UNESCO Digital Library [UNESDOC]
0000154025 Roads to independence: the African liberation heritage programme.

University of Dar es Salaam [UDSM] Library, Tanzania
Sunday News (newspaper)
Daily News (newspaper)

University of Namibia [UNAM] Archives
PA1/1/5 Shipanga, Esme and Bishop Winter on arrested husband, Andreas: 1976, 1978.
PA1/14/1/1 Namibia Today, Lusaka, Zambia (official organ of SWAPO).
PA1/16/8/15 Memo on South African forgery plot against SWAPO in Namibia. 2 April 1984.
PA1/20/13 SWAPO, internal documents: 1965–196.
PA3/3/1/1 SWAPO Monographs: Comrade DR Agostinho Neto Namibia mourns you, honour and glory to comrade Neto - Luanda: SWAPO Information and Publicity Department, approx. 1979.
PA3/5/3/273 Pyongyang review. Pyongyang: Foreign Languages Publishing House, 1988.
PA3/6/117 Study of the Juche Idea. Tokyo: International Institute of the Juche Idea, 1982.
PA3/6/121 Third World Forum. Quebec: Third World Forum, 1974/75.
PA3/6/67 Korea today. Pyongyang: The Foreign Language Magazines, 1992;
PA3/6/89 Newsletter [Non-Aligned countries]. Harare: The COMINAC II Secretariat, 1987–1990.
PA4/1/2/73/22 Report of the delegation of the United Nations Council for Namibia to the extraordinary ministerial conference of the movement of non-aligned countries on South-South co-operation, held at Pyongyang from 9 to 13 June 1987.
PA4/5/138, Foreign Trade of the Democratic People's Republic of Korea: 1987
PA4/5/421 Study of the Juche Idea: 1979–1990.
PA44/1/4/115 (iii) Leader of Democratic People's Republic of Korea. Pledges Support for SWAPO, 21/86.

PRIMARY SOURCES

University of South Africa [UNISA] Archives
Spotlight on Zimbabwe, Vol. 2, No. 4, August/September 1981.

University of the Free State [UFS] Archives, South Africa
M.B.4/750 Memorandum. Discussion with the United States Ambassador.

University of the Western Cape [UWC] Special Collections, South Africa
Allen Isaacman Collection, FRELIMO, Você da Revolução, No. 59, July 1978.

Wilson Center Digital Archive [WCDA]

TELEGRAM 066.712	Romanian Embassy in Pyongyang to the Romanian Ministry of Foreign Affairs, June 3, 1978. AMAE, Folder 784/1978, Issue 220. [Obtained and translated by Eliza Gheorghe].
BStU, MfS, HA II/10	Information About the State Visit of the General Secretary of the WPK CC and President of the DPRK, Kim Il Sung, to the GDR, June 7, 1984. [Obtained and translated by Thomas Stock].
MOL, XIX-J-1-j 1977, 24	Hungarian Embassy in Angola, Telegram, 15 June 1977. Subject: Angolan-North Korean relations, June 15, 1977. [Obtained and translated by Balázs Szalontai].
MOL, XIX-J-1-j Korea, 1982, 80	Hungarian Embassy in the DPRK, Report, 11 March 1982. Subject: North Korean activities in the Non-Aligned Movement, March 11, 1982. [Obtained and translated by Balázs Szalontai].

REFERENCES

Abebe, D. (2019) *Emperor's Own: Ethiopians in the Korean War*. Warwick: Helion & Company.

Abou-El-Fadl, R. (2019) 'Building Egypt's Afro-Asian Hub: Infrastructures of Solidarity and the 1957 Cairo Conference', *Journal of World History*, 30(1), pp. 157–92.

Adedze, A. (1995) 'Museums as a Tool for Nationalism in Africa', *Museum Anthropology*, 19(2), pp. 58–64.

Agarwala, P. N. (2014) *The New International Economic Order: An Overview*. New York: Pergamon Press.

Alexander, J. (2021) 'The Noisy Silence of Gukurahundi: Truth, Recognition and Belonging', *Journal of Southern African Studies*, 47(5), pp. 763–85.

Alexander, J., Israel, P., Larmer, M. and Oliveira, R. S. de (2020) 'Liberation Beyond the Nation: An Introduction', *Journal of Southern African Studies*, 46(5), pp. 821–8.

Alexander, J., McGregor, J. and Tendi, B.-M. (2017) 'The Transnational Histories of Southern African Liberation Movements: An Introduction', *Journal of Southern African Studies*, 43(1), pp. 1–12.

Allgemeine Zeitung (2011) 'Kommentar: Die Vergessenen des Wohlstands', 8 December.

Ang, I. (2017) 'What Are Museums For? The Enduring Friction Between Nationalism and Cosmopolitanism', *Identities*, 24(1), pp. 1–5.

Armstrong, C. K. (2004) *The North Korean Revolution, 1945–1950*. Ithaca: Cornell University Press.

Armstrong, C. K. (2013) *Tyranny of the Weak: North Korea and the World, 1950–1992*. Ithaca: Cornell University Press.

Armstrong, S. (1989) *In Search of Freedom: Andreas Shipanga Story as Told to Sue Armstrong*. Gibraltar: Ashanti Publishing.

REFERENCES

Arriola, L. R., Rakner, L., Walle, N. van de, Arriola, L. R., Rakner, L. and Walle, N. van de (eds) (2022) *Democratic Backsliding in Africa? Autocratization, Resilience, and Contention*. Oxford: Oxford University Press.

AsiaNews (2014) 'North Korea Is World's Largest Manufacturer of Statues of Dictators', 25 March.

Atlas Obscura (2014) 'Monument to African Dictator Laurent Kabila', 25 August. https://www.atlasobscura.com/places/monument-to-african-dictator-laurent-kabila.

Baas, R. (2022) 'The Rider and the Coffee Maker: Sites and Practices of Remembrance in Contemporary Namibia', *Journal of African Cultural Studies*, 34(1), pp. 48–67.

Bacon, J. (2018) 'Oops! Mike Pompeo refers to North Korean leader Kim as "Chairman Un"', *USA Today*, 9 May.

Baines, G. and Vale, P. (eds) (2008) *Beyond the Border War: New Perspectives on Southern Africa's Late-Cold War Conflicts*. South Africa: Unisa Press.

Ball, J. (2019) '"From Cabinda to Cunene": Monuments and the Construction of Angolan Nationalism since 1975', *Journal of Southern African Studies*, 45(5), pp. 821–40.

Ballbach, E. J. (2022) *Moving Beyond Targeted Sanctions: The Sanctions Regime of the European Union Against North Korea*. 4. Berlin: German Institute for International and Security Affairs.

Bartels, L. M., Daxecker, U. E., Hyde, S. D., Lindberg, S. I. and Nooruddin, I. (2023) 'The Forum: Global Challenges to Democracy? Perspectives on Democratic Backsliding', *International Studies Review*, 25(2), pp. 1–27.

BBC News (2016) 'North Korea's "Biggest" Export - Giant Statues', 16 February.

BBC News (2022) 'Angola Election: The MPLA Defeats Unita in Closest-Ever Election', 29 August.

Bechtol, B. E. (2018) *North Korean Military Proliferation in the Middle East and Africa: Enabling Violence and Instability*. Lexington: The University Press of Kentucky.

Becker, H. (2011) 'Commemorating Heroes in Windhoek and Eenhana: Memory, Culture and Nationalism in Namibia, 1990-2010', *Africa*, 81(4), pp. 519–43.

Becker, H. (2015) 'From "To Die a Tribe and Be Born a Nation" Towards "Culture, The Foundation of a Nation": The Shifting Politics and Aesthetics of Namibian Nationalism', *Journal of Namibian Studies*, 18, pp. 21–35.

Becker, H. (2020) 'Writing Genocide: Fiction, Biography and Oral History of the German Colonial Genocide in Namibia, 1904–1908', *Matatu*, 50(2), pp. 361–95.

Berger, A. (2016a) 'Disrupting North Korea's Military Markets', *Survival*, 58(3), pp. 101–30.

Berger, A. (2016b) *Target Markets: North Korea's Military Customers in the Sanctions Era*. London: Routledge.

Bermudez, J.S. (1990) *Terrorism, the North Korean Connection*. New York: Crane Russak.

REFERENCES

Bernstorff, J. von and Dann, P. (eds) (2019) *The Battle for International Law: South-North Perspectives on the Decolonization Era*. Oxford: Oxford University Press.

Bianchini, P., Sylla, N. S. and Zeilig, L. (eds) (2023) *Revolutionary Movements in Africa: An Untold Story*. London: Pluto Press.

Birmingham, D. (1978) 'The Twenty-Seventh of May: An Historical Note on the Abortive 1977 "Coup" in Angola', *African Affairs*, 77(309), pp. 554–64.

Blaauw, L. (2015) 'African Agency in International Relations: Challenging Great Power Politics?', in P. H. Bischoff, K. Aning and A. Acharya (eds) *Africa in Global International Relations: Emerging Approaches to Theory and Practice*. London: Routledge, pp. 85–107.

Blaauw, L. and Zaire, D. (eds) (2023) *Dominant Parties as Governments in Southern Africa: Their Changing Nature and Its Implications for Democracy and Democratic Consolidation*. Windhoek: Konrad Adenauer Foundation.

Bloomberg (2014) 'North Korea Bags $5 Million for Building Two Mugabe Statues', 27 March.

Bobiash, D. (1992) *South-South Aid: How Developing Countries Help Each Other*. London: MacMillan—St. Martin's Press.

Boman, T. (1960) *Hebrew Thought Compared with Greek*. London: Westminster Press.

Bongmba, E. K. (2004) 'Reflections on Thabo Mbeki's African Renaissance', *Journal of Southern African Studies*, 30(2), pp. 291–316.

Brazinsky, G. A. (2017) *Winning the Third World: Sino-American Rivalry during the Cold War*. Chapel Hill: The University of North Carolina Press.

Breckenridge, K. (2014) 'The Politics of the Parallel Archive: Digital Imperialism and the Future of Record-Keeping in the Age of Digital Reproduction', *Journal of Southern African Studies*, 40(3), pp. 499–519.

Bremer, I. (2022a) 'North Korea Pursues Medical Cooperation with African Countries during Pandemic', *NK News*, 31 March.

Bremer, I. (2022b) 'North Korea to Send 30 "Technicians" to Guinea for Agricultural Cooperation', *NK News*, 19 April.

Bremer, I. (2023) 'New North Korean Firm Boasts of Role in Building Library at Zambian University', *NK News*, 24 May.

Breuker, R. (2018) *De B.V. Noord-Korea: Een Kernmacht in de Marge*. Amsterdam: Prometheus.

Breuker, R. B. and Van Gardingen, I. B. L. H. (2016) *Slaves to the System: North Korean Forced Labour in the European Union: The Polish Case*. Leiden: Leiden Asia Centre.

Breuker, R. B. and Van Gardingen, I. B. L. H. (2018) *People for Profit: North Korean Forced Labour on a Global Scale*. Leiden: Leiden Asia Centre.

Brown, W. (2012) 'A Question of Agency: Africa in international politics', *Third World Quarterly*, 33(10), pp. 1889–908.

Brown, W. and Harman, S. (eds) (2013) *African Agency in International Politics*. London: Routledge.

Brzezinski, Z. and Dallin, A. (1963) *Africa and the Communist World*. Stanford: Stanford University Press.

REFERENCES

Burton, E. (2019) 'Hubs of Decolonization. African Liberation Movements and "Eastern" Connections in Cairo, Accra, and Dar es Salaam', in L. Dallywater, C. Saunders and H. A. Fonseca. (eds) *Southern African Liberation Movements and the Global Cold War 'East': Transnational Activism 1960–1990*. Berlin: De Gruyter Oldenbourg, pp. 25–56.

Buzo, A. (1999) *The Guerilla Dynasty: Politics and Leadership in North Korea*. Boulder: Routledge.

Catholic Commission for Justice and Peace in Zimbabwe and The Legal Resources Foundation (1997) *Breaking the Silence, Building True Peace: A Report on the Disturbances in Matabeleland and the Midlands, 1980 to 1988*. Harare.

Central Intelligence Agency (1978) *Korea: The Economic Race Between the North and the South*. Washington, D. C.: National Foreign Assessment Center.

Chan, S. (2021) *African Political Thought: An Intellectual History of the Quest for Freedom*. London: Hurst.

Chang, Y. (2020) *South Korea's Engagement with Africa*. London: Palgrave Macmillan.

Che, O. (2022) *International Friendship: The Gifts from Africa*. Heidelberg: Kehrer Verlag.

Che, O. (2015) *Mansudae Master Class: The Monumental Gifts from North Korea*.

Cheeseman, N. and Tendi, B.-M. (2010) 'Power-Sharing in Comparative Perspective: The Dynamics of "Unity Government" in Kenya and Zimbabwe', *Journal of Modern African Studies*, 48(2), pp. 203–29.

Chestnut, S. (2007) 'Illicit Activity and Proliferation: North Korean Smuggling Networks', *International Security*, 32(1), pp. 80–111.

Chipaike, R. and Knowledge, M. H. (2018) 'The Question of African Agency in International Relations', *Cogent Social Sciences*, 4(1), 1487257.

Chitando, E. and Tarusarira, J. (2017) 'The Deployment of a "Sacred Song" in Violence in Zimbabwe: The Case of the Song "Zimbabwe Ndeye Ropa Ramadzibaba" (Zimbabwe was/is Born of the Blood of the Fathers/Ancestors) in Zimbabwean Politics', *Journal for the Study of Religion*, 30(1), pp. 5–25.

Cho, J. (2018) *South Korea's Foreign Policy Towards Africa, Examining the DRC, Rwanda, Uganda, and Ethiopia in Comparison with China, Japan, and North Korea: Being Realist with Soft-Romanticism*. PhD. SOAS, University of London.

Choi, L. and Jeong, I. (2017) 'North Korea and Zimbabwe, 1978–1982: From the Strategic Alliance to the Symbolic Comradeship Between Kim Il Sung and Robert Mugabe', *Cold War History*, 17(4), pp. 329–49.

Christie, I. (1989) *Samora Machel: A Biography*. London: Panaf.

Clapham, C. (2008) 'Fitting China In', in C. Alden, D. Large and R. Soares de Oliveira (eds) *China Returns to Africa: A Superpower and a Continent Embrace*. London: Hurst, pp. 361–70.

Clough, R. N. (1987) *Embattled Korea: The Rivalry for International Support*. Boulder: Westview.

REFERENCES

Correia, P. and Verhoef, G. (2009) 'Portugal and South Africa: Close Allies or Unwilling Partners in Southern Africa during the Cold War?', *Scientia Militaria: South African Journal of Military Studies*, 37(1), pp. 50–72.

Costa, J.C.V. (2013) 'A Literatura Africana Como Pedagogia Libertadora na Prática do Ensino de História', *Educação Unisinos*, 17(2), pp. 137–44.

Cumings, B. (1997) *Korea's Place in the Sun: A Modern History*. New York: W. W. Norton & Company.

Dabengwa, D. (2017) 'Relations Between ZAPU and the USSR, 1960s–1970s: A Personal View', *Journal of Southern African Studies*, 43(1), pp. 215–23.

Dallywater, L., Saunders, C. and Adegar, F. H. (2019) *Southern African Liberation Movements and the Global Cold War 'East', Transnational Activism 1960–1990*. Berlin: De Gruyter Oldenbourg.

Davidson, B. (1992) *The Black Man's Burden: Africa and the Curse of the Nation-state*. Oxford: James Currey.

David-West, A. (2006) 'Nationalist Allegory in North Korea: The Revolutionary Opera "Sea of Blood"', *North Korean Review*, 2(2), pp. 75–87.

Denney, S., Green, C. and Cathcart, A. (2016) 'Kim Jong-un and the Practice of Songun Politics', in A. Cathcart, R. Winstanley-Chesters and C. Green (eds) *Change and Continuity in North Korean Politics*. New York: Routledge, pp. 53–64.

Dersso, S. A. (2012) 'The Quest for Pax Africana: The Case of the African Union's Peace and Security Regime', *African Journal on Conflict Resolution*, 12(2), pp. 11–48.

Diop, C. A. (2000) *Towards the African Renaissance: Essays in African Culture and Development, 1946-1960*. Trenton: Red Sea Press.

Dobrzeniecki, I. (2019) 'Juche Ideology in Africa: Its Origins & Development', *Acta Asiatica Varsoviensia*, (32), pp. 117–38.

Doran, S. (2017a) *Kingdom, Power, Glory: Mugabe, ZANU and the Quest for Supremacy, 1960-1987*. Midrand: Sithatha.

Doran, S. (2017b) 'Robert Mugabe—the Power of Lies, and the Lies of Power', *Daily Maverick*, 25 October.

Douek, D. (2020) *Insurgency and Counterinsurgency in South Africa*. London: Hurst.

Drew, A. (2015) 'Visions of Liberation: The Algerian War of Independence and its South African Reverberations', *Review of African Political Economy*, 42(143), pp. 22–43.

DuPre, A., Kasprzyk, N. and Stott, N. (2016) *Cooperation Between African states and the Democratic People's Republic of Korea*. Pretoria: Institute for Security Studies.

Elago, H. I. (2015) 'Colonial Monuments in a Post-Colonial Era: A Case Study of the Equestrian Monument', in J. Silvester (ed.) *Re-Viewing Resistance in Namibian History*. Windhoek: University of Namibia Press, pp. 276–97.

Ellis, S. (1996) 'Africa and International Corruption: The Strange Case of South Africa and Seychelles', *African Affairs*, 95(379), pp. 165–96.

REFERENCES

Ellis, S. (2000) 'Africa's Wars of Liberation: Some Historiographical Reflections', in P. Konings, W. van Binsbergen, and G. Hesseling, *Trajectoires de Libération en Afrique Contemporaine: Hommage à Robert Buijtenhuijs*. Paris: Karthala, pp. 69–92.

Ellis, S. (2002) 'Writing Histories of Contemporary Africa', *Journal of African History*, 43(1), pp. 1–26.

Ellis, S. (2011) 'The Genesis of the ANC's Armed Struggle in South Africa 1948-1961', *Journal of Southern African Studies*, 37(4), pp. 657–76.

Emmett, T. (1999) *Popular Resistance and the Roots of Nationalism in Namibia, 1915-1966*. Basel: P. Schlettwein Publishing.

Erdmann, G., Elischer, S. and Stroh, A. (2011) *Can Historical Institutionalism be Applied to Political Regime Development in Africa?* Hamburg: German Institute of Global and Area Studies.

Fan, J. (2009) 'Could Taiwan emulate N Korea?', *Taipei Times*, 18 August.

Fanon, F. (1961) *The Wretched of the Earth*. Paris: François Maspero.

Fisher, J. (2018) 'African Agency in International Politics', in *Oxford Research Encyclopedia of Politics*. Oxford: Oxford University Press.

Frank, R. (ed.) (2012) *Exploring North Korean Arts*. Nürnberg: Verlag für moderne Kunst.

Franklin, D. P. (1996) *A Pied Cloak: Memoirs of a Colonial Police Officer (Special Branch), Kenya, 1953-66, Bahrain, 1967-71, Lesotho, 1971-75, Botswana, 1976-81*. London: Janus.

Freeman, C.W. (1989) 'The Angola/Namibia Accords', *Foreign Affairs*, 68(3), pp. 126–41.

Friedman, J. (2015) *Shadow Cold War: The Sino-Soviet Competition for the Third World*. Chapel Hill: The University of North Carolina Press.

Gann, L. H. (1983) *Africa Between East and West*. Cape Town: Tafelberg.

Geingob, H. (2015) 'Heroes Day Speech', 26 August.

Geldenhuys, D. (2005) 'Pretoria and Pyongyang: Supping with Sinners', *South African Journal of International Affairs*, 12(2), pp. 143–56.

Getachew, A. (2019) *Worldmaking After Empire: The Rise and Fall of Self-Determination*. Princeton: Princeton University Press.

Gewald, J.-B. (2014) *To Grahamstown and Back: Towards a Socio-Cultural History of Southern Africa*. Leiden: Leiden University.

Gewald, J.-B., Hinfelaar, M. and Macola, G. (eds) (2008) *One Zambia, Many Histories: Towards a History of Post-Colonial Zambia*. Leiden: Brill.

Godwin, K. (2016) 'Gedenkstätten und Waffen. Nordkorea und Namibia Blicken auf Enge Beziehungen Zurück', *iz3w 357*, pp. 10–13.

Gordon, D. (2008) 'Rebellion or Massacre? The UNIP-Lumpa Conflict Revisited', in J.-B. Gewald, M. Hinfelaar and G. Macola (eds) *One Zambia, Many Histories: Towards a History of Post-Colonial Zambia*. Leiden: Brill, pp. 45–76.

Greig, I. (1977) *The Communist Challenge to Africa: An Analysis of Contemporary Soviet, Chinese and Cuban Policies*. London: Foreign Affairs Publishing.

REFERENCES

Grilli, M. (2018) 'Nkrumah's Ghana and the Armed Struggle in Southern Africa (1961–1966)', *South African Historical Journal*, 70(1), pp. 56–81.

Grilli, M. (2020) 'Southern African Liberation Movements in Nkrumah's Ghana', in *Oxford Research Encyclopedia of African History*. Oxford: Oxford University Press, pp. 1–31.

Guimaraes, F. A. (2016) *The Origins of the Angolan Civil War: Foreign Intervention and Domestic Political Conflict, 1961-76*. London: Palgrave Macmillan.

Gurney, C. (2000) '"A Great Cause": The Origins of the Anti-Apartheid Movement, June 1959-March 1960', *Journal of Southern African Studies*, 26(1), pp. 123–44.

Gyimah-Boadi, E. (2015) 'Africa's Waning Democratic Commitment', *Journal of Democracy*, 26(1), pp. 101–13.

Harrison, G. (2023) 'Wagner in Africa—Political Excess and the African Condition', *Review of African Political Economy*, 13 July.

Henriksen, T. H. (1981) *Communist Powers and Sub-Saharan Africa*. Stanford: Hoover Institution Press.

Higgins, E. (2021) *We Are Bellingcat: The Online Sleuths Solving Global Crimes*. London: Bloomsbury Publishing.

Hirai, H. (2023) *Comrade Kim Jong-Un's Revolutionary Thought*. FY 2022-#1. Tokyo: The Japan Institute of International Affairs.

Hobsbawm, E. and Ranger, T. (1983) *The Invention of Tradition*. Cambridge: Cambridge University Press.

Holtland, J. J. (2021) *De Koerier van Maputo: Een Nederlander in de Zuid-Afrikaanse Revolutie*. Amsterdam: Uitgeverij Podium.

Hoog, T. A. van der (2018) 'Uncovering North Korean Forced Labour in Africa: Towards a Research Framework', in R. B. Breuker and I. B. L. H. van Gardingen, *People for Profit: North Korean Forced Labour on a Global Scale*. Leiden: Leiden Asia Centre, pp. 67–83.

Hoog, T. A. van der (2019a) *Monuments of Power: The North Korean Origin of Nationalist Monuments in Namibia and Zimbabwe*. Leiden: African Studies Centre Leiden.

Hoog, T. A. van der (2019b) 'The Heroes of History: African Liberation Through a North Korean Lens', in T. H. Yoon and B. Klein Zandvoort, *Decoding Dictatorial Statues*. Eindhoven: Onomatopee, pp. 194–203.

Hoog, T. A. van der (2020) 'Three Ways to Conduct Historical Research on Africa in Times of Corona', *Africa at LSE*, 3 June.

Hoog, T. A. van der (2022a) 'A New Chapter in Namibian History: Reflections on Archival Research', *History in Africa*, pp. 1–26.

Hoog, T. A. van der (2022b) *Defying United Nations Sanctions: Three Reasons for African Engagement with North Korea*. Washington, D. C.: Korea Economic Institute of America.

Hoog, T. A. van der (2022c) 'Microphone Revolution: North Korean Cultural Diplomacy During the Liberation of Southern Africa', in C. Stolte and S. L. Lewis (eds) *The Lives of Cold War Afro-Asianism*. Leiden: Leiden University Press, pp. 265–90.

REFERENCES

Hoog, T. A. van der (2022d) 'On the Success and Failure of North Korean Development Aid in Africa', *NKEF Policy and Research Paper Series*, pp. 31–42.

Hoog, T. A. van der (2022e) 'Research Note: The Nordic Africa Institute (NAI) Pamphlet Collection', *Cold War History*, 22(3), pp. 363–8.

Hoog, T. A. van der (2023) *A Monumental Relationship: North Korea and Namibia*. Washington, D. C.: East-West Center.

Hoog, T. A. van der (2024) 'Pyongyang as a Crossroads for Afro-Asian Cooperation', *IIAS The Newsletter*, (97), pp. 4–5.

Hoog, T. A. van der and Moore, B. C. (2022) 'Paper, Pixels, or Plane tickets? Multi-Archival Perspectives on the Decolonisation of Namibia', *Journal of Namibian Studies*, 32, pp. 77–106.

Howard, K. (2020) *Songs for 'Great Leaders': Ideology and Creativity in North Korean Music and Dance*. New York: Oxford University Press.

International Court of Justice (no date) *South West Africa (Liberia v. South Africa)*. Available at: https://www.icj-cij.org/case/47 (accessed: 29 July 2023).

Jager, S. M. (2013) *Brothers at War: The Unending Conflict in Korea*. New York: W. W. Norton & Company.

Jang, J. (2014) *Dear Leader: From Trusted Insider to Enemy of the State, My Escape from North Korea*. London: Rider.

Jentzsch, C. (2022) *Violent Resistance: Militia Formation and Civil War in Mozambique*. New York: Cambridge University Press.

Jopela, A. P. de J. (2017) *The Politics of Liberation Heritage in Postcolonial Southern Africa, With Special Reference to Mozambique*. PhD. University of the Witwatersrand.

Kangumu, B. (2011) *Contesting Caprivi: A History of Colonial Isolation and Regional Nationalism in Namibia*. Basel: Basler Afrika Bibliographien.

Karekwaivanane, G. H. (2017) *The Struggle over State Power in Zimbabwe: Law and Politics since 1950*. Cambridge: Cambridge University Press.

Kerkhoff, N. (2020) 'North Korea and the Non-Aligned Movement: From Adulation to Marginalization', *Journal of American-East Asian Relations*, 28(1), pp. 41–71.

Khadiagala, G. M. (1994) *Allies in Adversity: The Frontline States in Southern African Security, 1975-1993*. Athens: Ohio University Press.

Kickert, W. J. M. and van der Meer, F.-B. (2011) 'Small, Slow, and Gradual Reform: What can Historical Institutionalism Teach us?', *International Journal of Public Administration*, 34(8), pp. 475–85.

Kiely, J. (2009) 'Memories of an African Student Forced to Study in North Korea During the 1980s', *Free Korea*, 28 May.

Kim, C. H. (2021) 'Pyongyang Modern: Architecture of Multiplicity in Postwar North Korea', *Journal of Korean Studies*, 26(2), pp. 271–96.

Kim, I. S. (1984) 'The Present Situation and the Tasks of Our Party', in *Works*. Pyongyang: Foreign Languages Publishing House, pp. 313–408.

Kim, I. S. (1985) 'Let Us Itensify the Anti-Imperialist, Anti-US Struggle', in *Works*. Pyongyang: Foreign Languages Publishing House, pp. 344–50.

REFERENCES

Kim, I. S. (1987a) 'Speech Delivered at the Ceremony Conferring an Honorary Doctorate at Algiers University', in *Works*. Pyongyang: Foreign Languages Publishing House, pp. 293–8.

Kim, I. S. (1987b) 'Talk to the President of the Liberation Front of Mozambique', in *Works*. Pyongyang: Foreign Languages Publishing House, pp. 122–45.

Kim, I. S. (1990) 'For the Development of Agriculture in African Countries', in *Works*. Pyongyang: Foreign Languages Publishing House, pp. 218–30.

Kim, I. S. (1991) 'The Life of a Revolutionary Should Begin with a Struggle and End with Struggle', in *Works*. Pyongyang: Foreign Languages Publishing House, pp. 128–33.

Kim, I. S. (1996) 'Talk to a Delegation of the Revolutionary Party of Tanzania', in *Works*. Pyongyang: Foreign Languages Publishing House, pp. 90–6.

Kim, I. S. (1997) 'Young People and Students, be the Vanguard of Our Times: Speech of Congratulations at the Opening Ceremony of the 13th World Festival of Youth and Students, July 1, 1989', in *Works*. Pyongyang: Foreign Languages Publishing House, pp. 54–7.

Kim, I. S. (2022a) 'Let Us Develop South-South Cooperation, Congratulatory Speech at the Extraordinary Ministerial Conference on Non-Aligned Countries on South-South Cooperation', in *For Achieving Global Independence*. Pyongyang: Foreign Languages Publishing House, pp. 49–61.

Kim, I. S. (2022b) 'Talk to the Delegation of the Zimbabwean Parliament, January 19, 1987', in *For Achieving Global Independence*. Pyongyang: Foreign Languages Publishing House, pp. 39–48.

Kim, J. I. (1989) *On the Art of the Cinema*. Pyongyang: Foreign Languages Publishing House.

Kim, S. (1983) 'Pyongyang, the Third World, and Global Politics', in T.-H. Kwak, W. Patterson and E. A. Olsen (eds) *The Two Koreas in World Politics*. Seoul: Kyungnam University Press, pp. 59–86.

Kim, S. (2014) *The Political Economy of Aid-Oriented Foreign Policy Change: Elite Perspectives on Mercantilism in Korea and Ghana*. PhD. University of the Western Cape.

Kim, S.-Y. (2010) *Illusive Utopia: Theater, Film, and Everyday Performance in North Korea*. Ann Arbor: University of Michigan Press.

Kim, U. J. and Rim, O. (eds) (2022) *International Friendship Exhibition House: Gifts Presented to Chairman Kim Jong Il*. Pyongyang: Foreign Languages Publishing House.

Kirby, J. (2020) 'Between Two Chinas and Two Koreas: African Agency and Non-Alignment in 1970s Botswana', *Cold War History*, 20(1), pp. 21–38.

Kirkwood, M. L. E. (2013) 'Postindependence Architecture through North Korean Modes', in *A Companion to Modern African Art*. Hoboken, New Jersey: John Wiley & Sons, pp. 548–71.

Knox, B. M. W. (1994) *Backing into the Future: The Classical Tradition and Its Renewal*. New York: W. W. Norton & Company.

REFERENCES

Ko, R. S. (2022) *An Exploratory Analysis of North Korea's Relationship with Africa: From the Cold War to Now*. Nairobi: Sochin Research Institute.

Koh, B. C. (1969) *The Foreign Policy of North Korea*. Westport: Praeger Publishers.

Koh, B. C. (1984) *Foreign Policy Systems of North and South Korea*. Berkeley: University of California Press.

Kornes, G. (2010) 'Whose blood waters whose freedom?' *Gegenerinnerungen in der namibischen Interniertenfrage*. Mainz: Johannes Gutenberg-Universität.

Kornes, G. (2019) 'Nordkorea Transnational: Arbeiten des Mansudae Art Studios in Frankfurt und Windhoek', in J. Beek, K. N'Guessan and M. Späth (eds) *Zugehörigkeiten: Erforschen, Verhandeln, Aufführen - im Sinne von Carola Lentz*. Cologne: Köppe, pp. 121–45.

Kriger, N. (2005) 'ZANU(PF) Strategies in General Elections, 1980–2000: Discourse and Coercion', *African Affairs*, 104(414), pp. 1–34.

Kriger, N. (2006) 'From Patriotic Memories to "Patriotic History" in Zimbabwe, 1990—2005', *Third World Quarterly*, 27(6), pp. 1151–69.

Kriger, N., Ranger, T. and Bhebe, N. (1995) 'The Politics of Creating National Heroes: The Search for Political Legitimacy and National Identity', in *Soldiers in Zimbabwe's Liberation War*. Oxford: James Currey.

Kwak, T., Patterson, W. and Olsen, E. A. (1983) *The Two Koreas in World Politics*. Seoul: Kyungnam University Press.

Kwon, H. and Chung, B.-H. (2012) *North Korea: Beyond Charismatic Politics*. Lanham: Rowman & Littlefield Publishers.

Kwon, P. B. (2020) 'Building Bombs, Building a Nation: The State, Chaeböl, and the Militarized Industrialization of South Korea, 1973–1979', *Journal of Asian Studies*, 79(1), pp. 51–75.

Landau, P. S. (2022) *Spear: Mandela and the Revolutionaries*. Johannesburg: Jacana.

Lankov, A. (2007) 'Juche: Idea for All Times', *Korea Times*, 27 November.

Lankov, A. (2013) *The Real North Korea: Life and Politics in the Failed Stalinist Utopia*. Oxford: Oxford University Press.

Larmer, M. (2008) 'Enemies Within? Opposition To the Zambian One-Party State, 1972–1980', in J.-B. Gewald, M. Hinfelaar and G. Macola (eds) *One Zambia, Many Histories: Towards a History of Post-Colonial Zambia*. Leiden: Brill, pp. 98–125.

Lee, C. (2010) *Making a World after Empire: The Bandung Moment and Its Political Afterlives*. Athens: Ohio University Press.

Leistner, G. M. E. (1983) 'Lesotho and South Africa: Uneasy Relationship', *Africa Insight*, 13(3), pp. 209–12.

Lekgoathi, S. P. and Mukonde, K. T. (2024) 'Zambia's Support for the African National Congress's Radio Freedom in Lusaka, 1967–1992', *Journal of African Cultural Studies*, 36(1), pp. 24–40.

Lessing, P. (1962) *Africa's Red Harvest*. New York: The John Day Company.

Lewis, S. L. and Stolte, C. (2019) 'Other Bandungs: Afro-Asian Internationalisms in the Early Cold War', *Journal of World History*, 30(1), pp. 1–19.

REFERENCES

Leys, C. and Saul, J.S. (1994) 'Liberation Without Democracy? The Swapo Crisis of 1976', *Journal of Southern African Studies*, 20(1), pp. 123–47.

Limb, P. (2018) 'Southern African Liberation Struggles 1960–1994: Contemporaneous Documents', *South African Historical Journal*, 70(1), pp. 270–80.

Lister, G. (2014) 'Political Perspective', *The Namibian*, 1 October.

Lodge, T. (2022) *Red Road to Freedom: A History of the South African Communist Party 1921—2021*. London: James Currey.

Machel, S. (1985) *Samora Machel, an African Revolutionary: Selected Speeches and Writings*. London: Zed Books.

Macías, M. (2013) 나는 평양의 모니카입니다. 예담.

Macías, M. (2023) *Black Girl from Pyongyang: In Search of My Identity*. London: Duckworth.

Macmillan, H. (2017) '"Past History Has Not Been Forgotten": The ANC/ZAPU Alliance—the Second Phase, 1978–1980', *Journal of Southern African Studies*, 43(1), pp. 179–93.

Macpherson, F. (1974) *Kenneth Kaunda of Zambia: The Times and the Man*. Lusaka: Oxford University Press.

Malaba, B. (2023) 'Zimbabwe | No Human Rights For "Bad Apples"', *ZAM*, 18 January.

Mallory, K. (2021) *North Korean Sanctions Evasion Techniques*. RAND Corporation.

Manatsha, B.T. (2018) 'Geopolitical Implications of President Seretse Khama's 1976 State Visit to North Korea', *Botswana Notes and Records*, 50, pp. 138–52.

Mandela, N. (1995) *Long Walk to Freedom: The Autobiography of Nelson Mandela*. New York: Back Bay Books.

Marmon, B. (2022) 'Research Notes: Negotiating South African ministerial archives (Defence & Foreign Affairs)', *Cold War History*, 22(3), pp. 359–62.

Marmon, B. (2023) 'The Federation of Rhodesia and Nyasaland 1953–1963: A Retrospective at its Unattained Platinum Jubilee', *South African Historical Journal*, pp. 1–6.

Martins, V. and Cardina, M. (2019) 'A Memory of Concrete: Politics of Representation and Silence in the Agostinho Neto Memorial', *Kronos*, 45(1).

Mattera, D. (2011) *Azanian Love Song*. Johannesburg: African Perspectives Publishing.

Mazarire, G. C. (2010) 'Rescuing Zimbabwe's "Other" Liberation Archives', in C. Saunders, *Documenting Liberation Struggles in Southern Africa*. Uppsala: Nordic Africa Institute, pp. 95–106.

Mbathera, E. (2024) 'Mbumba Confers National Hero Honour on Geingob', *The Namibian*, 16 February.

Melber, H. (2002) 'From Liberation Movements to Governments: On Political Culture in Southern Africa', *African Sociological Review / Revue Africaine de Sociologie*, 6(1), pp. 161–72.

Melber, H. (ed.) (2004) *Limits to Liberation in Southern Africa: The Unfinished Business of Democratic Consolidation*. Cape Town: HSRC Press.

REFERENCES

Melber, H. (2009) 'Southern African Liberation Movements as Governments and the Limits to Liberation', *Review of African Political Economy*, 36(121), pp. 451–9.

Melber, H. (2010) 'On the Limits to Liberation in Southern Africa', in C. Saunders (ed.) *Documenting Liberation Struggles in Southern Africa*. Uppsala: Nordic Africa Institute, pp. 39–47.

Melber, H. (2020) 'Namibia's Parliamentary and Presidential Elections: The Honeymoon is Over', *The Round Table*, 109(1), pp. 13–22.

Melber, H. (2021) '"One Namibia, One Nation"? Social Cohesion under a Liberation Movement as Government in Decline', *Stichproben. Wiener Zeitschrift für kritische Afrikastudien*, 21(41), pp. 129–58.

Meuser, P. (ed.) (2012) *Architectural and Cultural Guide Pyongyang*. SLP edition. Berlin: DOM Publishers.

Michishita, N. (2010) *North Korea's Military-Diplomatic Campaigns, 1966-2008*. London: Routledge.

Miller, J. (2013) 'Yes, Minister: Reassessing South Africa's Intervention in the Angolan Civil War, 1975–1976', *Journal of Cold War Studies*, 15(3), pp. 4–33.

Ministry of Foreign Affairs, Republic of Korea (1971) *Korea and its Relation with the United Nations*. Seoul: Ministry of Foreign Affairs, Republic of Korea.

Mitchell, D. M. (2021) *An African Memoir: White Woman, Black Nationalists*. Self-published.

Mnangagwa, E. (2017) 'My Life in Politics', *The Herald*, 24 November.

Moorcraft, P. (2011) *Mugabe's War Machine: Saving or Savaging Zimbabwe*. Barnsley: Pen & Sword Military.

Moore, G. and Beier, U. (eds) (2007) *The Penguin Book of Modern African Poetry: Fourth Edition*. 4th edition. London: Penguin Classics.

Mubako, S. (1975) 'The Quest for Unity in the Zimbabwe Liberation Movement', *African Issues*, 5(1), pp. 7–18.

Munguambe, C. V. L. (2017) 'Nationalism and Exile in an Age of Solidarity: Frelimo–ZANU Relations in Mozambique (1975–1980)', *Journal of Southern African Studies*, 43(1), pp. 161–78.

Mupawaenda, O. T. (1987) 'A Zimbabwean Librarian Visits North Korea', *Information Development*, 3(1), pp. 44–5.

Museveni, Y. K. (1997) *Sowing the Mustard Seed: The Struggle for Freedom and Democracy in Uganda*. London: Macmillan Publishers.

Mushingeh, C. (1993) 'The Evolution of One-Party Rule in Zambia, 1964-1972', *Transafrican Journal of History*, 22, pp. 100–21.

Myers, B. R. (2010) *The Cleanest Race: How North Koreans See Themselves - And Why It Matters*. Brooklyn, N.Y: Melville House.

Myers, B. R. (2015) *North Korea's Juche Myth*. Busan: Sthele Press.

Mytelka, L. K. (1989) 'The Unfulfilled Promise of African Industrialization', *African Studies Review*, 32(3), pp. 77–137.

Ndeyanale, E. (2024) 'Geingob to Rest in his Own Room at Heroes' Acre', *The Namibian*, 22 February.

REFERENCES

Ndhlovu, F. (2021) 'Reading Robert Mugabe Through the Third Chimurenga: Language, Discourse, Exclusion', *International Journal of Politics, Culture, and Society*, 34(1), pp. 85–103.

Ndlovu-Gatsheni, S. J. (2007) 'Re-Thinking the Colonial Encounter in Zimbabwe in the Early Twentieth Century', *Journal of Southern African Studies*, 33(1), pp. 173–91.

Ndlovu-Gatsheni, S. J. (2012) 'Rethinking "Chimurenga" and "Gukurahundi" in Zimbabwe: A Critique of Partisan National History', *African Studies Review*, 55(3), pp. 1–26.

Nganje, F. (2016) 'Historical Institutionalism and the Development of Sub-State Diplomacy in South Africa', *Journal for Contemporary History*, 41(1), pp. 149–68.

Nujoma, S. (2001) *Where Others Wavered*. London: Panaf Books.

Nyathi, P. (2018) *My Story: Joseph Khumo Nyathi (Dickson Khupe): Serving on ZPRA and ZNA's 5 Brigade*. Bulawayo: Amagugu Publishers.

Oberdorfer, D. and Carlin, R. (2013) *The Two Koreas: A Contemporary History*. New York: Basic Books.

O'Carrol, C. (2023) 'What to Make of North Korea's Closure of Multiple Embassies Overseas', *NK News*, 1 November.

O'Malley, A. (2018) *The Diplomacy of Decolonisation: America, Britain and the United Nations During the Congo Crisis 1960-1964*. Manchester: Manchester University Press.

Owoeye, J. (1991) 'The Metamorphosis of North Korea's African Policy', *Asian Survey*, 31(7), pp. 630–45.

Pak, C.Y. (2000) *Korea and the United Nations*. Leiden: Brill.

Pambi, J. M. M. P. U. (2023) *L'imaginaire politique Nord-Coréen: Un plaidoyer pour la souveraineté des États africains*. Paris: Harmattan RDC.

Park, C. (2021) 'The Namibian Heroes Acre Created by North Korea's Mansudae Art Studio', *Journal of Northeast Asian Studies*, 26(3), pp. 161–81.

Park, J. K. (1983) 'North Korea's Policy Toward the Third World: The Miliary Dimension', in T.-H. Kwak, W. Patterson and E. A. Olsen (eds) *The Two Koreas in World Politics*. Seoul: Kyungnam University Press, pp. 87–102.

Park, J. K. (1987) 'North Korea's Foreign Policy toward Africa', in J. K. Park, B. C. Koh and T.-H. Kwak (eds) *The Foreign Relations of North Korea: New Perspectives*. Boulder: Westview, pp. 437–9.

Park, S.-S. (1978) 'Africa and Two Koreas: A Study of African Non-Alignment', *African Studies Review*, 21(1), pp. 73–88.

Park, W. G. (2009) 'The United Nations Command in Korea: Past, Present, and Future', *Korean Journal of Defense Analysis*, 21(4), pp. 485–99.

Parsons, N. (2006) 'Unravelling History and Cultural Heritage in Botswana', *Journal of Southern African Studies*, 32(4), pp. 667–82.

Parsons, N., Henderson, W. and Tlou, T. (1995) *Seretse Khama, 1921-1980*. Gaborone: The Botswana Society.

REFERENCES

Passemiers, L. (2019) *Decolonisation and Regional Geopolitics: South Africa and the 'Congo Crisis', 1960-1965*. London: Routledge.

Pearce, J. (2015) 'Contesting the Past in Angolan Politics', *Journal of Southern African Studies*, 41(1), pp. 103–19.

Pearson, J. L. (2017) 'Defending Empire at the United Nations: The Politics of International Colonial Oversight in the Era of Decolonisation', *Journal of Imperial and Commonwealth History*, 45(3), pp. 525–49.

Phimister, I. (2012) 'Narratives of Progress: Zimbabwean Historiography and the End of History', *Journal of Contemporary African Studies*, 30(1), pp. 27–34.

Pohamba, H. (2014) 'Statement on the Occasion of the Inauguration of the Genocide Memorial Statue, the Sam Nujoma Statue and the Independence Memorial Museum', Windhoek, 20 March.

Portal, J. (2005) *Art Under Control in North Korea*. London: Reaktion Books.

Post, T. J. (2023) 'Megawati touts North Korea as model for nuclear program', *The Jakarta Post*, 13 June.

Potgieter, D. W. (2007) *Total Onslaught: Apartheid's Dirty Tricks Exposed*. Cape Town: Zebra Press.

PPLAAF (no date) 'Gradi Koko & Navy Malela: Sentenced to Death for Doing Their Job', *Plateforme de Protection des Lanceurs d'Alerte en Afrique*.

Prashad, V. (2007) *The Darker Nations: A People's History of the Third World*. New York: New Press.

Pritchard, J. (2019) 'Negotiating Research Access: The Interplay Between Politics and Academia in Contemporary Zimbabwe', in L. Johnstone (ed.) *The Politics of Conducting Research in Africa: Ethical and Emotional Challenges in the Field*. Cham: Springer International Publishing, pp. 171–90.

Rademeyer, J. (2016) *Beyond Borders: Crime, Conservation and Criminal Networks on the Illicit Rhino Horn Trade*. Geneva: The Global Initiative Against Transnational Organized Crime.

Rademeyer, J. (2017) *Diplomats and Deceit: North Korea's Criminal Activities in Africa*. Geneva: The Global Initiative Against Transnational Organized Crime.

Ranger, T. (1968) 'Connexions Between "Primary Resistance" Movements and Modern Mass Nationalism in East and Central Africa. Part I', *Journal of African History*, 9(3), pp. 437–53.

Ranger, T. (2004) 'Nationalist Historiography, Patriotic History and the History of the Nation: The Struggle over the Past in Zimbabwe', *Journal of Southern African Studies*, 30(2), pp. 215–34.

Reuters (2017) 'In Pakistan, North Korean diplomat's alcohol stash raises bootlegging suspicions', 8 November.

Reuters (2020) 'Hostel at North Korea's Berlin embassy must close, German court rules', 28 January.

Ri, J. C. (2012) *Songun Politics in Korea*. Pyongyang: Foreign Languages Publishing House.

REFERENCES

Rim, O. (2022) *International Friendship Exhibition House: Gifts Presented to Chairman Kim Jong Il*. Edited by U. J. Kim. Pyongyang: Foreign Languages Publishing House.

Roberts, G. (2021) *Revolutionary State-Making in Dar es Salaam: African Liberation and the Global Cold War, 1961–1974*. Cambridge: Cambridge University Press.

Roberts, G. (2023) 'The Rise and Fall of a Swahili Tabloid in Socialist Tanzania: *Ngurumo* Newspaper, 1959–76', *Journal of Eastern African Studies*, 17(1–2), pp. 1–21.

Robinson, D. (2006) *Curse on the Land: A History of the Mozambican Civil War*. PhD. The University of Western Australia.

Robinson, J. (1965) 'Korean Miracle', *Monthly Review*, pp. 541–9.

Rodney, W. (1972) *How Europe Underdeveloped Africa*. London: Bogle-L'Ouverture Publications.

Rotberg, R. I. (2012) *Transformative Political Leadership: Making a Difference in the Developing World*. Chicago: University of Chicago Press.

Ryang, S. (2012) *Reading North Korea: An Ethnological Inquiry*. Cambridge: Harvard University Asia Center.

Salisbury, D. (2021) 'Spies, Diplomats and Deceit: Exploring the Persistent Role of Diplomatic Missions in North Korea's WMD Proliferation and Arms Trafficking Networks', *Asian Security*, 17(3), pp. 313–30.

Sanders, E. (2009) 'Historical Institutionalism', in S. A. Binder, R. A. W. Rhodes and B. A. Rockman (eds) *The Oxford Handbook of Political Institutions*. Oxford: Oxford University Press, pp. 39–55.

Sapire, H. (2009) 'Liberation Movements, Exile, and International Solidarity: An Introduction', *Journal of Southern African Studies*, 35(2), pp. 271–86.

Sasman, C. (2013) 'Herero en Khoisan moet betoog oor monumente', *Die Republikein*, 18 October.

Sasman, C. (2014) 'NUDO-jeug kwaad oor 'SWAPO-museum'', *Die Republikein*, 23 April.

Saunders, C. (2003) 'Liberation and Democracy: A Critical Reading of Sam Nujoma's "Autobiography"', in H. Melber (ed.) *Re-Examining Liberation in Namibia. Political Culture Since Independence*. Uppsala: Nordic Africa Institute, pp. 87–98.

Saunders, C. (2007) 'The Role of the United Nations in the Independence of Namibia', *History Compass*, 5(3), pp. 737–44.

Saunders, C. (2010) *Documenting Liberation Struggles in Southern Africa*. Uppsala: Nordic Africa Institute.

Saunders, C. (2018a) 'Namibia's Liberation Struggle: The Mbita Version', *South African Historical Journal*, 70(1), pp. 281–90.

Saunders, C. (2018b) 'SWAPO, Namibia's Liberation Struggle and the Organisation of African Unity's Liberation Committee', *South African Historical Journal*, 70(1), pp. 152–67.

Scalapino, R. A. and Lee, H. (eds) (1986) *North Korea in a Regional and Global Context*. Berkeley: University of California.

REFERENCES

Schildkrout, E. (1995) 'Museums and Nationalism in Namibia', *Museum Anthropology*, 19(2), pp. 65–77.

Schmidt, W. (2009) "Neues Museum: Von "Grotesk" bis "toll"', *Allgemeine Zeitung*, 23 October.

Scholtz, G. (2014) 'It is a Privilege to be Namibian', *Die Republikein*, 31 March.

Schubert, J. (2015) '2002, Year Zero: History as Anti-Politics in the "New Angola"', *Journal of Southern African Studies*, 41(4), pp. 835–52.

Scott, G. (2018) *Adventures in Zambian Politics: A Story in Black and White*. Boulder, Colorado: Lynne Rienner Publishers.

Segal, D. (2017) 'Hosting Proms and Selling Cows: North Korean Embassies Scrounge for Cash', *The New York Times*, 7 October.

Serpell, N. (2019) *The Old Drift*. London: Vintage.

Shen, Z. and Xia, Y. (2018) *A Misunderstood Friendship: Mao Zedong, Kim Il-Sung, and Sino-North Korean Relations, 1949-1976*. New York: Columbia University Press.

Shillington, K. (2014) *Albert Rene: The Father of Modern Seychelles, a Biography*. Crawley: UWA Publishing.

Shitumpabo, K. P. (2014) 'Museum of Narcissism and Self-Glorification', *The Namibian*, 4 April.

Shubin, V. (2008) *The Hot 'Cold War': The USSR in Southern Africa*. London: Pluto Press.

Silvester, J. (2015) 'Introduction: Re-Viewing Resistance, Liberating History', in J. Silvester, *Re-Viewing Resistance in Namibian History*. Windhoek: University of Namibia Press.

Snyder, T. (2017) *On Tyranny: Twenty Lessons from the Twentieth Century*. New York: Crown.

Son, H. (2022) 'North Korean capital Pyongyang cracks down on citizens illegally moving downtown', *Radio Free Asia*, 28 March.

Song, J. (2011) *Human Rights Discourse in North Korea: Post-Colonial, Marxist and Confucian Perspectives*. London: Routledge.

Soulé-Kohndou, F. (2013) 'Histoire Contemporaine des Relations Sud-Sud. Les Contours d'une Évolution Graduelle', *Afrique contemporaine*, 248(4), pp. 108–11.

Southall, R. (2013) *Liberation Movements in Power: Party and State in Southern Africa*. Martlesham: Boydell & Brewer.

Steiner, C. B. (1995) 'Museums and the Politics of Nationalism', *Museum Anthropology*, 19(2), pp. 3–6.

Steiner, G. (1995) *After Babel: Aspects of Language and Translation*. Oxford: Oxford University Press.

Stiles, T. J. (2019) 'America Is Losing Its Memory', *Washington Post*, 7 May.

Strödike, F. O. (2013) 'Party of the History', *Allgemeine Zeitung*, 10 October.

Stueck, W. (1995) *The Korean War: An International History*. Princeton: Princeton University Press.

Stueck, W. (2002) *Rethinking the Korean War: A New Diplomatic and Strategic History*. Princeton: Princeton University Press.

REFERENCES

Suh, D. S. (1988) *Kim Il Sung: The North Korean Leader*. New York: Columbia University Press.

Suttner, R. (2008) *The ANC Underground in South Africa*. Auckland Park: Jacana Media.

SWAPO (1981) *To Be Born a Nation: The Liberation Struggle for Namibia*. London: Zed Books.

Szalontai, B. (2005) *Kim Il Sung in the Khrushchev Era: Soviet-DPRK Relations and the Roots of North Korean Despotism, 1953-1964*. Redwood City: Stanford University Press.

Telepneva, N. (2022) *Cold War Liberation: The Soviet Union and the Collapse of the Portuguese Empire in Africa, 1961–1975*. Chapel Hill: The University of North Carolina Press.

Temu, A. J. and Tembe, J. das N. (eds) (2014) *Southern African Liberation Struggles: Contemporaneous Documents, 1960-1994*. Dar es Salaam: Mkuki na Nyota.

Tendi, B.-M. (2010) *Making History in Mugabe's Zimbabwe: Politics, Intellectuals, and the Media*. Oxford: Peter Lang.

Tendi, B.-M. (2020) *The Army and Politics in Zimbabwe: Mujuru, the Liberation Fighter and Kingmaker*. Cambridge: Cambridge University Press.

The Institute for East Asian Studies (1974) *North Korea's Policy Toward the United Nations*. Seoul: The Institute for East Asian Studies.

The Namibian (2022) 'Keep Swapo in Power Until Jesus Comes', 25 April.

The Namibian (2023a) 'Namibia Not a Republic of Homosexuals—Ekandjo', 8 June.

The Namibian (2023b) 'Schlettwein Breaks Rank Over Same Sex Bill', 10 July.

The Nationalist (1966a) 'Friendship Between Tanzania, Korea', 13 January.

The Nationalist (1966b) 'Korean Stand on Rhodesian Issue', 8 January.

The Sentry (2020) *Overt Affairs*. Washington, D. C. Available at: https://thesentry.org/reports/overt-affairs/ (accessed: 29 September 2021).

The Sentry (2021) *Artful Dodgers*. Washington, D. C. Available at: https://thesentry.org/reports/artful-dodgers/ (accessed: 29 September 2021).

Thörn, H. (2006) 'Solidarity Across Borders: The Transnational Anti-Apartheid Movement', *Voluntas: International Journal of Voluntary and Nonprofit Organizations*, 17(4), pp. 285–301.

Tlhage, O. (2023) 'McLeod-Katjirua Would Scrap Democracy If She Could', *Namibian Sun*, 31 July.

Todd, J. G. (2007) *Through the Darkness: A Life in Zimbabwe*. Cape Town: Struik Publishers.

Todorović, M. (2022) 'Heritage in and as Diplomacy: A Practice Based Study', *International Journal of Heritage Studies*, 28(7), pp. 849–64.

Trewhela, P. (2009) *Inside Quatro: Uncovering the Exile History of the ANC and SWAPO*. Johannesburg: Jacana.

Tsoubaloko, F. H. (2016) 'Songs as A Tool of Resistance in The Namibian Path to Freedom', *Applied Science Reports*, 16(2), pp. 122–6.

Ukrainska Pravda (2023) 'Prigozhin Suggests that Russia Follow North Korea's Example So the Country Isn't "Screwed Up"', 24 May.

REFERENCES

United Nations (1950) *Korea and the United Nations*. New York: Department of Public Information.

United Nations Panel of Experts (2010) *S/2010/571, Final Report of the Panel of Experts Submitted Pursuant to Resolution 1874 (2009)*.

United Nations Panel of Experts (2012) *S/2012/422, Final Report of the Panel of Experts Submitted Pursuant to Resolution 1985 (2011)*.

United Nations Panel of Experts (2013) *S/2013/337, Final Report of the Panel of Experts Submitted Pursuant to Resolution 2050 (2012)*.

United Nations Panel of Experts (2014) *S/2014/147, Final Report of the Panel of Experts Submitted Pursuant to Resolution 2094 (2013)*.

United Nations Panel of Experts (2015) *S/2015/131, Final Report of the Panel of Experts Submitted Pursuant to Resolution 2141 (2014)*.

United Nations Panel of Experts (2016) *S/2016/157, Final Report of the Panel of Experts Submitted Pursuant to Resolution 2207 (2015)*.

United Nations Panel of Experts (2017) *S/2017/150, Final Report of the Panel of Experts Submitted Pursuant to Resolution 2276 (2016)*.

United Nations Panel of Experts (2018) *S/2018/171, Final Report of the Panel of Experts Submitted Pursuant to Resolution 2345 (2017)*.

United Nations Panel of Experts (2019) *S/2019/171, Final Report of the Panel of Experts Submitted Pursuant to Resolution 2407 (2018)*.

United Nations Panel of Experts (2020) *S/2020/151, Final Report of the Panel of Experts Submitted Pursuant to Resolution 2464 (2019)*.

United Nations Panel of Experts (2021) *S/2021/211, Final Report of the Panel of Experts Submitted Pursuant to Resolution 2515 (2020)*.

United Nations Panel of Experts (2022) *S/2022/132, Final Report of the Panel of Experts Submitted Pursuant to Resolution 2569 (2021)*.

United Nations Panel of Experts (2023) *S/2023/171, Final Report of the Panel of Experts Submitted Pursuant to Resolution 2627 (2022)*.

United Nations Panel of Experts (2024) *S/2024/215, Final Report of the Panel of Experts Submitted Pursuant to Resolution 2680 (2023)*.

Urquhart, B. (1991) *A Life in Peace and War*. New York, New York: W. W. Norton & Company.

Venzke, I. (2019) 'The International Court of Justice During the Battle for International Law (1955–1975): Colonial Imprints and Possibilities for Change', in J. von Bernstorff and P. Dann (eds) *The Battle for International Law: South-North Perspectives on the Decolonization Era*. Oxford: Oxford University Press.

Villiers, C. F. D., Metrowich, F. R. and Plessis, J. A. D. (1975) *The Communist Strategy*. Pretoria: Department of Information.

Visser, W. (2004) 'The Production of Literature on the "Red Peril" and "Total Onslaught" in Twentieth-Century South Africa', *Historia*, 49(2), pp. 105–28.

Wada, H. (2013) *The Korean War: An International History*. Lanham: Rowman & Littlefield.

REFERENCES

Walker, L. (2019) 'Decolonization in the 1960s: On Legitimate and Illegitimate Nationalist Claims-Making', *Past & Present*, 242(1), pp. 227–64.

Walker, P. (2010) 'Senegalese President Unveils £17m African Renaissance Statue', *The Guardian*, 4 April.

Wallace, M. (2011) *History of Namibia: From the Beginning to 1990*. Oxford: Oxford University Press.

Walsh, D. (2018) 'Need a North Korean Missile? Call the Cairo Embassy', *The New York Times*, 3 March.

Werbner, R. (1998a) 'Introduction', in R. Werbner (ed.) *Memory and the Postcolony: African Anthropology and the Critique of Power*. London: Zed Books.

Werbner, R. (1998b) 'Smoke from the Barrel of a Gun: Post-Wars of the Dead, Memory and Reinscription in Zimbabwe', in R. Werbner (ed.) *Memory and the Postcolony: African Anthropology and the Critique of Power*. London: Zed Books, pp. 71–102.

Wessels, A. (2017) 'Half a Century of South African "Border War" Literature: A Historiographical Exploration', *Journal for Contemporary History*, 42(2), pp. 24–47.

White, L. (2009) '"Heading for the Gun": Skills and Sophistication in an African Guerrilla War', *Comparative Studies in Society and History*, 51(2), pp. 236–59.

White, L. (2015) *Unpopular Sovereignty: Rhodesian Independence and African Decolonization*. Chicago: University of Chicago Press.

White, L. (2021) *Fighting and Writing: The Rhodesian Army at War and Postwar*. Durham, NC: Duke University Press.

White, L. and Larmer, M. (2014) 'Introduction: Mobile Soldiers and the Un-National Liberation of Southern Africa', *Journal of Southern African Studies*, 40(6), pp. 1271–4.

Wilkins, H. (2023) 'North Korean Company Behind Benin "Woman King" Statue', *VOA*, 12 January.

Williams, C. (2015) *National Liberation in Postcolonial Southern Africa: A Historical Ethnography of SWAPO's Exile Camps*. New York: Cambridge University Press.

Williams, C. A. and Mazarire, T. (2019) 'The Namibian Independence Memorial Museum, Windhoek, Namibia', *The American Historical Review*, 124(5), pp. 1809–11.

Wimmer, A. and Schiller, N. G. (2003) 'Methodological Nationalism, the Social Sciences, and the Study of Migration: An Essay in Historical Epistemology', *The International Migration Review*, 37(3), pp. 576–610.

Xinhua (2020) 'Botswana Commemorates Fallen Heroes Day', 28 February.

Yoon, M. K. (2014) *Aestheticized Politics: The Workings of North Korean Art*. PhD. Leiden University.

Youcef, A. L. (2014) 'The Algerian Army Made Me a Man', *Transition*, (116), pp. 67–79.

Young, B. R. (2018) *Guerilla Internationalism: North Korea's Relations with the Third World, 1957-1989*. PhD. George Washington University.

REFERENCES

Young, B.R. (2020) 'Cultural Diplomacy with North Korean Characteristics: Pyongyang's Exportation of the Mass Games to the Third World, 1972–1996', *The International History Review*, 42(3), pp. 543–55.

Young, B.R. (2021a) *Guns, Guerillas, and the Great Leader: North Korea and the Third World*. Stanford, California: Stanford University Press.

Young, B.R. (2021b) *North Korea in Africa: Historical Solidarity, China's Role, and Sanctions Evasion*. Washington, D. C.: United States Institute of Peace.

Yu, C.-A. (2007) 'The Rise and Demise of Industrial Agriculture in North Korea', *Journal of Korean Studies*, 12(1), pp. 75–109.

Zeller, J. (2008) 'Symbolic Politics: Notes on the German Colonial Culture of Remembrance', in J. Zimmerer and J. Zeller (eds) *Genocide in German South-West Africa: The Colonial War of 1904-1908 and its Aftermath*. London: The Merlin Press, pp. 231–51.

Zeller, W. and Melber, H. (2019) 'United in Separation? Lozi Secessionism in Zambia and Namibia', in L. de Vries, P. Englebert and M. Schomerus (eds) *Secessionism in African Politics: Aspiration, Grievance, Performance, Disenchantment*. Cham: Springer International Publishing, pp. 293–328.

Zuern, E. (2012) 'Memorial Politics: Challenging the Dominant Party's Narrative in Namibia', *Journal of Modern African Studies*, 50(3), pp. 493–518.

Zwirko, C. (2019) 'UN Ban on North Korean Overseas Workers Comes into Effect', *NK News*, 22 December.

Zwirko, C. (2020) 'UN: Angola Deported 296 North Korean Workers, Some After Sanctions Deadline', *NK News*, 5 August.

INDEX

African Development Bank, 92
African Regional Committee for the
  Study of the Juche Idea, 74
African Renaissance Monument, 181,
  237
AAPSO (Afro-Asian People's Solidarity
  Organisation), 32, 33, 34, 39,
  46–8, 53, 54, 90
  Havana conference (Cuba), 29,
    133
  membership, 47
Afro-Asian solidarity, 24, 30–3, 46–50
Age of Juche, 77
agriculture, 86–7
Agro-Scientific Research Centre, 92
AK-47, 103, 104, 171
  Kalashnikovs, reverse-engineered,
    123
Algeria, 130–2
  Afro-Asian Conference, 131
Algerian Revolution, 130–2
Algiers, 59, 129
All-African Peoples' Conference
  (1958), 132
ANC (African National Congress), 6,
  20, 44–5, 52, 110, 132, 219–20,
  236, 239
  armed resistance, roots of, 207
  exile camp, 25–6

gun appearance, 103
leadership, 126
military doctrine, 128
MK (Umkhonto we Sizwe), 207,
  208
notion of family, 197
Angola in Arms, 53
Angola, 2, 24, 30, 45, 111, 163, 192,
  200–2
  ANC camps, 139
  freedom and blood, 19
  imports, 165
  nation building, 201
  North Korean aid, 89
  North Korean training camp, 137
Angolan Civil War, 112
Angolan War of Independence, 112,
  113
Anti-Apartheid Movement (AAM), 32
anticolonial campaigns, 23–7
April Spring Friendship Art Festival, 58
Arc of Triumph, 61
Arduous March (famine), 4
AREMA (*Antoko Revolisionera Malagasy*),
  150, 151
Arirang Mass Games, 58
armed struggle, embracing, 108–11
arms embargo (United Nations, 2006),
  163

INDEX

Arusha Declaration (1967), 91
assassinations, 155
Aveyime Rice Project, 94–5

Banda, Hastings, 40
Bandung Conference (1955), 32, 46
Banner of Independence, 77
Battle of Blood River (1838), 207
Battle of Isandlwana, 208
Battle of Ismailia Monument, 205
battlefields of Africa, 111–14
Ben Bella, Ahmed, 115, 131
Benin, 181
Biko, Steve, 155
blood
    comradeship, 20
    a symbol of sacrifice, 19–20
BNP (Basotho National Party), 150,
    152, 153
boipelego principle, 71
Botswana, 2, 21, 44, 62–4, 114, 155
Boumédiène, Houari, 59
Brazzaville, 42
British Foreign Office, 38, 60, 62, 67,
    78
British High Commission, 77
Bulgaria, 59, 232
Bureau of African Affairs, 90, 126–7,
    132

Capitol Cinema (Gaborone), 78
Castro, Fidel, 133
CCM (*Chama Cha Mapinduzi*), 6, 236
Centre of Revolutionary Instruction,
    134
ch'ongdae Kamun ('barrel-of-the-gun
    philosophy'), 124, 211–12
ch'ung (loyalty to the sovereign or
    country), 199
Chimurenga, 113, 161–62, 209–10, 212
China, 6, 41, 98, 117, 120, 130
Chitepo, Herbert, 155
Chollima Agricultural Science Institute,
    90, 92, 95

CIA (Central Intelligence Agency), 87,
    123
Communist Bloc, 41
comrades, term, 20
Congo, Republic of, 2, 42, 83, 168,
    171–2, 177, 231
    national history museum, 183
consciencism, 71
Corée Populaire, 53
Covid-19 pandemic, 9, 11, 173
Cuba, 6, 113–14

Dabengwa, Dumiso, 124
Dakawa Rice Irrigation Project, 92
Dar es Salaam Declaration (1975), 109,
    111
Dar es Salaam, 26–7, 47
    hub for African liberation, 136
    North Korean embassy,
    trade show, 92
Davidson, Basil, 158
decolonisation, 3, 4, 12, 24, 26–7,
    98–9, 248
democratic backsliding, 240–3
democratic elections (South Africa,
    1994), 24
DPRK (Democratic People's Republic
    of Korea, *see* North Korea)
Dingane, Zulu king, 207
Diop, Cheikh Anta, 181
Distelheim, Lisa, 25
dos Santos, José Eduardo, 20, 44

Eastern Bloc, 3, 31, 32–3
Egypt, 133, 205, 233
Ekandjo, Jerry, 235
'elite memorialism', 217
El-Sharkawi, Abdel Rahman, 47
Eritrean Liberation Front, 136
Ethiopia, 109, 120
Ethiopian Airlines, 168
Ethiopian Kagnew Battalion, 120
ethnic nationalisms, 21
exile camps, 25–6

328

INDEX

exiled African guerrilla fighters, 134–5

F-7 fighter jets, 169
Fanon, Frantz, 33, 132
Fifth Brigade (Zimbabwe), 14, 142,
   143–50, 152, 153, 249
First, Ruth, 155
FLN (*Front de Libération Nationale*),
   130–2
FNLA (*Frente Nacional de Libertação de
   Angola*), 41, 45, 113, 134
Foreign Trade of DPR Korea, 227, 231
FRELIMO (*Frente de Libertação de
   Moçambique*), 6, 11, 20, 53, 64,
   128, 136, 138, 150, 161, 221, 236,
   239, 243, 244
   gun appearance, 103
   liberation struggles, 26
   notion of family, 198
   RENAMO challenged, 113, 149

Gaborone, 62, 64, 77
Geingob, Hage, 154, 223–4
German Democratic Republic, 62
Ghana Juche Farm, 90, 95
Ghana, 133
   military support, 130, 132
   North Korean aid projects, 90–1
   technical aid, 93–5
Ghana–DPRK Friendship Society, 91
global paper trail, 9–12
Great National Bereavement, 222
Green Pine Associated Corporation,
   165
Guebuza, Armando, 216, 221
Guinea, 69–70, 83
Gukurahundi Memorial Centre, 149
Gukurahundi, 147, 148, 149, 176, 242
guns, 103, 104

Haegeumgang Trading Corporation,
   164, 165
Hallstein Doctrine, 42, 54
Hani, Chris, 155

Harare
   military advisors in, 66
Heroes Days, 219
Ho Dam, 144
Hoare, James, 11
Honwana, Fernando, 150
hyo (filial piety), 199
hyŏngmyŏng yesul (revolutionary art),
   221

Ibrahim, Abdullah, 103
Independence Memorial Museum, 2,
   185, 186, 188–91, 193–4
International Court of Justice, 109
International Friendship Exhibition
   House, 55, 62, 69
International Institute of the Juche
   Idea, 77
International Seminar of the Juche
   Idea, 80

Jang Jin Sung, 104, 222
Japanese Empire, 37
Jonathan, Leabua, 152
Jong Jun Gi, 95
Journal of African Marxists, 127
Juche farming, 87, 88, 93–4
Juche ideology, 13–14, 46, 52, 71–83,
   98
   film shows, 78–9
   inspiration for postcolonial rule,
     80–2
   Juche agriculture, 87, 88, 92
   Kim Il Sung's persona, 72
   soft power, 76–80
   term, 71
Juche Study Centres, 72–3, 74–5, 82,
   83, 98, 158
Juche Tower, 61

Kabila, Laurent-Désiré, 216, 237
Kapuuo, Clemens, 155
Kasavubu, Joseph, 216
Kasrils, Ronnie, 45, 133

329

INDEX

Katjavivi, Peter, 196
Kaunda, Betty, 62
Kaunda, Kenneth, 28, 33, 49, 61, 68,
    69, 108, 125–6, 196, 200, 202–3,
    218, 242, 245
    Kim Il Sung's birthday party
       (1982), 1–2, 61, 62
    and Kim Il Sung relations, 155, 157
    Zambian humanism, 71, 108
Kawawa, Rashidi, 93
Khama III, 64
Khama, Ian, 63
Khama, Ruth, 63
Khama, Seretse, 61, 63
Kim Hyung Jik, 212
Kim Il Sung
    56th birthday, 78
    agricultural production, 87, 88–9
    anticolonial guerrilla warfare, 193
    anti-imperialist hero, 176
    artistic revolution, 222
    attainment of political
       independence, 141
    birthday party, 1–2, 58, 61
    concerned about Southern Africa,
       44
    death of, 222, 247
    desire for reunification, 54
    dictatorship, 41–2
    'the gift of the gun', 104, 123
    Indonesia visit, 46
    Khama letter to, 63
    on liberation struggle, 34
    Nyerere and, 91–2
    Pyongyang Conference (1987), 10,
       50–2
    Sea of Blood, 20, 21
    South–South cooperation, 87–8
    speeches, 76
    support of NAM members, 49–50
    vision of Pyongyang, 52
    'world tour' (1975), 59–60
    Zimbabwean parliament delegation
       and, 52–3

Kim Il Sung Agricultural Research
    Centre, 96
Kim Jong Il, 4, 59, 72, 73, 104, 124,
    211, 212
Kim Jong Suk, 212
Kim Jong Un, 83, 167
Kim Yong Nam, 163
Kinshasa, 56
KOMID (Korea Mining Development
    Trading Corporation), 166, 229
Korea Paekho Trading Corporation,
    231, 232, 233
Korea Today or Foreign Trade of the
    Democratic People's Republic, 77
Korea Today, 78
Korean peninsula
    diplomatic competition, 39–40,
       53–4
    division of, 3–4, 37, 46
    reunification support, 44
Korean People's Army, 119, 135, 165
Korean War, 30, 37, 46, 53, 86, 119–
    24, 175
    post-war reconstruction, 122–4
Kounoutcho, Sossa, 80
Kozonguizi, Fanuel, 29
Kumsusan Palace, 61

L'imaginaire politique Nord-Coréen, 83
Lesotho, 41, 89, 152
LGBT rights, 235
Li Jong Ok, 144
'Liberalism 101', 158
Liberia, 109
Lisbon military coup (1974), 111
Luanda skyline, 195
Lubowski, Anton, 155
Lumumba, Patrice, 109, 155, 216
Lusaka Manifesto (1969), 28, 109,
    110

MAAN (*Memorial António Agostinho*
    Neto), 195, 196, 201, 202, 203
Machel, Graça, 64–5

INDEX

Machel, Samora, 20, 25–6, 28–9, 44, 49, 61, 132, 150, 155, 221
   monument, 215, 216–17, 220
   Pyongyang visits, 64–5
   'The Weapons That Brought Us Victory' speech, 128
Madagascar, 151–2
Maji, 208
Malagasy defence forces, 151
Malawi, 40, 43, 113
Mali, 74, 78–9
Mandela, Nelson, 131–2, 219
Mansudae Art Projects, 201
Mansudae Art Studio, 182–3
MOP (Mansudae Overseas Projects), 166, 182–3, 188, 229, 230, 231
Mao Zedong, 103, 105
Maputo, 215
Marley, Bob, 143
Marxism–Leninism, 71, 126
Matabeleland, 142, 147, 148
Mau Mau rebellion (Kenya), 109
Mauritania, 59
McLeod-Katjirua, Laura, 242–3
Melber, Henning, 5, 34, 220, 237
Microphone Revolution, 97–9
military exports, 123
military mindsets, 133–6
minority rule, 24–5
MK (*Umkhonto we Sizwe*), 207, 208
Mnangagwa, Emmerson, 82, 148
Mogadishu Declaration (1971), 109, 110
Mogae, Festus, 63, 64
Moksong Overseas Construction & Economic Technology Cooperation Company, 231, 232, 233
Mondlane, Eduardo, 132
Moshoeshoe I, 208
Mozambican Civil War, 112, 113
Mozambican War of Independence, 112
Mozambique, 2, 24, 26, 30, 111, 192
   Clean Brigade, 150–1
   freedom and blood, 19

independence struggle, 161
Kalashnikov features, 105
nation building, 201
'natural alliance' between socialist countries, 128
North Korean aid, 89
North Korean arms deal, 164–5
Samora's Pyongyang visits, 64–5
MPLA (*Movimento Popular de Libertação de Angola*), 6, 11, 46, 53, 113, 124, 134, 137, 138, 198, 202, 217, 236, 239
   blood, 20
   members' Sierra Leone visit, 75
Msungu, Peter, 76–7
Mugabe, Robert, 19–20, 30, 40, 47, 56, 59, 61, 143, 154, 155, 176, 242, 243, 249
   Fifth Brigade, 14, 142, 143–50, 152, 153, 249
   Pyongyang visits, 65–6, 68
Mugabe, Sally, 220
MINUSCA (Multidimensional Integrated Stabilisation Mission in the Central African Republic), 177
Mulungushi Club, 28
Mupawaenda, O. T., 80
Museveni, Yoweri, 170
Mushi, E. S., 80
Mwaanga, Vernon, 97–8, 99
Mwanza Air Force Base, 164

Non-Aligned Movement (NAM) Film Festival, 79
Namibia Press Agency, 104
Namibia, 108, 111, 126, 163, 195–7, 230, 247
   anthem/Independence Day, 19
   arms deal, 166
   decolonisation, 32
   Heroes Day, 219
   Juche Study Centres, 73, 74
   Mansudae Overseas Projects (MOP), 166, 182–3

INDEX

museum, 2
North Korean museum, 186
occupation and liberation of, 24, 29
and Pyongyang cooperation, 66–7
UN support, 31
weapons for the armed struggle, 129
Namibian Defence Force, 166
Namibian Ministry of Defence, 166
Namibian War of Independence, 112, 113
Nasionale Party (South Africa), 24
National Committee (Mali), 74
National Heroes' Acre (Namibia), 69, 205, 210, 218, 223, 228
National Heroes' Acre (Zimbabwe), 203, 205, 206, 209, 210, 218, 219, 220, 238
National Meeting on Socialist Revolutionary Charter of Madagascar-Juche Idea, 75
nationalism, 128
NATO (North Atlantic Treaty Organization), 32
Ncome River, 207
Neto, Agostinho, 132, 133–4, 172, 195, 201, 244
memorialisation of, 217–18
Neto, Agostinho, 21, 27
New International Economic Order, 88
NK News, 231
Nkomo, Joshua, 30, 115–16, 125, 146–7, 216
Nkrumah, Kwame, 90, 115
NAM (Non-Aligned Movement), 32, 33, 34, 40, 44, 46, 48–50, 54, 66, 88, 97, 123, 142
Action Program for Economic Cooperation, 49
events in Pyongyang, 57
membership, 48–9
Pyongyang Conference (1987), 10, 50–2

Non-Aligned Summit (Zimbabwe, 1986), 20, 50–1
North Korea (DPRK, Democratic People's Republic of Korea)
formation of, 4
African visits and North Korean heritage role, 60
agricultural production, 87
anti-South Korea events, 47–8
arms industry, 122
bookshops and libraries in Africa, 77
construction projects, 228–9
embassy system, 173
ethnic nationalism, 21
family state, 198–200
films, 78–9
from communism to Juche, 71
gun and political culture, 104
illicit North Korean transport, 168
importance of literature, 76–7
independent image, 86
investments, 231
'military first' idea, 212
military experience, 119–28
military incursion into South Korea, 37
military training, 136–8
non-military sources of income, 169
pragmatism, 45–6
training facilities, 138
UN and, 31
UN resolution, 38–9
UN sanctions, 162–6
United Nations sanctions, 4–5, 14
weapons systems, 122–3
North Korean army, 37
North Korean foreign policy, 6–8
military exports, 14
North Korean Ministry of Foreign Affairs, 44, 59, 167
Nujoma, Sam, 25, 61, 66–7, 139, 153, 170, 189, 190

INDEX

'General Agreement' with North Korea, 67
memorialisation of, 217
weapons, 129, 130
Nujoma, Utoni, 242
Nyerere, Julius, 3, 28, 49, 55–6, 58, 90, 91, 93, 97, 108, 111–12, 114, 116, 124–5, 127, 156
monument, 216
Nyerere, Mwalimu, 115
Nyerere, Wangazi, 93
Nzo, Alfred, 112, 125

OAU (Organisation of African Unity), 28, 29–30, 34, 44, 97, 110
OAU Liberation Committee, 24, 28–30, 34, 90, 97, 108, 110, 111, 115, 131, 132
limits, 30
Old Drift, The (Serpell), 23
Open-source intelligence techniques (OSINT), 12
Ould Daddah, Moktar, 59

Palmer, Major General, 145
Party–Military Complex, 175–7
People's Weekly, The, 77
periodization, 247–8
PLAN (People's Liberation Army of Namibia), 66, 132, 137, 153
'Poem of Return' (Rocha), 179, 184
Pohamba, Hifikepunye, 188, 193, 213
Portugal, 32
Portuguese Empire, 24, 111, 154
Prigozhin, Yevgeny, 245
Pyongyang
African presidents in, 55–70
African presidents to, 13
cultural diplomacy, 39
foreign policy, 43–4
'good-will missions', 38
ideological training in, 79–80
invitation diplomacy, 56–7, 63–4, 67–70

Mugabe's visit to Pyongyang, 143, 144
multilateral conferences in, 60
patriotic history from, 185–94
portrayal, 57
Pyongyang Conference (1987), 10, 50–2, 88, 248
Pyongyang Foreign Languages House, 76
Pyongyang Review, 78
Pyongyang Times, 53
Pyongyang Zoo, 167

race, 21
Radio Botswana, 78
Radio Freedom, 103
Ranger, Terence, 187–8, 191–2
Ratsiraka, Didier, 151
Rebelo, Jorge, xiii, 101, 103
RENAMO (*Resistência Nacional Moçambicana*), 113, 150, 151
René, France-Albert, 68, 151
ROK (Republic of Korea, *see* South Korea)
Revolutionary Martyrs' Cemetery, 210, 221
Rhodesia (modern Zimbabwe), 24, 113
'Robben Island' (poem), 17, 32
Robben Island, 235, 239
Rocha, Jofre, xiii, 179, 184
Rodney, Walter, 85
Romania, 59

SACP (South African Communist Party), 20, 207
sacrifice and comradeship, 20–21
Samora Machel Centre for Knowledge and Development, 216
Scott, Guy, 69
self-determination, 3, 33
self-reliance. *See* Juche ideology
Senegal, 181, 237
The Sentry, 231, 232
Serpell, Namwali, 23

333

INDEX

Seychelles, 89, 151–2
Shamuyarira, Nathan, 28
Sharpeville massacre (1960), 109
Shipanga, Andreas, 29, 31–2, 114–15,
  123, 126, 139, 199, 236
  Congo visit, 132–3
Shirihuru, Edson, 81, 82
Sierra Leone, 75
Sino-Soviet split (1961), 41, 86
Smith, Ian, 24
socialism, 72
solidarity, 23–35
  African, 27–30
  global, 30–3
  tangible, 114–16
South Africa, 8, 30, 32, 83, 109, 114,
  120–1, 154
  North Korean football team, 148
  occupation and liberation of, 24–5
South African Defence Force, 113, 116
South Korea (ROK, Republic of Korea)
  13, 42–3, 183
  American troops in Seoul, 42
  and non-aligned African states, 42
  connection to South Africa, 121
  dependence on US and UK, 42–3
  diplomatic competition, 39–40,
    53–4
  formation of, 3–4
  international recognition, 38
  Ministry of Foreign Affairs, 47
  solid position within the UN, 38
  'visitation diplomacy', 56
Southern African Liberation Struggles
  project, 237
South–South cooperation, 14, 50–2,
  85–96, 248
  aim of, 88–9
  development aid as foreign policy,
    86–9
  failure and success, 95–6
  strategic hubs, 90–5
Soviet Union, 6, 41, 62, 98, 119, 126,
  130

sŏn'gun (military first), 124, 211–2,
  220
SPUP (Seychelles People's United
  Party), 150, 152
Standard, The (newspaper), 156
State Department, 43, 121
Study Group of the Works of Comrade
  Kim Il Sung, 74
Study of the Juche Idea (journal), 73, 74,
  77, 78, 79–80, 81, 88
Suppression of Communism Act, 76
surface-to-air missile Pechora (S-125),
  164
Suttner, Raymond, 197, 219–20
SWANU (South West Africa National
  Union), 29
SWAPO (South West Africa People's
  Organisation), 6, 19, 20, 25, 29,
  45, 46, 52, 66–7, 69, 103, 109,
  113, 116, 138, 150, 176, 190, 217,
  223, 236, 239, 242, 243
  armed struggle, 114–15
  freedom fighters, 134–5
  leadership, 125
  military budget, 30
  military camps, 31
  MOP and, 186, 189
  notion of family, 197–8
  People's Liberation Army of
    Namibia (PLAN), 66, 132,
    137, 153
  political programme for its military
    cadres, 135
  rely on public history, 191
  rise to power, 188
  roots of its resistance, 208–9
  UN and, 30
  weapons, 129

Tambo, Oliver, 207, 208
TANU (Tanganyika African National
  Union), 137
  Policy on Socialism and Self-
    Reliance, 91

334

INDEX

Youth League, 137, 209
Tanzania Development Bank, 92
Tanzania, 3, 41, 44, 83, 133
  agricultural scientists, 88
  decolonisation, 26–7
  film industry, 79
  NAM, 49–50
  North Korean aid projects, 90–3, 96
  North Korean arms deals, 164
  North Korean diplomats, 27
  North Korean embassy, 136
  North Korean training camp, 137
  self-reliance, 91
  weapons, 129
Tanzania–Korea Friendship Society, 91
Tanzanian Ministry of Foreign Affairs, 156
Tanzanian People's Defence Force, 137, 164
Third World Forum, 85
Three Dikgosi Monument, 64
Tiyende Pamodzi (liberation song), 1, 61, 62
Tjitendero, Mose Penaani, 78
To be Born a Nation: The Liberation Struggle for Namibia, 196, 197
Toivo ya Toivo, Andimba, 52

Ujamaa, 71, 83
UN African Group, 109
UN Command, 120, 121
UN General Assembly, 31, 38–9, 54, 56
UN Panel of Experts, 164, 169, 229–30, 233
UN Security Council resolution 2397 (2017), 230
UN Trusteeship Council, 108
UNESCO, 192
ungjangsŏng (grandness), 201
Union of the Peoples of Cameroon, 136
UNIP (United National Independence Party), 6, 20, 81, 157, 199–200, 218, 236, 239, 245
  gun appearance, 103
UNITA (*União Nacional para a Independência Total de Angola*), 45, 53, 113
United Kingdom, 32, 145
UN (United Nations), 3, 30–1, 34, 37, 187
  African UN members, 38
  decolonisation, 24
  Korean competition, 46
  limits, 31
  on North Korean arms trade, 177
  sanctions, 162–6, 230, 234, 249
United Nations Institute for Namibia, 73
UNSC (United Nations Security Council), resolution 1874, 163
US (United States), 9, 32, 37, 40, 120, 131, 177, 187
University of Lusaka, 231
University of Namibia, 73
University of Zimbabwe, 81

Victorious Fatherland Liberation War Museum, 194
Victorious Fatherland Liberation War, 211

Wade, Abdoulaye, 181
Wagner Group, 158
Western Bloc, 3, 31, 32
Windhoek, 69, 166
  Independence Memorial Museum, 2, 185, 186, 188–91, 193–4
Woman King, The (movie), 181
Workers' Party of Korea (WPK), 80–1, 222, 244
  35th anniversary, 65
  Propaganda and Agitation Department, 76
World War II, 3, 23, 37, 109
Wretched of the Earth, The (Fanon), 132

INDEX

Yang Hyong Sop, 44
yŏnggu chusŏk (eternal president), 221
Yugoslavia, 59
yuhun chŏngch'i (legacy politics), 218, 224

Zaire (modern Democratic Republic of Congo), 41, 49, 243
Zambia, 41, 44, 62, 81, 97, 113, 217, 227
  bilateral relationships, 157
  North Korean aid, 89
  one-party state, 200
Zambian humanism, 71, 108
ZANLA (Zimbabwe African National Liberation Army), 134, 146
ZANU (Zimbabwe African National Union), 20, 30, 45–5, 53, 81, 113, 133, 134, 136, 138, 161, 203, 209–10, 239, 242
  authoritarian turn, 162
  DPRK supported, 65
  gun appearance, 103, 104
  military cooperation between North Korea and, 142–9
  weapons usage, 129
ZANU–North Korean relations, 6

ZANU-PF (Zimbabwe African National Union-Patriotic Front), 6
Zanzibar, 91
ZAPU (Zimbabwe African People's Union), 30, 45–6, 81, 113, 116–17, 124, 136, 143, 144, 148, 161
Zimbabwe Ndeye Ropa, 20
Zimbabwe People's Army, 135
Zimbabwe, 2, 40, 41, 44, 81, 108, 111, 154, 187–8, 247
  anti-ROK agenda, 51
  freedom and blood, 19
  Kalashnikov features, 105
  liberation struggle, 30
  North Korean aid, 89
  North Korean bookshops in, 77
  patriotic history, 192
  and Pyongyang cooperation, 65–6
  'savage killings', 142
Zimbabwean War of Independence, 112–13
ZIPRA (Zimbabwe People's Revolutionary Army), 148
Zulu Kingdom, 208
Zulu, Alexander Grey, 138
Zuma, Jacob, 44
Zuze, Peter, 52